ENTREPRENEURSHIP AND SMALL BUSINESS MANAGEMENT

by

Dr. P. SRINIVAS SUBBA RAO

M. Com, M.A., M. Phil., B.L, Ph.D.

Faculty, Dept. of Management Studies,
M.R.A. College - P.G. Courses
Vizianagaram - Andhra Pradesh

DISCOVERY PUBLISHING HOUSE

New Delhi—110002

Edition – 2017

ISBN: 978-81-7141-589-2

Entrepreneurship and Small Business Management

Published by:

DISCOVERY PUBLISHING HOUSE PVT. LTD.
4383/4B, Ansari Road Darya Ganj
New Delhi - 110 002 (India)
Phone: +91-11-23279245, 43596064-65
Fax: +91-11-23253475
E-mail: discoverypublishinghouse@gmail.com
sales@discoverypublishinggroup.com
web: www.discoverypublishinggroup.com

Printed at:
Infinity Imaging Systems
Delhi

PREFACE

The recent years have witnessed a dramatic expansion in the small scale sector in almost all parts of the World. It is not only the developing countries that have experienced such a phenomenon but a similar experience has also been gathered by a large number of industrially developed countries like United States of America, United Kingdom, Germany and Japan.

India, a developing country which is in economic reforms through liberalisation should give more importance to Small scale sectors. Which is highly suitable for the economic conditions prevailing in the country. This sector plays a key role in the industrial development of developing country like India. This is because they provide immediate large-scale employment and have on comparatively high labour-capital ratio. They need a shorter gestation period and relatively smaller markets to be economic. They also need lower investments, offer a method of ensuring a more equitable distribution of national income and facilitate an effective mobilisation of resources of capital and skill, which might otherwise remain unutilised. Further, they stimulate the growth of industrial entrepreneurship and promote a more diffused pattern of ownership and location. They also constitute a key link in the process of socio economic transformation of underdeveloped social structures. Considering all these aspects, they are accorded top priority in our country to ensure economic development with social justice to which the nation is seriously committed.

The Government of India and State Governments initiated several promotional measures for the development of small scale industries in the country. They have attained a significant growth in terms of their number, employment, investment, output and exports. But still these industries suffer from various problems. In this context the present study seeks to highlight the problems of small scale industrial units of Vizianagaram, Srikakulam and Visakhapatnam districts in Andhra Pradesh as it is evident that they have been suffering from various problems on several fronts such as production, Labour, Marketing, Finance etc., In fact, the growth and performance of these units would have been better had they been free from these problems. This study is largely based on the primary data collected from small scale industrial units of these three districts.

The study has been divided into 8 chapters. The first chapter deals with the role, development, institutional setup and problems of small scale sector in the Indian economy. The second chapter describes the objectives of the study and the methodology followed. The third chapter outlines the development of small scale industries in Andhra Pradesh in general and Vizianagaram, Srikakulam and Visakhapatnam districts in particular. The fourth chapter discusses the growth and organisation of sample units of these three districts. The fifth chapter analyses the various problems faced by the sample units. The sixth chapter brings out the causes for sickness with particular reference to sample units in these three districts which have fallen sick. Seventh chapter concentrates on the comparative analysis of the problems of sample units and the eight chapter summarises the findings and conclusions drawn from the study. Besides, suggestions made to the Government, Financial Institutions and small entrepreneurs to enable them to play their respective roles in resolving the various problems faced by small scale industrial units.

P. Srinivas Subba Rao

ACKNOWLEDGMENTS

I express my sincere and deep sense of gratitude to my revered research guide Prof. A. K. Khadrekar, Faculty, Department of Commerce and former Head of the Department, Department of Management Studies and Research, Dhanwate National College. Nagpur for his consistent and invaluable guidance and continued encouragement throughout the course of the compilation and the preparation of this thesis.

I owe my special gratitude to the Principal Prof. G. G. Fukey and Prof. A. H. Vajre and Prof. Babun Taiwad of Commerce Department for their valuable advice during my study.

I am also thankful to Dr. K. Hanumantha Rao, Principal, M.R. V. G. P. G. Centre for his valuable advice during my study.

My sincere thanks to Mr. K. V. Sri Rama Rao, M. S., M/s. Sun Systems, Hyderabad for the qualitative and meticulous computer word processing.

P. Srinivas Subba Rao

CONTENTS

Preface

Acknowledgements

I.	**Introduction**	1
II.	**Objectives and Methodology**	36
III.	**Development of Small Scale Industries**	60
IV.	**Growth and Organisations of Sample Units**	98
V.	**An analysis of the Problems of Sample Units**	139
VI.	**Sickness in Small Scale Sector**	186
VII.	**Comparative Analysis of Problems of Sample Units**	211
VIII.	**Findings, Conclusions and Suggestions**	261
	Select Bibliography	271
	Index	

CHAPTER—I

INTRODUCTION

"Small Industry seems to fit into the economic and social conditions of most Asian countries better than large scale production."

I.L.O.

The recent years have witnessed a dramatic expansion in the small scale sector in almost all parts of the world. It is not only in developing countries that have experienced such a phenomenon but a similar experience has also been gathered by a large number of industrially developed countries like Japan, U.K, Germany, U.S.A, Switzerland, etc.

Japan for instance, achieved rapid industrialisation through the small scale sector in the latter half of the 19th century. The small scale sector in this country plays a catalytic and predominant role in the accelerated growth of the economy.

Even in the developed countries of western Europe, United Kingdom and United States of America there is a recognition that small and rural industries play a significant role in complementing the large industry and in providing opportunities for creative energies of the skilled people. The watch industry in Switzerland—the largest in the World—is based on the work of a multitude of small, almost cottage industry, units. So important were small firms considered in United Kingdom that a report (Boiton Committee, 1971) parodised the famous saying of Voltaire that "if small business does not exist, it would be necessary to invent it." In the United States of America Small business administration, more than 30 years old, had been placed on a statutory footing reporting directly to the president.

SMALL SCALE SECTOR—INDIAN ECONOMY

The small-scale sector is the hub of many economic activities in a developing country like India. The role played by this sector in the economic activity of advanced industrialised countries in no less. The socio-economic transformation of India cannot be achieved without paying adequate attention to the development of this labour intensive and capital sparing sector.

The small-scale sector has emerged as a dynamic and vibrant sector of Indian economy. Today, it accounts for nearly 35% of the gross value of output in the manufacturing sector and over 40% of the total exports from the country. In terms of value added this sector accounts for about 40% in the manufacturing sector. Next to agriculture, this sector's contribution to employment in magnificent. It is an excellent sector in the country's economy.

The small-scale sector has been assigned a pride of place in the country's industrial development programme, as it has the capacity to achieve economic growth in small gestation period, high employment potential and relatively limited financial requirements. In a developing nation like India where population is high and incomes are low, it is inevitable to develop the small industrial sector, which absorbs more men with low capital. Because of these, Mahatma Gandhi and his followers favoured Small Scale Industries.

In a labour-abundant and capital-scarce country like India, small-scale industries have come to occupy a significant position in the planned industrialisation of the economy. Most small-scale industries have low capital and high potential for employment generation. Besides, they possess locational flexibility, which serve as an effective instrument for achieving a wide dispersal of industries. Small-scale industrial units also serve as an instrument in achieving a wide dispersal of industries. Small-scale industrial units also serve as a means of bringing forth indigenous entrepreneurship and savings laying dormant particularly in semi-urban and rural areas.

IMPORTANCE OF SMALL SCALE INDUSTRIES

The following points further explain the importance of Small Scale Industries.

1. Small units which are highly innovative though they do not maintain their own research and development wings.
2. Small firms are quick in studying changes in tastes and fashions of consumers and in adjusting the production process and production accordingly.

3. Small enterprises are almost always locally owned and controlled and they can strengthen rather than destroy the extended family and other social systems and cultural traditions that are perceived as valuable in their own rights as well as symbols of national identity.
4. People who work in small enterprises are happier in their work than those who work in large ones in spite of lower wages and poor standards of safety, comfort and welfare facilities.
5. Small enterprises and new entrepreneurs were at the forefront practically every business boom of the last decade, whether it was computers, television sets, consumer electronics, garments, diamond exports or advertising.
6. It is only small-scale units which have a tendency to disperse over wider areas. According to the second all-India census on small scale units, 62.19% of the units are located in backward areas.

ADVANTAGES OF SMALL-SCALE SECTOR

The small scale sector provides immediate large employment and have a comparatively higher labour capital ratio; they need a shorter gestation period and relatively smaller markets to be economic.

The small scale sector has been assigned a pride of place in the country's industrial development programme due to the following reasons:

1. Small scale industrial units create immediate and permanent employment at a relatively small capital cost.
2. Small scale enterprises can be based on processing of locally produced raw materials.
3. From small scale industrial enterprises knowledge and skill can be transferred to other enterprises small enterprises may grow into medium sized enterprises.
4. Small Scale units offer a method of ensuring more equitable distribution of national income which is socially desirable.
5. Small scale industrial (projects) units can be taken up in a short period and hence can increase production in a short run.
6. Small scale units can save and earn foreign exchange by producing and exporting goods from local resources.

7. The development of small scale enterprises will create jobs in the rural areas of the developing countries where unemployment and under employment are high.
8. Small scale industries are generally labour intensive and do not require a large amount of capital. The energy of unemployed and under employed people may be used for productive purposes in an economy where capital is scarce.
9. A part from the linages between agricultural rural development and small-scale industrial enterprises there is an essential linkage between large scale enterprises and small scale enterprises in the sense that the former create opportunities or facilities for the growth of the later.
10. Majority of small scale units do not require a high level of technology.
11. Small units bring integration with rural economy on the one hand and large scale enterprises on the other.
12. Small scale units facilitate mobilisation of resources of capital and skills which often would remain inadequately utilised.
13. Small scale industries assist in dispersal and avoid problem which unplanned urbanisation tends to create.
14. Small units meet a substantial part of increased demand for consumer goods including mass consumption goods.
15. Small scale industries in developing countries help to create economic stability in society by diffusing prosperity and by checking the expansion of monopolies.

DEVELOPMENT OF SMALL SCALE INDUSTRY IN INDIA

In a developing economy like India small-scale industry constitutes the backbone of its economic structure. Its development create last employment opportunities for the people, effects decentralisation of industries by the creation of industrial estates and makes possible a redistribution of economic power and income. However, the advent of modern large scale mechanised industry, the imposition of restrictions on Indian trade by the British rulers and deteriorating socio-economic conditions lead to the decline of small-scale industry. But, within the provisions of the nation's policy of economic development after the attainment of independence, it has staged a grand recovery and is now on the path of progress towards great expansion. A brief view of small scale sector before and after independence can be discussed as follows:

PRE-INDEPENDENCE:

Before independence only cottage industries, villages industries or Agro based industries. These industries flourished in India in early times. They were main sources for income and employment and their products were noted for their excellence and artistic skill. "At a time when the West of Europe, the birth place of the modern industrial system, was inhabited by uncivilised tribes, India was famous for the wealth of her fuels and for the high artistic skill of her craftsmen."[1]

Professor weber wrote, "The skill of the Indians in the production of delicate woven fabrics, in the mixing of colours, the working of metals and precious stones, the preparation of essence and in all manners of technical arts, has from very early times, enjoyed a world-wide celebrity."[2] "The muslims of Dacca were famous ages ago, throughout the civilised world. Textile fabrics of inimitable fineness tapestry glittering with gold gems, rich embroideries and brocades, carpets wonderful for the most brilliant hue, furniture most elaborately carved, swords of forms and excellent temper are among the objectives that prove the perfection of art in India."[3]

These de reservations signify the prominence and the glory of the products of the cottage and small scale industries. In the pre-independence period, as many as 18 million entrepreneurs have established enterprises in this sector and contributed to the advancement of industry in the country.

Gandhian Thought

The case of supporting small scale industries in the scheme of Indian planning is based partly on ideological and partly on economic grounds. The ideological stand of thought linking small scale industry to cottage and village industries is derived from Gandhian faith in the role of village crafts for the promotion of rural uplift and employment. Gandhian economics in the economics of the 'Whole Man' as against the economics of "the economic man". His economics is based on the revival of village crafts because he preferred 'bread for all before cake for some'. Gandhiji's hostility to Urbanisation and modern mechanised industry is well known, so is his glorification of self-employment. Gandhiji firmly believed that the economic conditions of all village-folk would be improved if village crafts were re-vitalised.

The decay of these industries has been accelerated after the advent of the British, though the seed was sown in the Moghul period itself. The causes worked towards this situations were follows:

1. The competition from machine made goods of the British industry resulted in the fall in the demand for the Indian goods.
2. The Indian artisans were forced to work in the East India company's workshops for their livelihood, as they could not find sufficient demand for their homemade goods.
3. Another reason for the closer of the small units was discouraging policy of the East India Company.
4. The low cost foreign products influence resulted in the decline of Swadeshi goods.
5. With the disappearance of the native courts in Mughal Period, the small and cottage industries lost their patronage.

The National Planning Committee, set up in 1938 under the chairmanship of Pandit Jawaharlal Nehru, constituted a panel to study this problem.

Some of the cottage and small industries have shown remarkable progress and have survived under the East India Company rule in India due to the following reasons.

Indian agriculturists needed supplementary occupation to absorb their idle time and to augment their low earnings. The cottage and village industries provided additional occupation for the idle agriculturists in the off season.

Therefore, a large number of repair services of different types that have followed in the wake of large scale industries, can be and are indeed carried on in small establishments in the vicinity of large industries.

The illiteracy and poverty, the lack of alternative means of employment, lack of demand for their products, home living and conservative nature and social and religious instructions have forced them to stick to their age-old ancestral profession.

After Independence :

Since independence, the Government of India, realising the socio-economic significance of the role of the small scale industries, has initiated several positive measures for their development. The industrial policy pronouncements, the progressive allocations made in Five Year Plans, the creation of different promoting and supporting organisations and the nationalisation of commercial banks reflect the spirit and effort of the Government towards the creation of a favourable climate for the growth and working of small industry. In fact, the progress and the performance achieved by small scale industry are the result of the various measures initiated by the Government for their growth and effective working.

SMALL SCALE INDUSTRIES AND FIVE-YEAR PLANS

***First Five Year Plan* (1951-56)** : To protect the small scale sector, the First Five Year Plan recommended 'common production programme to ensure that while large and small units both make their contribution to the total requirement of the community, the small units would fulfil the targets set for them.

An important landmark in the history of the development of small scale industry in 1953-54 which was jointly sponsored by the GOI and Ford Foundation. The team India was the visit of international perspective team in its report recommended the setting up of regional extension Institutes to provide services in areas of technical, marketing and financial matters. In pursuance of recommendation made by the team, four Regional Extension Institutes were set up at Bombay, Calcutta, Delhi, and Madras, to provide technical assistance to small industrialists. Two organisations constituted by the Government to extend further help and guidance were small Industries Development Organisation (SIDO), 1954 and National Small Industries Corporation (NSIC), 1955. Thus, the ground work was laid for the growth of small scale industry in India during the first plan period.

***Second Five Year Plan* (1956-61)** : The second Five Year Plan gave prominence to heavy and basic industries but did not neglect the small industries or the small producer. In fact, the basic philosophy of the plan was not only to encourage small industries, but to establish an economic order with the small producer at the center. The plan also endorsed the "Common Production Programme" the proposal for non-expansion of the capacity of selected large scale industries, the position of a cess or an excise duty on the production of some large industries, the development of industrial Co-operative and a scheme of special assistance to small industries.

***Third Five Year Plan* (1961-66) :** Third five year plan aimed at a greater diversification of the production in the small sector and a closer integration between the large and small sector in specified items. Another scheme of the plan was to reserve certain items exclusively for development in the small scale sector.

***Annual Plans* (1966-69) :** During the period from 1966-69 three annual plans were prepared and adopted before starting Fourth Plan. A considerable amount was allotted for the development of Small Scale Industries in these three years.

***Fourth Five Year Plan* (1969-74) :** One main objective of small industries programme has been to protect such industries. The Government failed in this objective. The Fourth Plan while admitting this fact cautioned the Government in the following words, "The operation of the industrial licensing system has not been effective in preventing competition from the large industries and in providing the required degree of initial protection. Nor has it been possible to prevent concentration of industries in large cities and towns."[4]

The estimated outlay in the public sector for village and small industries worked out to Rs. 251 crores in the fourth plan. Besides, the total amount of investment in the private sector exceeded the target of Rs. 560 crores envisaged in the plan.

***Fifth Five Year Plan* (1974-79) :** Fifth Five Year Plan rightly mentions: "A significantly large number of persons already dependent on traditional industries like handlooms, Agriculture, Coir, Khadi and village industries are living below the poverty time. Therefore, the principal objective of the programme for development of different small industries in the Fifth Plan are to facilitate the removal of poverty and inequality in consumption standards of their persons through creation of large scale opportunities for fuller and additional productive employment and Improvement of their skills so as to improve their level of earning."[5]

With this end in view, the revised Fifth Plan allocated a sum of Rs. 510 crores village and small industries in the public sector.

***Sixth Five Year Plan* (1980-85) :** During the Sixth Five Year Plan the programmes for the village and small industries sector would be so designed as to sub-service some objectives they are mentioned in the following paragraph.

Improvement in the level of production earning particularly of the artisans, though measures like upgradation of skills and technologies and producer oriented marketing etc. Creation of additional employment opportunities on a dispersal and decentralised basis. Significant contribution to growth in the manufacturing sector through *inter alia*, further utilisation of existing installed capacities. Establishment of a wide external base through appropriate training and package of incentives. Creation of viable structure of village and small sector so as to progressively reduce the role of subsidies and expand efforts in export promotion.

***Seventh Five Year Plan* (1985-90) :** Seventh plan laid down the following objectives for village and small scale industries:

1. to assist in the growth and wide spread dispersal of industries;
2. to increase the level of earning of artisans;
3. to ensure regular supply of goods and services through use of local skills and resources;
4. and to develop entrepreneurship is combination with improved methods of production.

The seventh plan made a provision of Rs. 2,752 crores for village and small industries which is 1.5 per cent of total outlay.

***Eighth Five Year Plan* (1992-97) :** Eighth plan clearly states "one of the areas of priority of the eighth plan is generation of adequate employment to achieve near full employment level by the turn of this century. Several activities pertaining to this sector like processing allied activities have been identified as critical goals in priority sectors. It is possible for detail programmes of khadi, village industries, handlooms, sericulture, and handicrafts to integrated local area development programmes for selected villages for poverty alleviation through increase in employment. It is also envisaged that entry into service sector which is expected to play a major role in generating employment during eighth plan and the 'informal ' sector will be made free of innumerable rules, regulations and bureaucratic controls. Further, research and innovation in the tools and techniques of traditional occupations, including those of rural artisans will be encouraged and their extensive adoptation will be induced."[6]

With this philosophy for the development of village and small scale industries, the Eighth plan allocates Rs. 6,334 crores i.e. per cent of the total public sector outlay for the development of village and small industries.

The Small Scale Sector crossed the plan estimates by the second year of the plan.

The following Table 1.1 shows the plan outlays Small Scale Industries from first five year plan to eighth five year plan.

Table—1.1 Outlays for the Development of Small Scale Industries in the Five Year Plans

Plans	*Plan Period*	*Total Outlays (Rs. in crores)*
First Five Year Plan	1951-56	42
Second Five Year Plan	1956-61	187
Third Five Year Plan	1961-66	241
Annual Plans	1966-69	132
Fourth Five Year Plan	1969-74	251
Fifth Five Year Plan	1974-79 1979-80	510
Sixth Five Year Plan	1980-85	1,780
Seventh Five Year Plan	1985-90	2,752

Source : Planning Commission, Government of India, Eighth Five Year Plan, 1992-97.

SMALL INDUSTRY—INDUSTRIAL POLICIES

That the small industries have a specific role to play was underlined by the *Industrial Policy 1948* which state that cottage and small scale industries are particularly suited for better utilisation of local resources and for the achievement of local self-sufficiency in respect of certain types of essential goods. After the formulation of First Five Year Plan, a committee was appointed by the planning commission with Professor D.G.Karve as chairman. The committee recommended that any development programme for small industry should be decentralised, should aim at gradual improvement in techniques without reducing job opportunities, should assure marketing through co-operatives, and aim at positive promotional support rather than enforce protection or reservation.

A small scale industries board was constituted in 1954 and a number of helping schemes such as supply of machinery on hire purchase, liberal and wider grants under the State Aid to Industries Act, and price preference in Government purchase were also initiated to provide support to the small sector.

The Government announced its second *Industrial Policy in 1956* which replaced the Industrial Policy Resolution of 1948. This Industrial Policy statement explicitly makes it clear that the "Small Scale Industries provide immediate large scale employment, offer a method of ensuring a more equitable distribution of national income and facilitate an effective mobilisation of resources of capital and skill which might otherwise remain unutilised."

The State had followed a policy of supporting small scale industries by restricting the volume of production in the large scale sector, by differential taxation, or by direct subsidies. While such measures continue to be taken wherever necessary, the aim of the State Policy is to ensure that the decentralised sector acquires sufficient vitality to be self-supporting and its development is integrated with that of large scale industry. The State will, therefore, concentrate on measures designed to improve the competitive strength of the small scale producer.

The Janata Government has given a fitting place to small scale sector through *New Industrial Policy 1977*. This policy puts its thus: The emphasis of industrial policy has so far been on large industries, neglecting cottage industries totally and giving small industries the minimum importance. It is the firm policy of this Government to change this approach. The main thrust of new industrial policy will be on effective promotion of cottage and small industries widely dispersed in rural areas and small towns.

To bring about this change the industrial policy statement has suggested six specific measures.

1. It is the policy of the Government that whatever can be produced by small, cottage industries, must only be so produced. The number of products reserved for small sector has been increased from 180 to 504 and again enlarging the list of reserved items to 807.
2. Special attention will be given to units in the "Tiny Sector", namely those with investment in machinery and equipment up to one lakh rupees and situated in towns and in villages with a population of less than 50,000.

3. Special legislation will be introduced to give due recognition and adequate protection to the self-employed in cottage and household industries.
4. The focal point of development for small sector and cottage industries will be taken away from big cities and state capitals to the district headquarters. In each district there will be one agency to deal with all requirements of small and village industries. This will be called "District Industries Centre,"
5. Special arrangements for the marketing of the products of the small sector will be made by providing services such as product standardisation quality control, marketing surveys etc.
6. Technical change will be encouraged in the traditional sector, as for instance the production of "Nai Khadi."

When the Congress Government re-captured power at the Centre in 1980, a New *Industrial Policy* was announced *in July 1980* based on the proposition that 'industrialisation is the *sine quanon* of economic progress." The salient features of the policy are mentioned hereunder:

1. to increase capital investment in small sector to Rs. 25 lakhs;
2. to increase capital investment in tiny sector from Rs. 1 lakh to Rs. 2 lakhs; and
3. to increase capital investment in ancillary units to Rs. 35 lakhs.

Besides, the Government intended to strengthen the existing arrangements to finance small scale units and make changes if necessary to ease the credit problems of the sector. Moreover, the system of reservation of items for exclusive production by small scale units would continue in future.

The industrial policy statement of 1985 was also accorded importance to the small scale sector and made some suitable policy changes.

The new Government announced new policy measures for promoting and strengthening of small tiny and village enterprises on August,6, 1991 through its *New Industrial Policy statement, 1991.*

The primary objective of this policy, during the nineties would be to impart more vitality and growth impetus to the sector so that the sector could contribute in terms of growth of output, employment and export, the other objectives of the policy are:

1. to decentralise and delicense the sector;
2. to deregulate and debureaucratise sector;
3. to review all statutes, regulations and procedures and effect suitable modification when necessary;
4. to promote small enterprises especially industries in tiny sector;
5. to motivate small and sound entrepreneurs to set up new green enterprises in the country;
6. to involve traditional and reputed voluntary organisations in the intensive development of Khadi village industries through area approach;
7. to maintain a sustained growth in productivity and attain competitiveness in the market economy especially in the international market;
8. to industrialise backward areas of the country; and
9. to accelerate the process of development of modern small and tiny enterprises and village industries through appropriate incentives, institutional support and infrastructure investments.

THE DEFINITION OF SMALL SCALE UNIT

The first official criterion for small-scale industry dates back to the second five Year Plan when it was in terms of gross investments in land, building, plant and machinery and the strength of the labour force. Subsequently, on the recommendation of the Federation of Association of Small Industries of India (FASII) an apex level organisation of small scale industry. Set up under the aegis of the Ford Foundation Team, only the investment in fixed assets in plant and machinery, whether held in ownership terms or by lease or by hire-purchase, instead of fixing the limit on overall investment, was considered for granting the status of Small Scale Industrial units. From time to time there have been many changes in the ceiling limit of investment in plant and machinery.

The term "small-scale industry" has been defined in three ways. The conventional definition includes cottage and handicraft industries which employ traditional labour-intensive methods to produce traditional products, largely in village households.

The operational definition for policy purpose includes all those undertakings having an investment in fixed assets in plant and machinery, whether held on ownership terms or by lease or hire-purchase, not exceeding Rs. 60 lakhs.

The third definition of small-scale industry relates to national income accounting. This includes all manufacturing and processing activities, including maintenance and repair services, undertaken by both household and non-household small-scale manufacturing units, which are not registered under the Factories Act.

Accordingly, a small industry is presently defined as "a unit engaged in manufacturing, servicing, repairing, processing and preservation of goods having investment in plant and machinery, at an original cost not exceeding Rs. 60 lakhs.

The following statements explains the evolutionary changes that took place in the definition of Small Scale Industry since 1948.

Evolution of the Definition of Small-scale Industries

Date	*Defining authority*	*Main features*	
		Capital investment in plant and machinery	*Number of persons employed*
1	*2*	*3*	*4*
April - 48	Industrial policy resolution	All industries in handlooms, handicrafts, coil, silk & khadi and village industries are grouped into the small sector.	
Jan-55	Small-Scale industries board	Rs. 5 lakhs	50 (if using power) or 100 (without the use of power) per shift.
Sep-57	Small-scale industries board	Rs. 5 lakhs	"Pershift" has been changed into "multiple shift" irrespective of the number of persons employed.

cont.

1	*2*	*3*	*4*
Jan-60	Small-scale industries board	Rs. 5 lakhs	Irrespective of the number of persons employed.
July-66	Ministry of industries, Government of India	Rs. 7.5 lakhs	Irrespective of the number of persons employed.
Nov-74	Small-scale industries board	Rs. 10 lakhs	Irrespective of the number of persons employed.
July--80	Industrial policy resolution, Government of India	Rs. 20 lakhs	Irrespective of the number of persons employed.
Mar-85	- od-	Rs. 35 lakhs	- do -
Aug-91	Small Scale industrial policy statement	Rs. 60 lakhs	- do - (Rs. 75 lakhs for export-oriented units).

Recent Definition

Based on the recommendation of Abid Hussian Committee during the year 1996-97 the National Front Government had increased the limit of investment in small Scale units from Rs. 60 lakhs to Rs. 3 crores. However the present BJP Government in thinking of reduction the investment limit in a Small Scale unit to Rs. 1 crore instead of Rs. 3 crores.

Liberalisation—Its impact

The new economic policies or the economic reform programmes encompass reforms in the industrial trade, fiscal and monetary policies. These will, of course, generate far-reaching changes in industry. The process of industrial restructuring has, however, just begun, the transition period has also seen recession and other adverse features such as credit squeeze, import compression, high interest rates etc., during the adjustment process. The impact of liberalisation on the small scale sector will be felt only in the coming years.

Given the waste industry/ economic base of the country and the many layered structures of demand, it is unlikely that this process will affect the small scale sector adversely in the long run. This will, however, depend on the ability of the small scale sector to take advantage of its inherent strengths of quick response, innovation and flexibility. It will also depend on the extent and efficacy of the institutional frame work responsible for its promotion and support.

To assess the response of Small Scale sector and its ability to reposition itself in the changed business environment, a SWOT (strengths, weaknesses, opportunities, threats) Analysis 7 of small scale sector is carried out. This analysis is presented in the next two pages.

Swot Analysis Opportunities

- impetus to quality, efficiency and better technology.
- "Big opportunities in small" Development commissioner, SSIs, New Delhi.
- dismantling of the controls regime.
- variety/availability of raw materials and components.
- access to hitherto, in accessible sectors.
- opportunity to restructure/diversity.
- integration and linkages with large/medium industry.

Strengths

- Quick response (immediacy of decision making)
- flexible production systems
- Innovation and specialisation
- Customised production

These advantages are realised in practice whenever these units depict a higher level of product innovation and technology/quality awareness.

Weaknesses

The major disadvantage of small enterprise in a competitive environment is that of lack of resources in terms of:

- limited access to and higher cost of capital
- limited access to information and markets.
- inadequate managerial resources
- external reliance for support services.

Therefore, a sustainable system for promotion of modern small scale units would involve setting up of adequate institutional arrangements to provide common support services to these units in their various requirements.

Threats

- increased competition particularly in the consumer goods sector.
- inadequate access to institutional credit/higher interest rates.
- natural disadvantages in backward areas.
- threat to employment opportunities.
- threat local/indigenous technologies, i.e., Tiny and village industries.
- vulnerability in terms of access to technology information and advanced management practices.
- inadequate standardisation of products, processes components, parts, subassemblies etc. in order to encourage linkage between small and large units.

Reservation of Items

The Government has been following a policy of reservation of items for exclusive development in small scale sector. During 1970-71 there were only 216 items in the reserved list, this number increased to 834 during 1980-81 and at present (1997) there are 822 items under reserved list. This is being continuously reviewed and revised. Number of items reserved for manufacturing of small scale industries from 1980-97 can be seen in the Table 1.2

Table—1.2 Reservation of Items for Exclusive Production in Small Scale Sector

Sl. No.	*Year*	*No.of items reserved (cumulative figures)*
1	1980	834
2	1990	836
3	1991	836
4	1992	836
5	1993	836
6	1994	836
7	1995	836
8	1996	836
9	1997	822

Source : Economic Survey, 1996-97.

CONTRIBUTION OF SMALL SCALE SECTOR TO INDIAN ECONOMY

The small scale sector which plays a pivotal role in the Indian economy in terms of unemployment and growth has recorded a high rate of growth link independence in spite of tough competition from large sector. It is now one of the fastest growing sectors in the country. It has made steady progress during recent years. The good performance of the small scale units is evident from their number, production, employment and foreign exchange earnings. During the last decade alone, the small sector has progressed from the production of simple consumer goods like soap, detergents, leather goods to the manufacture of many sophisticated products like electronic control systems, micro-wave components, electro medical equipment, T.V. sets etc.

According to the figures supplied by the office of the development commissioner, as shown in Table 1.3 Small Scale industries, there were a total of 8.74 lakh small scale units in 1980-81, 8.05 lakh units in 1979-80, 13.55 lakh units in 1985-86, 19.38 lakh units in 1990-91 and 27.24 lakh units in 1995-96 and 29.14 lakh units in 1996-97. The value of investment is also considerable, which was amounting to Rs. 24, 874 crores in 1994-95 i.e. about 400 per cent higher than what it was in 1980-81. Even after due allowances are made for the fairly steep increase in the price of investment goods, the fact remains that the phase of investment in this sector is quite heartening.

Contribution to Employment

The root cause for unemployment in India is the over growing population which has out paced the development of industry and agriculture. For a country oils, with limited financial resources and huge reservoir of human resources, small scale industry is the only means for solving the unemployment problem. With its inherent nature of labour intensiveness, small scale industry has been providing employment at an increased rate which is evident from Table 1.5.

It can be noticed from the table that employment generated by the small scale industry increased significantly to 153 lakhs by 1995-96 from 96 lakhs in 1985-86 with a growth rate of 50 per cent.

Table—1.3 Small-Scale Sector Growth over the years (Units, Production, Employment, Investment and Exports)

Year	*No. of units (in lakhs)*	*Employment (in lakhs)*	*Investment (in Rs. crores)*	*Production at current prices (Rs. crores)*	*Export (Rs. in crores)*	*Share in total exports (%)*
1980-81	8.74	71.00	5,850	28,060	1,643	24.5
1981-82	9.62	75.00	6,280	32,600	2,071	26.5
1982-83	10.59	79.00	6,000	35,000	2,045	23.2
1983-84	11.58	84.10	7,360	41,620	2,164	22.1
1984-85	12.42	90.00	8,380	50,520	2,553	21.7
1985-86	13.55	96.00	9,585	61,228	2,769	25.4
1986-87	14.76	101.40	10,975	72,250	3,617	29.3
1987-88	15.76	107.00	12,621	87,300	4,345	28.8
1988-89	17.12	113.00	15,229	1,06,875	5,681	28.1
1989-90	18.27	119.60	18,196	1,32,320	7,990	29.9
1990-91	19.38	124.30	19,302	1,55,340	9,100	28.2
1991-92	20.82	129.80	20,438	1,78,699	13,883	31.5
1992-93	22.35	134.10	21,816	2,09,300	17,785	33.1
1993-94	23.85	138.40	22,934	2,41,648	25,307	36.3
1994-95	25.71	146.56	24,874	2,93,990	29,068	35.2
1995-96	27.24	153.00	N.A.	3,37,207	36,470	32.0
1996-97	29.14	158.91	N.A.	4,03,824	40,355	34.0
1997-98	30.14	167.20		4,65171	44,442	35.2
(E) 1998-99	31.21	171.58		5,38,357	49,481	34.9

Source : Development Commissioner, Small Scale Industry.
Annual Report, Ministry of Industry 1996-97.
Economic Survey, 1996-97.

N.A : Not available

The growth of small scale industrial units in terms of their number, employment, production and exports are shorn graphically in GI,G2,G3 and G4 graphs respectively.

GRAPH—1 GROWTH IN NUMBER OF SMALL SCALE INDUSTRIAL UNITS

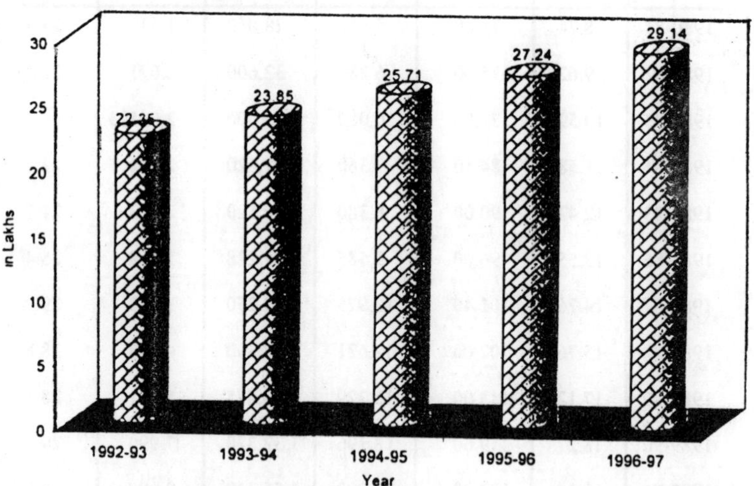

GRAPH—2 GROWTH OF EMPLOYMENT IN SMALL SCALE INDUSTRIAL UNITS

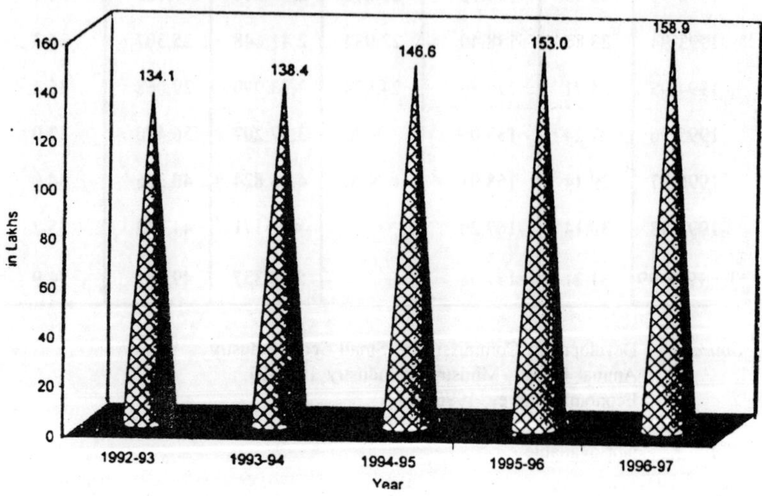

GRAPH—3 GROWTH OF PRODUCTION IN SMALL SCALE INDUSTRIAL UNITS

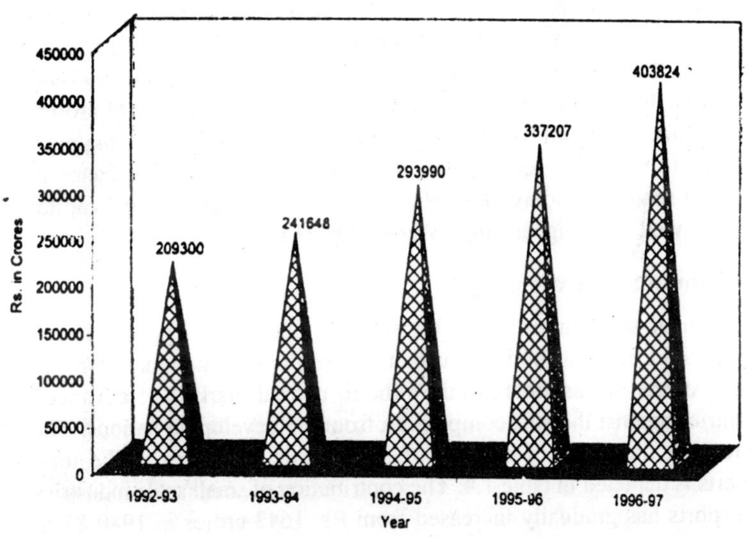

GRAPH—4 GROWTH OF EXPORTS IN SMALL SCALE INDUSTRIAL UNITS

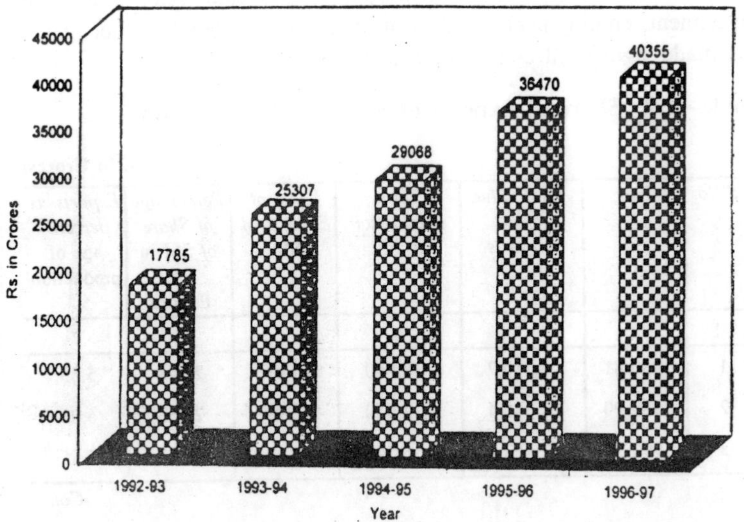

Contribution to Output

Small industry has been contributing significantly to the gross national product of the country. Table 1.3 shows that the total production of small industry was Rs. 28,060 crores in the 1980-81 which rose to Rs. 61,228 crores in 1985-86 and Rs. 3,37,207 crores in 1995-96. However, the output during 1996-97 came down to Rs.3,03,824 crores. Except this, during all the years the output was increasing. If a big push is given to the small scale sector, it can become a stabilising factor in a capital-scarce economy like India by providing a higher output capital ratio as well as a higher employment capital ratio.

Contribution to Exports

Small scale industry has registered a phenomenal growth in the export field by contributing substantially to the total national earnings from exports. It has entered into hitherto untried markets of advanced countries against the stiff competition from the developing nations. The increasing the share of exports of small scale industries in the total exports is depicted in table 1.4. The contribution of small scale industries to exports has gradually increased from Rs. 1643 crores in 1980-81 to Rs. 40,355 crores during 1996-97. It's share had progressively risen from 24.48 per cent in the year 1980-81 to about 33.97 per cent in the year 1996-97. However, the year to year changes are significant.

A view of the progress made by the small scale sector in terms of investment, employment, production and exports does bear out that it has made significant contribution to the economy.

Table—1.4 Share of Exports of Small Scale Industries

(Rs. In Crores)

S.No.	*Year*	*Total value of all Exports*	*Total Production in SSI*	*Value of Exports of SSI*	*Percentage of Share of SSI in* Total Exports	*Exports as percent-* age of production
1	2	3	4	5	6	7
1	1980-81	6,710.7	28,060	1,643	24.48	5.85
2	1989-90	27,681.4	1,32,320	7,990	27.55	6.03
3	1990-91	32,553.3	1,55,340	9,100	29.68	5.85

Cont...

1	2	3	4	5	6	7
4	1991-92	44,041.8	1,78,699	13,833	31.52	7.76
5	1992-93	53,688.3	2,09,300	17,785	33.12	8.49
6	1993-94	69,751.0	2.41,648	25,307	36.28	10.47
7	1994-95	82,675.6	2,93,990	29,068	35.16	9.88
8	1995-96	1,06,353.3	3.37,207	36,470	32.03	10.81
9	1996-97	1,17,250.0	4,03,824	40,355	33.97	10.00

Source : Annual Report, Development Commissioner, Small Scale Industry. *Ministry of Industry, 1996-97.*

SMALL SCALE SECTOR AND INSTITUTIONAL SET-UP

The department of small scale industries, Government of India sets out the policy framework for promotion and development of small scale industries. It monitors and evaluates the growth and performance of the sector and implements appropriate policies, programmes and schemes. Hence it is apex institution for supporting small scale industries. The small scale supported by a host of central/state Government institutions, autonomous institutions and non Government organisations. A brief details of these are provided here.

SMALL INDUSTRIES DEVELOPMENT ORGANISATION (SIDO)

It is a subordinate office of the department of Small Scale Industries. It is an apex body and is a nodal agency for formulation co-ordinating and monitoring the policies and programmes for promotion and development of small scale industries.

It also renders comprehensive service including consultancy in technical and managerial aspects; training, common facility services, testing and tool facilities, Marketing and Marketing assistance, for small scale units. These services are provided through a network of institutions and associate agencies created for specific purposes.

SERVICES OF SIDO

A variety of support services are available to small units from SIDO and its associate institutions. A brief description of the services being rendered is given below:

1. Entrepreneurship Development and Training;
2. Training and Extension Services;

3. Skills Development;
4. Assistance to entrepreneurs development institutes;
5. Preparation of project profiles;
6. Plant modernisation studies;
7. Testing services;
8. Subcontract exchanges;
9. Establishment of total rooms and product and process development centres.

SMALL INDUSTRIES SERVICE INSTITUTES (SISIs)

There are 28 SISIs and 31 branch institutes set up in state capitals and other places all over the country. Their main functions are as follows:

- Interface between Central and State Government;
- Technical support services and consultancy services;
- Entrepreneurial development programmes;
- Development efforts;
- Promotional programmes;
- Export promotion liaison.

NATIONAL SMALL INDUSTRIES CORPORATION (NSIC)

NSIC is a Government of India enterprise established in 1955. Over the years it has emerged as a premier institution for Small Scale Industries which provides technology and marketing support.

Its main functions are as follows:

- Machinery hire purchase scheme for small scale units;
- Equipment leasing scheme;
- Marketing support programmes under consortia marketing;
- Single point registration scheme for marketing;
- Technology assistance;
- Development and training activities;
- Raw material assistance.

NATIONAL INSTITUTE FOR ENTREPRENEURSHIP AND SMALL BUSINESS DEVELOPMENT (NIESBUD)

The NIESBUD was established in 1983 by Ministry of Industry, Government of India, as an apex body for co-ordinating and overseeing the activities of various institutions, agencies engaged in entrepreneurship development in the area of small industry and business.

It has the following objectives:

- to serve as an apex national level resource institute to accelerate the process of entrepreneurship development;
- to support other institutions in carrying out entrepreneurship development activities;
- to evolve standardised materials, process of selection, training support and sustenance to potential entrepreneurs;
- to provide information support to promoters, entrepreneurs;
- to organise courses and confer appropriate certifications;
- to provide national and international forums for interactions and exchange of ideas; and
- to train the trainers.

SMALL INDUSTRIES DEVELOPMENT BANK OF INDIA (SIDBI)

It is an apex bank set up to meet the credit needs of the small scale sector, the bank commenced operations on 2nd April, 1990. It performs the following functions:

- Refinance of term loans extended to small scale industries by banks and state financial institutions;
- Equipment refinance to Small Scale Industries Units;
- Special refinance schemes for in house quality control facilities DG sets, pollution control equipment, energy saving systems;
- Financial assistance to marketing organisations marketing Small Scale industries products;
- Loans to organisations/institutions to set up industrial estates for small scale industries;
- Equity type assistance schemes e.g. seed capital scheme, National Equity Fund Scheme;

- Single window scheme (SWS) to provide both term loan and working capital to Small Scale Industries through one agency;
- Special reference schemes for women entrepreneurs;
- Bills rediscounting scheme for sale/acquisition of machinery on deferred payment terms;
- Direct discounting scheme for equipment and components;
- Pre-shipment credit in foreign currency to EOUs;
- Venture capital fund with a corpus of Rs. 20 crores. Resource support to factoring companies and other institutions promoting Small Scale Industries.

Up to the year 1993-94 SIDBI has sanctioned an aggregate assistance of Rs. 13795 Crores and made disbursements of Rs. 10960 Crores. Among the new schemes started/assisted by SIDBI are 'Factoring services' for small scale industries and a venture capital fund.

There are other Autonomous Institutions Extending Support to Small Scale Industries. A brief study regarding those institutions is also given here.

1) ***National Institute of Small Industry Extension and Training (NISIET)*** Two such institutes are located at Hyderabad and Gauhati; These provide Training, Development, Management documentation support to various agencies concerned with Small Scale Industries.

2) ***National Institute of Design, Ahmedabad*** is a premium design School of the nation. It also provides specialized course in product design in areas of furniture ceramics, Textile printing, leather plastics and metal forming to small scale industries.

3) ***National Productivity Council (NPC)*** and its local branches provide help in improving productivity in small scale industrial units.

4) ***Seven product cum process development centres*** in areas of ceramics, foundry, sports goods, electrical appliances, electronics, glass and essential oils.

5) ***Ten tool rooms*** located in different parts of the country.

6) ***Four central Footwear Training Centres*** for training manpower in leather and footwear products.

INDUSTRY ASSOCIATIONS

The Industry Associations provide the small scale industries with common platform to voice their needs to indicate co-operative efforts in promoting small scale industries—Governments, policies in recent years have stressed the increasing role of the Industry Associations and the Non-Gazetted Officers in setting up common facilities and other co-operative ventures in areas of Technology, Marketing and other support services.

MAJOR NATIONAL LEVEL ASSOCIATIONS

There are 8 major national level associations which are formed to protect the interests of small Scale Industries. Their names are given hereunder:

- Federation of Association of Small Industries of India (FASII);
- Indian Council of Small Industries;
- Indian Federation of Tiny Enterprises;
- World Association of Small and Medium Enterprises;
- All India Manufacturers Organisation;
- Federation of Indian Chamber of Commerce and Industry;
- PHD Chamber of Commerce and Industry;
- Confederation of Indian Industry.

Industry associations also exist at State levels. Product specific associations look after the interests of their member units.

SMALL SCALE INDUSTRIES BOARD

The range of development work in small scale industries involves several department/Ministries and several organs of the central/state Governments. To facilitate co-ordination and inter institutional linkages, the Small Scale Industries Board has been constituted.

It is a apex advisory body constituted to render advice to the Government on all issues pertaining to the small scale sector. The industries Minister of the Government of India is the chairman and the Board comprises among others, state industry ministers, some members of parliament, secretaries of various departments of Government of India, financial institutions, public sector undertakings, Industry associations and eminent experts in the field.

INCENTIVES AND FACILITIES

Central as well as State Governments have evolved numerous schemes to provide incentives and facilities for small enterprises. These relate to the areas of fiscal concessions, credit allocations and instruments of preference and protection.

The following are the package of incentives and facilities provided by Central Government:

Excise Exemption

Excise duty concessions have been given to the small scale industries in what is called the Excise Duty Exemption Scheme for Small Industries. This is to enable the Small Scale Industries to compete on favourable terms with their counterparts in the large and medium sector.

Excise Duty Exemption Scheme: As of now, the Excise Duty Exemption Scheme applies to the entire small scale industries spectrum. The relief is as follows:

Clearance Slab (Rs. in lakhs)	*Rate of Duty*
0-30	Nil
30-50	Normal duty less 10% points subject to minimum of 5%.
50-75	Normal duty less 5% points subject to minimum of 5%.

The scheme is applicable to all Small Scale Industries whether registered or not with annual turnover limit of up to Rs. 200 lakhs.

Direct Taxes

- At present there does not exist any exclusive scheme of direct tax concessions for small scale industries .
- Like any other industrial unit, new small scale units can avail income tax rebate by way of deduction equal to 25% of their

profits for a period of 10 years (section 80-IA of Income Tax Act) provided the unit employs more than 10 persons.

Tax Holiday Scheme

In the union Budget for 1993-94 a five year tax holday has been granted for new industrial undertakings located in all of the North Eastern States, Jammu and Kashmir, Himachal Pradesh, Sikkim, Goa and U.T. of Andaman and Nicobar Islands, Dadar and Nagar Haveli, Daman and Diu, Lakshadweep and Pondicherry. This has now been extended to backward districts from the year 1994-95.

CREDIT POLICIES

The Government has had a focussed credit policy for small scale industries. The components of the credit policies, as at present, are stated below:

Priority Sector Lending: Credit flow to the small scale sector is ensured as part of the priority sector lending by banks.

Institutional Arrangements: Small industries Development Bank of India (SIDBI) is the apex refinance bank. Term loans are provided by State Financial Corporations (SFCs), Scheduled Banks to Small Industries.

National Equity Fund Scheme (NEFS)

Under the scheme, Small Scale units are given equity type seed capital assistance to meet the margin money requirements of small units. Servicing is charged at nominal rate of 1%. The NEFS was setup with a corpus of Rs. 10 Crores and is administered by SIDBI. The scope of the scheme includes projects with outlays upto Rs. 10 lakhs and the quantum of assistance available is upto Rs. 1.5 lakhs.

Infrastructural Development Schemes and Special Programmes

Both the central and state Governments have conceived and implemented a multitude of schemes for development of infrastructure conducive for growth of Small Scale industries. Also to attain the cherished objective of equity and income distribution, the SIDO and its associate institutions help to implement special programmes for employment generation. The following are some of the development schemes and special programmes.

Growth Centre Scheme

In order to promote industrialisation of backward areas, the Central Government announced in June 1988 the scheme for establishing 70 growth centers though out the country, Each growth center would be bestowed with the best of infrastructural facilities to facilitate and promote industrial growth.

About 65 Growth Centers have been identified. An important criteria for identification of Growth Center is that is sphere of influence should cover an area of about 40 to 800 hectares.

About 28 Growth Centers are in various stage of completion. The total central assistance released till 1993-94 was Rs. 68.25 crores.

Industrial Estate Programme

Industrial estate programme in India is perhaps the biggest programme undertaken by any developing country. The programme started in 1992 when the first such estate was established at Hadapsat in Maharashtra. The main objective of the programme is to encourage and support the creation, expansion and modernisation of small scale industries through provision of factory accommodation, common service facilities and assistance and servicing throughout, all stages of establishments and operation and developing sub contracting relationships within the small scale and large scale industries and specialised manufacturing activities. Subsequently, the programme also assumed the role of regional development through provision of built-in factory accomodation with the requisite facilities and services in semi-urban, rural and backward areas.

Integrated Infrastructural Development Scheme

The scheme is envisaged to augment infrastructural facilities in the rural and backward areas with special emphasis on linkages between agriculture and industry. The schemes will cover those centrally declared backward districts which have not been given coverage under the growth centre scheme.

Transport Subsidy

This scheme provides an incentive to industries setup in hilly, remote and inaccessible areas. Under the scheme subsidy ranging from 50% to 90% is admissible on transport costs incurred for movement of raw materials and finished goods from designated rail heads/ports up to the location of the industrial unit and vice versa.

Details of Areas Eligible for Transport Subsidy

S. No.	*Name of State—UT*	*Areas Eligible*	*Designated railbased/ port*
1.	Jammu & Kashmir	Whole state	Pathankot/Jammu Whichever is Nearer
2.	North Eastern States Assam, Meghalaya, Manipur, Nagland Tripura, Arunachal Pradesh, Mizoram and Sikkim.	Whole of the Areas of the State listed.	Siliguri
3.	Hilly areas of Uttar Pradesh	Dehradun, Chamoli, Nainital, Garhwal Uttarkashi, Pithorgarh	Dehradun, Rishikesh, Moradabad, Bareilly, Kotdwara, Shajhanpur, Rampur.
4.	Andaman & Nicobar	Whole of the Union territory	Madras
5.	Lakshadweep	Whole of the Union territory	Cochin
6.	Darjeeling Dist.of West Bengal	Whole of District	Siliguri.

Ancillary Development Programme

Up to 1970, there was no systematic development of ancillary industry in the country. A separate cell was created in the office of DC (SSI) for planning and development of Small Scale Industrial units as ancillaries. The programme began with Public Sector Undertakings which started developing ancillaries to help them in souring sub-assemblies or components. By 1980 more than 2000 captive ancillary units were set up for various public sector undertakings. In order to develop ancillary units and to keep their technology updated in line with the requirement of parent units, the definition of ancillary units provides a higher investment limit of Rs. 75 lakhs in plant and machinery against Rs. 60 lakhs for other Small Scale Industrial units.

Entrepreneurship Development Programmes

The Government of India had well recognised the importance and the need for systematic implementation of EDPS way back in early 1970 for the benefit of technically qualified youngsters. SIDO took pioneering steps to conduct EDPS throughout the country. Then a set of Governmental and non-Governmental EDOs (Entrepreneurship Development Organisations) came into being, which included Technical Consultancy Organisations (TCOs) also.

The 1980s saw the establishment of resource institutions in the field of Entrepreneurship Development such as NIESBUD, in Delhi and EDI in Ahmedabad. SIDO has recently launched a 'A bare foot manager' scheme to create a cadre of personnel occupying man responsible position in SSI.

Quality Certification Scheme

In order to promote modernisation and technology upgradation in Small Scale Industries, the units are assisted in improving the quality standard of their products.

A new scheme has been launched to assist about 100 Small Scale units in obtaining ISO-9000 or an equivalent international quality standard. Subject to an upper ceiling of Rs. 75 lakhs, each unit is given financial assistance equal to 50% of the cost incurred in acquiring the quality standard.

The small scale industrial units are also encouraged to participate in quality awareness and learning programmes organised specially for their benefit.

PROBLEMS OF SMALL INDUSTRY

Certain problems of small scale industries arise out of difficulties which are inherent in small units. Some of the major handicaps are briefly given as follows:

Raw Materials: The availability of raw materials has been a great problem in our country. Some of them are chronically in short supply; some are very scarce at times and abundant at others; and there are great price variations. Manufacturers and suppliers very frequently create artificial scarcities and rig up prices. Even the government is at fault, some time deliberately, because it is politically motivated, and often throws the trade into complete confusion by frequent changes in policy, especially in regard to controls.

Shortage of the right type of raw material at standard prices has affected the entire industrial sector. Because of their smallness and weak financial position, small scale industries have to utilise the services of middlemen to get raw materials on credit. Such an arrangement however, result in higher costs and in particularly disadvantageous when raw-materials are imported, for the profit margins of middlemen are rather high. Their meagre resources induce small industrialists to use cheap and inferior materials, which naturally affect the quality of their finished products. Moreover, the irregular supply of certain raw-materials adversely affects their production programmes.

Production: Small units suffer from poor infrastructure facilities shortage of power, proper lighting and ventilation at work place and absence of sanitary and safety measures etc. These shortcomings have tended to endanger the health of workman and have adversely affected the rate of production. One of the major handicaps of the small-scale sector has been the absence of the latest technology which alone can ensure quality and high rate of productivity.

Marketing: Marketing is one of the major stumbling blocks for small-scale industries. Lack of standardization, poor designing, poor quality, lack of quality control, lack of precision, poor finish, poor bargaining power, lack of service after scales, scale of production, brand preferences, distribution contacts, lack of knowledge of marketing, competition, ignorance of potential markets, unfamiliarity with export activities (procedure and market know-how), financial weakness are the main constraints in the marketing, techniques of the small scale industrial units. Often small entrepreneurs are dependent on middlemen who have monopoly over the markets.

Managerial: Small scale industries in our country have suffered from the lack of entrepreneurial ability to develop initiative and undertake risks in the unexplored industrial fields. The inefficiency in management comes first among managerial problems. The poor training imbibed by the owner-manager leads the concern to the brink of ruin. As the capital invested is very low, there is no scope for specialisation in any discipline. Hereditary entrepreneurship, often lacking proper planning and forecasting and involving family feuds, brings down the efficiency of the management.

Financial: The shortage of finance affects the ability of the small units severely. Every kind of problem whether of raw material, power, transport or marketing faced by an entrepreneur in its ultimate analysis turns out to be a problem of finance. The small industry gets elbowed out by the large and medium scale industries in the procurement of bank finance and institutional credit. Commercial banks suspect the stability of small industries and are not interested in lending the small amounts these industries require. This problem of finance is vitally related to the problems of production technical and managerial competence and marketing. Non-availability of timely finance has been the root cause of the above problems.

Sickness: A serious problem which is hampering small scale sector has been sickness. Many small units have fallen sick due to one problem or the other. Research has shown that sickness is broadly caused by two sets of factors internal factors and external factors. From among the various internal and external causes of sickness the important ones are—bad management, lack of accounting and management information systems, high rate of capital gearing, failure of the management to respond adequately to changing economic, social political and technological environments, delays and cost escalations, inadequacy of finance, shortage of raw materials, outdated plant and machinery, low labour productivity, labour unrest, inflation and demand recession etc. Besides these factors, some aggregate economic behaviours of the country, such as growth in Gross National Product, availability of credit, volume of money supply, capital market activity or level of investment and price level fluctuations, may have important bearing on industrial sickness in the country.

Organisation of the Study

From the foregoing description, it is evident that the Small Scale Sector is given a pride of place in the country's strategy for the development. The small scale sector could perform well realising the expectations of the people. This sector's performance would have been far better then what is attained already in the past, had it has been problem free. In the light of this backdrop the present study is undertaken to highlight the problems of small scale industrial units and there by to suggest some measures to resolve them. The study in organised in the manner given below.

Chapter—II Out lines the objectives and methodology of the study. Besides, it provides a brief survey of literature and it also explains the limitation of the study.

Chapter—III Deals with the development of small scale industries in Andhra Pradesh with particular reference to Vizianagaram, Srikakulam and Visakhapatnam districts.

Chapter—IV Presents the growth and organisation of sample units in Vizianagaram, Srikakulam and Visakhapatnam districts. It also evaluates the performance of these units with reference to investment, output and utilisation of capacity.

Chapter—V Analyses the various problems faced by the sample Small Scale Industrial Units of Vizianagaram, Srikakulam and Visakhapatnam districts.

Chapter—VI Deals with the sickness in Small Scale Sector. It analyses the various causes for the sickness in sample units.

Chapter—VII Deals with the sickness inn Small Scale Sector. It analyses the various causes for the sickness in sample units.

Chapter—VII Concentrates on comparative analysis of various problems of sample units of Vizianagaram, Srikakulam and Visakhapatnam districts.

Chapter—VIII Out lines the findings and conclusions. It also points out the suggestions made to the small entrepreneurs, financial agencies and various small industry promotion agencies in the light of the findings and conclusions made out in the study.

—Reference

1. Government of India, *Report of the Industrial Commission 1918,* P. 1
2. Government of India, *Report of the Industrial Commission 1918,* P. 295.
3. Mamoria, C.B., *Organisation and Financing of Industries in India* (Allahabad:Kitabmahal, 1960).
4. *Fourth Five Year Plan 1969-74 Draft,* PP. 21-22.
5. *Planning Commission, Draft Fifth Five Year Plan 1974-79* Part III P. 164.
6. *Planning Commission, Eighth Five Year Plan (1991-92)* Vol. II, P. 133.

CHAPTER—II

OBJECTIVES AND METHODOLOGY

The main purposes of this chapter are to describe the objectives of the study and to discuss the methodology followed. Besides, efforts are also made to outline the problem of the study and survey of literature. Further, the chapter enlightens the significance of the study and limitation.

PROBLEM OF THE STUDY

It is very clear from the descriptions made in the previous chapter that small scale industries occupy prominent place in the economic development of a country like India, mainly because of their special suitable features as explained in the chapter. In fact Small Scale industries have to play major role in countries like India where the capital formation is very low, and the growth of population in very high. Realising the importance of this Small Scale sector, the Government of India took several measures for the growth and development of Small Scale sector since independence. The allocations made in Five Year Plans, the policy measures taken in industrial statements and setting up of various national level and state level institutions show the interest of the government in supporting the development of Small Scale sectors inspite of various measures taken by the government, the Small Scale units in the country have been suffering due to various problems with various reasons. In the light of this background the present study has been taken up to identify the problem area of this sector and thereby to suggest appropriate measures in order to resolve the problems faced by them. To carry out the study on smooth and sound lines it is hypothesized that the Small Scale units are suffering from several problems like production, marketing, labour, financial and managerial etc.

To test the validity of hypothesis the Small Scale industrial units of Vizianagaram, Srikakulam, Visakhapatnam districts of coastal Andhra Pradesh are selected for the study. To avoid ambiguity and to organise the survey on sound lines the objectives of the study are clearly defined as follows:

OBJECTIVES

The objectives of the study are given hereunder with a view to identify the problems faced by Small Scale units and suggest suitable measures to resolve the same.

1. to study the origin, growth and working of Small Scale industries in India along with a description of industrial policies, five year plans, institutional set up etc;
2. to describe the growth and working of Small Scale industries in the state of Andhra Pradesh and in Vizianagaram, Srikakulam and Visakhapatnam districts;
3. to examine the working performance of sample units in Vizianagaram, Srikakulam and Visakhapatnam districts;
4. to ascertain and analyse various problems faced by the sample units of the study;
5. to investigate into the reasons for sickness in Small Scale units in order to suggest the suitable measures for revival or sick units;
6. to make a comparative analysis as the problems of different sample units of these three districts; and
7. finally to suggest suitable measures based on the findings in the problem areas.

METHODOLOGY

The study is empirical in nature and it is based on the data personally collected with the help of an elaborate schedule which can be seen in appendix. Before collecting the relevant data and set of schedule have been presented and adjustments are made according to requirement. The researcher visited all the sample units personally and collected data from entrepreneurs of Vizianagaram, Srikakulam, Visakhapatnam districts. This really helped the researcher in exploring the required data from the respondents. To obtain qualitative data the researcher used to have discussions with sample respondents wherever necessary. All attempts have made to extract the correct information though informal discussion with the entrepreneurs. While collecting the data the researcher often visited industrial centers of Vizianagaram, Srikakulam and Visakhapatnam and got the help from the industrial promotion officers in collecting the data from the sample units.

Besides the primary data, the researcher gathered secondary data through consulting the libraries of Nagpur University and Andhra University. He went through the published material in the field of Small Scale sector reasonably well before he finalising the problem of the study.

PERIOD OF THE STUDY

The study covers a period from 1980-81 to 1995-96. This period of one and half decade has taken with a view to reflect the actual position of Small Scale units taking all ups and downs into consideration. However, for the sake of convenience a period from 1991-92 to 1995-96 is considered to be a reasonable period to analyse the various problems of Small scale industrial sector.

SELECTION OF THE SAMPLE

For any smooth and sound sample survey accurate and representative sample selection is essential. As far as Vizianagaram, Srikakulam, and Visakhapatnam districts are concerned a systematic record relating to Small Scale industrial units are not available. As registration of Small Scale units is only optional it is found that some of the units operating in these districts are functioning without registration. No information is obtained regarding total number of such units and their locations. A study has, therefore, being confined to those small units which are registered through the district industry centers of these three districts which maintain registers for Small Scale units and tiny units. The researcher found very difficult to separate Small Scale units from the total small and tiny industrial units. However, due care has taken in identifying the Small Scale units of the districts. As on 31st March 1996, it is found that there are 464 Small Scale units out of 3039 small and tiny industrial units in Vizianagaram district. Similarly 484 Small Scale units out of 5374 total (small and tiny) industrial units in Srikakulam district, and 1116 Small Scale units out of 15098 total units in Visakhapatnam district. The following table 2.1 gives the particulars of small and tiny industrial units covered under study and tiny units of Vizianagaram, Srikakulam, and Visakhapatnam districts as on 31st March, 1996.

Table—2.1 Small Scale and Tiny Industrial Units of Vizianagaram Srikakulam and Visakhapatnam Districts as on 31-3-96

S.No.	*Name of the district*	*S.S.I. units*	*Tiny units*	*Total units*
1	Vizianagaram	464	2,575	3,039
2	Srikakulam	484	4,890	5,374
3	Visakhapatnam	1,116	13,982	15,098

Source : District Industries Centres of Vizianagaram, Srikakulam and Visakhapatnam Districts.

The total Small Scale industrial units identified as on 31st March 1996 as classified as Agro based, Chemical based, Forest based, Mineral and Building material based, Engineering and Allied based, Textile based and miscellaneous categories. The following table 2.2 &2.3&2.4 show the category wise total number of Small Scale units available in the respective three districts as on 31st March, 1996.

Table—2.2 Number of Small Scale Industrial Units in Different Categories of Industries in Vizianagaram District as on 31-3-96

S.No.	*Category of units*	*Number of units*
1	Agro based	230
2	Forest based	83
3	Chemical based	19
4.	Mineral and Building material based	68
5	Engineering and allied based	39
6	Textile based	5
7	Miscellaneous	20
	Total	464

Source –: Records of district industries center, Vizianagaram.

Table—2.3 Number of Small Scale Industrial Units in Different Categories of Industries in Srikakulam District as on 31-3-1996

S.No.	Category of units	Number of units
1	Agro based	304
2	Forest based	26
3	Chemical based	24
4	Mineral and building material based	40
5	Engineering and allied based	50
6	Textile based	13
7.	Miscellaneous	27
	Totel	484

Source : Records of district industries centre, Srikakulam.

Table—2.4 Number of Small Scale Industrial Units in Different Categories of Industries in Visakhapatnam District as on 31-3-96

S.No.	Category of units	Number of units
1	Agro based	178
2	Forest based	224
3	Chemical based	132
4	Mineral and building material based	220
5	Engineering and allied based	244
6	Textile based	42
7	Miscellaneous	80
	Total	1,116

Source : Records of district industries center, Visakhapatnam.

For smooth conduct and accurate sample survey the less numbered textile units and service based miscellaneous units are excluded from the study. And 10 per cent of sample units of each category at random are taken for study. For the purpose of the study a Small Scale unit is defined as a unit in which investment on machinery and equipment installed does not exceed Rs. 60 lakhs irrespective of the inputs on buildings, working capital and number of workers employed in the unit.

Following this procedure 44 Small Scale units from Vizianagaram, Srikakulam districts each and 100 units from Visakhapatnam district are selected from all the strata taken together. A picture of the sample size of different categories is given in the following three tables 2.5,2.6. and 2.7.

Table—2.5 Sample Size of Different Categories of Small Scale Units of Vizianagaram District

S.No.	*Category of units*	*Total no. of S.S.I. units*	*Sample Size*
1	Agro based	230	23
2	Forest based	83	8
3	Chemical based	19	2
4	Mineral and building material based	68	7
5	Engineering and allied based	39	4
6	Textile based	5*	—
7	Miscellaneous	20*	—
	Total	464	44

'*': *sTextile and miscellaneous units are excluded from sample.*

Table—2.6 Sample Size of Different Categories of Small Scale Units of Srikakulam District

S.No.	*Category of units*	*Total no. of S.S.I. units*	*Sample Size*
1	Agro based	304	30
2	Forest based	26	3
3	Chemical based	24	2
4	Mineral and building material based	40	4
5	Engineering and allied based	50	5
6	Textile based	11*	—
7	Miscellaneous	27*	—
	Total	482	44

'*': *Textile miscellaneous units are excluded from sample.*

Table—2.7 Sample Size of Different Categories of Small Scale Units of Visakhapatnam District

S.No.	*Category of units*	*Total no. of S.S.I. units*	*Sample Size*
1	Agro based	178	18
2	Forest based	224	22
3	Chemical based	132	13
4	Mineral and building material based	220	22
5	Engineering and allied based	244	25
6	Textile based	42*	—
7	Miscellaneous	80*	—
	Total	1,106	100

'*': *Textile and miscellaneous units are excluded from sample.*

The researcher identified 8,6 and 22 sick units in Vizianagaram, Srikakulam and Visakhapatnam districts respectively. The Small Scale units of these three districts are categorised on the basis of items of production.

Agro Based

The units under this category are mainly established at Vizianagaram, Parvathipuram, Gajapathinagaram, Balijipeta, S.Kota mandals of Vizianagaram district. There are 230 Agro based units engaged in various activities like rice mills, cold storage house, agricultural implements, food products and confectionery, flour mills, dall mills dairy products, jute and mesta and oil mills. It is observed that out of 23 sample units 4 units are found sick.

The main Agro based units in Srikakulam district are rice mills, flour mills, cashew kernal processing, coir based units, jute stick powder and particle board from jute stick powder. The majority of units are situated in the Mandals of Sompeta, Rajam, Ponduru, Amadalavalasa Mandals. Out of 30 sample units 4 units are found sick.

Forest Based

The forest based units are mainly concentrated in Vizianagaram, S.Kota, Saluru, Bobbili Mandals of Vizianagaram district. There are 83 units in this category which are engaged in manufacturing of plywood and venner sheets, bobbins spools, mill boards, paper cones, sawing and planning of wood. Out of 8 units of sample 2 units become sick.

The units in this category are mainly located in rural areas of Palakonda, Palasa Mandals of Srikakulam district. The main activity of these units are sawing and planning of wood and manufacturing of wooden furniture.

There are 224 forest based units in Visakhapatnam District. Which are engaged in furniture saw mills plywood etc. Most of these units concentrated in Visakhapatnam, Paderu, and Araku Mandals. It is noticed that out of 22 sample units 5 are sick.

Chemical Based

The units in this category are mainly located in Vizianagaram and Parvatipuram mandals of Vizianagaram district. There are 19 units of this type which are engaged in manufacturing chemicals, basic inorganic chemicals, dyes and allopathic pharmaceutical preparations. Two sample units taken from Vizianagaram and Parvathipuram Mandals are working well.

There are 26 chemical based units are established in industrial estates of Amadalvalasa, Kusumpuram and Pydibheemivaram industrial development areas of Srikakulam district which are manufacturing chlarinated parafin wax, starch, dye sulphate, oxygen and acytylin gases. Two units are selected for the study.

The 132 units of Visakhapatnam district in this category are mainly concentrated in Visakhapatnam industrial estates, Autonagar, Anakapalli, and Tuni Mandals of Visakhapatnam district. The chief activity of this strata are engaged in preparation of magnisium sulphate, hydrochloric acid, sulphuric acid, H.acid, zinc sulphate etc. Out of 13 sample units selected for survey 2 of them are sick. As chemical units are being used in some plastic, leather and pharmaceutical units, for the sake of convenience these units are also included under chemical based category.

Mineral and Building Material Based

The units of this category are mainly concentrated at Kottavalasa, Alamanda Vizianagaram, Bogapuram Mandals of Vizianagaram district. There are 68 units in this strata, and 7 were selected for the study out of which one unit is found sick. The chief activities of these units are making of tiles, slabs, stone chips, slag cement, quick lime, slaked lime and hydraulis.

The units of this strata in Srikakulam District are mainly established at Tekkali, Amadalavallasa, Srikakulam, Rajam Mandals. There are only 40 units in this category which are involved in making granite slabs, polishing tiles, slag cement, spun pipes, asphaltic corrugated roof sheets, stone chips etc., 4 units are selected for study in this category, out of which one unit is found sick.

Based on the Visakhapatnam Steel Plant, Coromondal Fertiliser, Hindustan Zinc Limited there are many slag cement plants, fly ash brick plants, gypsum based units besides tiles, spun pipes, hallow brick units established in Visakhapatnam industrial estate, Autonagar, Kottavalasa Mandal and Anakapalli Mandal of Visakhapatnam district. Out of 220 units in this sector 22 units are selected as sample and 6 of them are found sick.

Engineering and Allied Based

The units in this category in Vizianagaram District, spread throughout the district. The chief activities of these units are general engineering works, manufacturing of machinery for other Small Scale units, casting of iron, aluminium utensils, manufacturing of other non-metalic mineral products and wire drawings of steel. Out of 39 units in this category 4 units are selected for study and out of which one unit is found to be sick.

The units of this industry in Srikakulam District are mainly concentrated all industrial estates and industrial development areas besides, Palasa, Ichapuram and Srikakulam Mandals. Out of 50 units of this category 5 units are selected for study and out of which one unit is found sick. The activities of these units are manufacturing of ferrous and non-ferrous castings, making of steel furniture, stainless steel pots, aluminium utensils, welding electrodes etc.

There are a large number of Engineering and Allied based units 244 in Visakhapatnam District which have been engaged in a diversified activities like steel and aluminium fabrication, material handling equipment, manufacturing of spares of heavy earth moving equipment, steel wire ropes which are mainly established in Visakhapatnam Gajuwaka industrial estates, and Autonagar of Visakhapatnam. Besides these, general engineering workshops, casting of ferrous and non-ferrous metals brass and aluminium utensils and re-rolling mills, are spread atAnakapalli, Narsipatnam, Tuni Mandals of Visakhapatnam district. 25 units under this category are selected for study and 5 of them are found sick.

Profile of Respondents

The profile of respondents of Vizianagaram, Srikakulam and Visakhapatnam districts are depicted in the following three tables i.e. 2.8,2.9 and 2.10 whose detailed communications have helped to formulate the study in a systematic way. The detailed profile of 44 respondents each of Vizianagaram and Srikakulam districts and 100 respondents of Visakhapatnam district is shown in these tables.

Table—2.8 Profile of Respondents of Different Strata of Vizianagaram District

Details of Respondents	*Agro Based*	*Forest Based*	*Chemical .based*	*Mineral & Building Material Based*	*Engg. & Allied Based*	*Total*
1	*2*	*3*	*4*	*5*	*6*	*7*
Total no.of units	23	8	2	7	4	44
Type of Ownership						
Proprietorship	10	2	—	1	1	14
Partnership	6	4	1	3	2	16
Private Limited	7	2	1	3	1	14
Educational Background						
Below Graduation	6	6	—	2	—	14
Graduation	8	1	—	2	2	13
Post-graduation	6	1	1	2	1	11
Technical	1	—	1	—	1	3
Professional	2	—	—	1	—	3
Experience						
Without experience	8	2	—	1	1	12
0-2 years	3	2	1	1	1	8
2-5 years	2	—	1	2	—	5
Trade Experience	10	4	—	3	2	19
Social Status						
O.C.	16	4	2	5	2	29
B.C.	5	3	—	2	1	11
S.C.	2	1	—	—	1	4

cont.

1	*2*	*3*	*4*	*5*	*6*	*7*
Gender(sex)						
Man	18	7	2	5	3	35
Woman	5	1	—	2	1	9
Family Background						
Business	12	3	1	2	2	20
Industry	2	1	1	2	1	7
Agriculture	6	2	—	1	—	9
Others	3	2	—	2	1	8
Source of idea estd.						
Past Experience	10	3	—	—	1	17
Trade Connection	4	2	—	2	1	9
Occupation	2	—	—	—	—	2
Tech. Education	2	—	1	1	1	5
Industrial Consul. advice	3	—	—	1	1	5
Friends & Relatives advice	2	3	—	1	—	6
Position						
Healthy Unit	19	6	2	6	3	36
Sick Unit	4	2	—	1	1	8
Location/Place of Unit						
Town Unit	8	3	1	5	3	20
Village	15	5	1	2	124	

Table—2.9 Profile of Respondents of Different Strata of Srikakulam District

Details of Respondents	*Agro Based*	*Forest Based*	*Chemical based*	*Mineral& Building Material Based*	*Engg. & Allied Based*
1	*2*	*3*	*4*	*5*	*6*
Total no.of units	30	3	2	4	5
Type of Ownership					
Proprietorship	18	2	—	1	2

cont.

1	*2*	*3*	*4*	*5*	*6*
Partnership	8	1	1	1	2
Private Limited	4	—	1	2	1
Educational Background					
Below Graduation	15	2	—	1	2
Graduation	7	1	—	—	1
Post-graduation	3	—	1	2	1
Technical	3	—	1	1	1
Professional	2	—	—	—	—
Experience					
Without	12	1	—	1	1
0-2 years	5	1	—	1	2
2-5 years	4	—	1	—	—
Trade Experience	9	1	1	2	2
Social Status					
O.C.	18	2	2	2	3
B.C.	8	1	—	2	2
S.C.	4	—	—	—	—
Gender(sex)					
Man	26	2	2	3	4
Woman	4	1	-	1	1
Family Background					
Business	10	2	1	2	2
Industry	5	—	1	1	—
Agriculture	10	—	—	—	1
Others	5	1	—	1	2
Source of idea established					
Past experience	8	2	1	2	1
Trade connection	10	1	1	1	1
Occupation	6	—	—	—	—
Tech.Education	1	—	—	—	1

cont.

1	2	3	4	5	6
Industrial consultants advice	3	—	—	—	1
Friends and relatives advice	2	—	—	1	1
Position					
Healthy unit	26	3	2	3	4
Sick unit	4	—	—	1	1
Location of the Unit					
Within town limits	12	1	—	2	4
Village	18	2	2	2	1

Table—2.10 Profile of Respondent of Different Strata Visakhapatnam District.

Details of Respondents	*Agro Based*	*Forest Based*	*Chemical based*	*Mineral& building material based*	*Engg & allied based*	*Total*
1	*2*	*3*	*4*	*5*	*6*	*7*
Total no.of units	18	22	13	22	25	100
Type of Ownership						
Proprietorship	3	6	3	7	4	23
Partnership	8	8	3	3	8	30
Private Limited	7	8	7	12	13	47
Educational Background						
Below Graduation	6	10	2	6	4	28
Graduation	6	6	3	3	9	27
Post-graduation	2	2	4	3	8	19
Technical	2	2	4	5	2	15
Professional	2	2	-	5	2	11
Experience						
Without	7	8	-	2	6	23
0-2 years	3	4	3	6	6	22

cont.

1	*2*	*3*	*4*	*5*	*6*	*7*
2-5 years	2	4	5	10	10	31
Trade Experience	6	6	5	4	3	24
Social Status						
O.C.	12	13	6	14	17	62
B.C.	6	7	5	7	6	31
S.C.	0	2	2	1	2	7
Gender(sex)						
Male	14	17	12	18	17	78
Female	4	5	1	4	8	22
Family Background						
Business	8	9	3	12	10	42
Industry	8	5	4	3	8	28
Agriculture	-	2	3	2	3	10
Others	2	6	3	5	4	20
Source of idea established						
Past experience	6	8	4	6	6	30
Trade connection	6	6	1	8	8	29
Occupation	-	4	3	2	2	11
Tech.Education	-	-	2	-	4	6
Industrial consultants advice	4	2	2	3	4	15
Friends and relatives advice	2	2	1	3	1	9
Position						
Healthy unit	14	17	11	16	20	78
Sick unit	4	5	2	6	5	22
Location of the Unit						
Within town limits	10	10	8	13	16	57
Village	8	12	5	9	9	43

Data Analysis

The data collected from both primary and secondary sources are processed systematically, applying growth rates and percentages to evaluate the working of Small Scale industrial units and analyses the problem in order to draw meaningful inferences and conclusions.

Survey of literature

Before selection of the present topic that is, the role organisation and problems of Small Scale sector, a survey of literature is done so as to ensure that the selection process does not lead to any duplication. Efforts are made to study and analyse literature on the subject matter and observations are made as under.

The total literature available on the Small Scale sector is of various types i.e., research reports (both published and unpublished dissertations) reports of the government and the papers published in various highly reputed journals. The researcher has gone through these sources which made him finally to select the present problem for his doctoral degree which has not been undertaken by any individual or institution in the recent past.

There are some surveys conducted by many individuals on the general aspects of Small Scale sector which highlighted their attention on the role, growth and place of the Small Scale sector in a developing economy like India. They gone through various aspects of Small Scale sector at macro level viz., Growth, organisation working problems, contribution to national economy etc., The studies of Brahme, [1] De Hann, [2] Desai[3], Jain[4], Joshi,[5] Mohanty [6], Niranjundun[7], Rao[8], Staly[9] and Uma Maheswar Rao[10] are important among them.

Some of the research studies at macro level relate to various regions of the country. These studies mainly concentrated on the problems faced by Small Scale sector of the concerned regions. The problems faced by Small Scale industries in different regions are differ, because of differences in the geographical features. For example, the Small Scale sector of backward regions have more problems than the Small Scale sector of developed regions. Moreover, the nature of problems in the backward regions differ from that of developed regions. As such the regional studies are relevant because of the differences in the regional features. Banerjee[11], Sandesara [12], Shamboo Prasad[13], and Upadhyaya[14] have concentrated on such studies.

Some studies are carried out with special emphasis on specified regions. Those regional studies are organised by Domman[15],Agarwal[16], Agarwal[17], Gangole[18], Gopal[19], Gupta[20], Manjundhar[21], Moosa Baker[22], Mathur[23], Nirmal Camera[24], Oommen[25], Rastogi[26], and Varma[27]

There are studies which focused their attention on specific problems besides general problems such as financial, marketing, personnel and managerial. Bala Krishna[28], Gopal[29], Kaveri[30], Mishra[31] Mohammed Sayed[32], Murthy[33], Navrang[34], Panda[35] Perikh[36], Ramakrishna[37] have concentrated on financial problems. Azmtali[38], Gudgil[39] and Sohgal[40] have dealt with marketing problems. Acharya[41], Athreya[42], Dhameja[43], Deshpande[44], Navnihal Singh[45], Padmanabhan[46], Raj [47] and Sharma[48] have dealt with other managerial and entrepreneurial problems in Small Scale industry. Besides these, some researchers concentrated their attention on general problems like production, investment, employment, and output in small scale sector. Do Shushil Kumar[49], Gambhir[50], Kapardikar,[51] Mitra[52], Namdeo[53], Satyapal[54] and Saxena[55] have dealt with investment, output and employment in the small scale industries. Further more-many have conducted studies on the problems of small scale industries. Further more many have conducted studies on the problems of small scale industrial units. They are Agarwal[56], Anselm[57], Bahader Singh[58], Banerjee[59], Barooah[60], Dey[61], Gurcharan[62], Nisar Ahmed[63], Patel[64], Rastogi[65], Sharma[66], Sharma[67], and Siya Ram [68] there are some studies which have paid their attention on specific areas like rice, leather, bidi and slate industries respectively.

There are some studies which have paid their attention for state level industrial corporations, institutional finances and commercial banks. The studies of Iyer[69], Parikh[70], Rama Krishna[71], and Sudeshran Lal[72] are some of them stressed more on institutional and bank finances. The studies of Apparao[73],, Balmohandas[74], Brahmanadham[75], Ramandaham[76], Rama Krishna Sarma[77], Sadasiva Reddy[78], Somusundaram[79], Suryanarayana[80], Venkatswamy[81] are concentrated on various aspects like growth, role problems finances and ancillary units pertaining to the Andhra Pradesh.

Appa Rao's study on small enterprises promotion in Andhra Pradesh examined the role played by Andhra Pradesh State Financial Corporation in the promotion and operation of small scale industrial units in the state of Andhra Pradesh. Balmohandas focussed his attention on ancillary industries in Visakhapatnam Brahmandam's study on financing small scale industries by commercial banks pertains to Guntur district. He identified various problems faced by the small units obtaining term loans and working capital loans.

Some research papers are published in the periodicals by the eminent researchers on sickness in small scale sector. They focussed attention on industrial sickness, prevention of sickness and rehabilitation of units which have fallen sick in small scale sector. The papers published on sickness by Aravind Bhandari[82], Asthana[83], Basant Kumar[84], Fareoq Khan[85], Patwardham[86], Singh[87], Sinha[88], Syed Amin Jafri[89], Sinhan[90], Shubhra Garg[91] are some of them.

The Government of India received few reports prepared by the committees appointed by them from time to time. Among them the reports of ford foundation team, Lokandham committee, Bhat committee, Japanese delegation, and Village and Small Industries committee, Abid Hussain committee, are important. Besides these, there are some publications of the small industry promotional organisations and State Governments on small sector also plays an important role. Ford foundation team expressed the need for establishing an apex organisation and extension of training institutes to provide training and technical assistance to the entrepreneurs. Lokanadham committee gave some guidelines for the implementation of industrial policy resolution of 1956 in respect of small scale sector. The Village and Small industries committee argued for the clear demarcation of the field of operation for small industry and suggested an increase in the expenditure for the development of the sector under five-year plans. Balachandan committee examined the problem of scarcity of raw-materials for small industries. Bhat committee prepared the draft legislation for the small scale industry to provide a legal frame work. Japanese delegation on small scale industries gave some guidelines for the development of small scale sector in India based on Japanese experience.

From the above survey of literature, it is obvious that a good number of research studies have been undertaken on various aspects of small scale sector. A few researchers have studied on the place and role of small industries in Indian economy and reviewed the contribution of Small Scale sector to Indian economy from time to time. A few researchers have worked on cottage industries. Some have done their research work on the problems faced by Small Scale sector. Some have specifically concentrated their attention on specific problems such as financial, managerial, marketing and personal. Some studies have dealt with Small Scale promotional agencies, finance corporations and banks, some researchers have studied the concepts confirming their scope to their concerned regions. They examined the contribution of Small Scale sector to the economic development of their respective regions. They also have outlined the various problems confronted by small scale sector in their respective regions. There are very little contributions pertaining to the state of Andhra Pradesh. All this gives an understanding that there is a dearth of works on the problems faced by Small Scale industries confined to a specific district.

It is in this context note worthy that there is no study of this type related to three districts viz., Vizianagaram, Srikakulam and Visakhapatnam districts of north coastal Andhra Pradesh. The present study is intended to explorate problems faced by these three developing, backward and developed districts of Andhra Pradesh respectively with a comparative study.

Significance of the Study

The study has great significance in the absence of similar study pertaining to problems of small scale industrial unit in Vizianagaram, Srikakulam and Visakhapatnam districts and their comparison. Further these three districts have three different status in industrial development. Visakhapatnam district is said to be an industrially forward district when compared to Srikakulam district which is said to be industrial backward district. The Vizianagaram district lies between these two districts, a comparative study of such districts is no doubt a meaningful one. Therefore, the importance of the present study need not be overemphasised. In the light of the fact, different problems are centered in this sector and that this study aims at the resolving of various problems of this sector. So far, many have organised several studies on several aspects of Small Scale sectors with reference to India. There has been little attention paid on the problems.

Most of the small sector units in the country are facing one problem or the other in their running. The Small Scale units could have achieved more if they are not free from different problems. Keeping these aspects in view, this study of role, organisation and problems of small scale industries in Vizianagaram, Srikakulam and Visakhapatnam districts is taken up. Besides, the study obtained significance as it deals with the comparative analysis among three districts of coastal Andhra Pradesh. Previously no study of this nature was taken up. The present study throw light on varied problems of small Scale units. Further the study helps the policy makers in the light of changing scenario. It forms a basis for further research dealing with different problems, promoting agencies, etc., Thus the study has a great relevance and significance in the present context of Small Scale sector in the Indian economy.

Limitation

Though proper care is taken in the successful completion of the Study is not free from the following limitation.

The researcher faced several problems in obtaining accurate data from the respondents. However, researcher made number of visits to the respondents and their units to collect reliable and accurate data. Inspite of best efforts put in by the researcher there are a little data constrains whose impact on the interpretations and conclusions of the study is negligible as sufficient care has taken to draw meaningful conclusions.

—References

1. Brahme, S., *Modern Small Scale industry: a wheel within a wheel.* ICSSR Project, 1979.
2. De Haan, H., *Small Scale industries in India. Their role in development.* Research project by institute of economic growth, New Delhi, 1982.
3. Desai Vasant, *Problems and prospects of small scale industries in India* Bombay, Himalaya Publishers.
4. Jain and Jain, *Small Scale industry. A guide and reference handbook.* New Delhi, Nabhi Publishers, 1973.
5. Joshi. N., *Cottage and Small Scale industry in India*, New Delhi: Sujana book centre, 1956.
6. Mohanty, Bedabati., *Economics of Small Scale industries*, New Delhi, Ashish publishing house, 1986.
7. Narijudan, S *"Economic research for small and industry development illustrated by India's experience.* New Delhi, Asia, 1962.
8. Rao, R.V., *Small industries and the developing economy in India.* Delhi, concept, 1979.
9. Staley. E., and Morser, *Modern small industries for developing countries*, (New York: Mc Graw Hill Book Company, 1965).
10. Uma Maheswa Rao, CH., *Some ecoreric aspects of small scale industries in India*, (Bombay: popular Prakasan, 1965).
11. Banerjee, Naresh Chemdara, *Small Scale industries: case study of old Gaya district*, (Thesis submitted to Magadha University 1974-76).

12. Sandesara, J.C., *Size and Capital Intensity*, (Bombay: University of Bombay, 1969).

13. Shamboo Prasad Singh, *Role of SSI in a developing region with special reference to Bihar.*

14. Upadhyaya, D.V., *Some aspects of household and small industries.*

15. Domman, M.A., *Small industry in Indian growth: A case of study in Kerala*, Delhi, The Author, 1972.

16. Agarwal and Shobhama, *An intensive study of Small and cottage industry in Aligarh district.* (Thesis submitted to Agra University, 1980).

17. Agarwal, Radharaman., *Small industry and economic growth: A study of Engineering and Electronic goods units in the Union Territory of Delhi.* (Thesis submitted to university of Rajastan, 1983)

18. Gongole, Arun Kumar, *State and to small scale and Cottage industries in Madhya Pradesh*, (Thesis submitted to University of Sauyar, 1967-74).

19. Gopal D.K., *A Techno-Economic study of Small Scale Engineering Industries of District Saharanpur.* (Thesis submitted to University of Roorkee, 1981).

20. Gupta, Vipin Chandra., Role of Small scale industry in industrial development of Uttar Pradesh since 1951. (Thesis submitted to Kanpur University, 1980).

21. Majumdhar, Soumendu, *Small Scale enterprises in West Bengal*, (Thesis submitted to University of Burwan, 1967-72)

22. Mossa Baker, A., Role of Small Scale industries in the economic development of Kerala, (Thesis submitted to University of Calicut, 1979).

23. Mathur, S.P., *Economic of Small Scale industries in Agra region*, (Thesis submitted to Agra University, 1978), (Sundeep Prakasan, 1979).

24. Nirmal Camera, *Small Scale manufacturing in Jammu and Kashmir State*, 1950-71, (Thesis submitted to University of Jammu, 1972-77).

25. Oomman, M.A., *Small Scale industries in Kerala*, (Thesis submitted to University of Kerala, 1960-68) Research publications in social sciences, Delhi, 1972).

26. Rastogi Chandramohan, *Promotion of small scale industries in Uttar Pradesh with special reference to Allahabad district.* (Thesis submitted to University of Allahabad, 1974-81).

27. Varma, N.S., *Cottage and Small Scale industries in Madhya Pradesh* (Thesis submitted to Sagar University, 1959).

28. Balakrishna, G., Financing small scale industries in India, (Poona: Gokhale Institute of Politics and Economics, 1972).

29. Gopal, Swaroop; *Advances of small scale industries and small borrower*: New Delhi, Sultan Chand Publishers.

30. Kaveri, V.S., *Financial rations as Predictors of borrowers health with reference to Small Scale industries in India*, (Thesis submitted University of Bombay, 1974-76) New Delhi: Sultan Chand & Sons, 1980).

31. Mishra, Gaya Prasad, *Financing in the small scale industries in the Union Territory of Delhi*, (Thesis submitted to University of Delhi 1974-81).

32. Mohammed Sayeed, *Financing of Small cottage industries in UttarPradesh*, (Thesis submitted to University of Allahabad, 196).

33. Murthy P.L.N.V.S.S.G.K., *Financing of Small Scale industry in Rayalaseema* (Thesis submitted to Sree Krishna Devaraya University, 1978-81).

34. Navarang, Sudhershanlal., *Loans to small industries and small borrowers*. Asich Publisher, Bombay, 1976.

35. Panda, Ganasyam *Working Capital in Small manufacturing companies in Orissa*, (Thesis submitted to Sambalpur University, 1967-80).

36. Pareek, Hanuman Sahai, *Financing of Small Scale industry in a developing Economy*, (New Delhi National Publishing House, 1978).

37. Rama Krishna, K.T., *Finances for Small Scale industry in India* (Bombay: Asia Publishing House, 1962).

38. Azmat Ali, S., *Marketing problems of small scale and cottage industries of Uttar Pradesh special with reference to Aligar district*, (Thesis submitted to Aligar Muslim University, 1973).

39. Gagil, Prabhakar Gopal, *Marketing of Turmeric in Sangli district*, (Thesis submitted to University of Poona, 1971-75).

40. Sohgal, Jag Mohan Lal, *A study of marketing practices and problems of Small Scale industries in Haryana*, (Thesis submitted to Kurukshethra University 1976-79).

41. Acharya, Sarthi; *Micro econometric analysis of short run managerial decision of small scale firms, Indian Institute of Technology*, (Thesis submitted to Kanpur University, 1973-77).

42. Athreya Nagan Harihar; *Small scale entrepreneurship development of Small manageable factors* (Thesis submitted to University of Bombay, 1974-78).

43. Dhameja N.L., *Management accounting problems in small industries*, New Delhi, K.W.A., 1975.

44. Deshpande, Manohar Uttam Rao, *Small scale industrial entrepreneurship in a developing region*, (Thesis submitted to Marathwada University, 1977-80).

45. Nau Nihal Singh; *Scientific management of small scale industries* (Bombay: Lalvani Publishing House 1970).

46. Padmanaban, D., *A Psychological Socio-economic study of entrepreneurship in Small scale industries in and around Coimbatore city*, (Thesis submitted to University of Madras, 1976-81).

47. Raj, P.K; *Industrial entrepreneurship in SSI's Orissa*, (Thesis submitted to Utkal University, 1978-83).

48. Sarma, Anil Kumar; *Management problems of Small industrial enterprises in Assam*, (Thesis submitted to Gauhati University, 1977).

49. De, Sushil Kumar; *Employment Potential of the village and small scale industries in India*, (Thesis submitted to Jadavpur University 1972-78).

50. Gambhir, Gurubachan Das; *Labour in Small scale industries in Madya Pradesh with special reference to women and child labour cotton ginning, bidi making, rice milling and shellac industries*, (Thesis submitted to Vikram University, 1963-70).

51. Kopardekar, S.D., *SSI's in Poona*, (Thesis submitted to University of Poona) Pune: G.Y. Rane Prasan, 1974).

52. Mitra Lalit Kumar, *Employment and output in small enterprises of India*, (Thesis submitted to University of Calcutta, 1966-680.

53. Namdeo, R.S., *Job motivation in Small industries : A case study of Chatishgar region*, (Thesis submitted Ravi Sankar University 1983).

54. Satyapal., *Labour in Small scale industries in Haryana*, (Thesis submitted to Kurukshetra University, 1970-73).

55. Saxena, K.K., *An input output model for registered Small scale industries in Rajasthan*, (Thesis submitted to University of Udaypur, 1975-8!).

56. Agarwal, Manik Chandra; *An analytical study of the problems of selected agricultural cottage industries in upper Narmada Valley*, (Thesis submitted to Vikram University, 1971).

57. Anselm, Mercy, *The problems and possibilities of growth of the Small scale Engineering industry of greater Bombay*, (Thesis submitted to University of Bombay, 1972-80).

58. Bahadar Singh; *Problems of innovations in Small scale and cottage industries of Jammu and Kashmir state*, (Thesis submitted to University of Jammu, 1977-81).

59. Benerjee, Sabita; *Some aspects of the problems of small and medium sized industry in India with special reference to West Bengal*, (Thesis submitted to University of Calcutta, 1957-60).

60. Barooah, Hem Kanta, *Prospects and problems of Small scale industries in Lakshmipur district*, (Thesis submitted to Gauhati University, 1981).

61. Dey, Kikhil Bhushan; *Small scale industries in Cachar district. Their growth, problems and prospects* (Thesis submitted to Gauhati University, 1981).

62. Gurucharan Kaur; *The problem of cottage industries*, (thesis submitted to Karnataka University, 1973-80).

63. Nisar Ahmed, *Problems and prospects of Small scale and cottage industries in Kashmir*, (Thesis submitted to Aligar Muslim University, 1969-76).

64. Patil, L.R., *Problems of Small Scale industries : A case study with special reference to metropolitan areas in Maharashtra*, (Thesis submitted to University of Bombay, 1975-79).

65. Rastogi, K.P., *Problems and prospects of Small scale industries in Meerut district*, (Thesis submitted to Meerut University 1973-79).

66. Sharma, Dau deyal; *Problems and prospects of small scale industries in Rajashtan*, (Thesis submitted to Agra University, 1978).

67. Sharma, Deo raj; *Problems and prospects of Small Scale industries in the bill region of Uttar Pradesh with special reference of Kamaun*, (Thesis submitted to Kumaun University, 1982).

68. Siyaram; *Problems of Small Scale industries in Uttar Pradesh* (Thesis submitted to University of Lucknow, 1973).

69. Iyer, T.N. Krishan, *Guidelines for financing of Small scale industries Bombay*, Vore & Co. Publication, 1976.

70. Parikh, Suryakant, M., *How to finance Small business enterprises*, Delhi, McMillan, Publishers, 1977.

71. Rama Krishna, K.T., *Finances for Small scale industry in India*, Ania Publishers, Bombay, 1962.

72. Sudershan Lal; *Loans to small industries and small borrowers*, Navrang Publishers, Delhi, 1976.

73. Apparao Balla, *Small enterprise promotion in Andhra Pradesh: role of Andhra Pradesh State Financial Corporation*, (Thesis submitted to Andhra University, 1982).

74. Bala Mohandas, Y., *Ancillary industrial development. A case study of ancillary industrial units in Visakhapatnam*, (Thesis submitted to Andhra University, 1972-77).

75. Bramanadham, G.N., *A study of financing small scale industry by commercial banks in Guntur district*, (Thesis submitted to Nagarjuna University, 1983).

76. Ramanadham, V.V., *Economy of Andhra Pradesh*, (Bombay: Asia Publishing House, 1959).

77. Rama Krishna Sarma, K., *Industrial Development of Andhra Pradesh regional analysis* (Thesis submitted to Osmania University, 1982).

78. Sadasiva Reddy, B., *Development of SSI's in Andhra Pradesh with particular reference to Cuddapah district*, (Thesis submitted to Sri Venkateswara University, 1982).

79. Soma Sunderam, G., *A study of the working of Small scale industrial units in Rayalaseema areas of Andhra Pradesh*, (Thesis submitted to University of Mysore, 1978-83).

80. Suryanarayana, C.V.A.S., *The corporate sector of Andhra Pradesh* (Thesis submitted to Osmania University for M.Phill).

81. Venkata Swamy G., *Performance of the state government undertakings in Andhra Pradesh,* (Thesis submitted to Osmania University for M. Phill., 1971).

82. Arvind Bhandari, *"Small industry: creeping sickness" Commerce,* December 20, 1980, p. 1156.

83. Asthana B.R.; *"Sickness in small industries," The Management Accountant,* Vol. 15, No.6, June, 1980.

84. Besanta Kumar, *"Some relevant issues regarding sick units in KVI sector,* "Khadi Gramodyog, Vol.31, No.9, June, 1985, p. 381.

85. Farooq Khan, A., *"Challenges of industrial sickness: diagnosis and remedies,* "Southern Economist, silver jubilee volume 25, October 1, 1986.

86. Patwardhan, M.S., *"Industrial sickness: Causes and the remedy,* "Economic Times, September, 28, 1981, p. 5.

87. Singh, Y.R., *"Small scale industries: Some problems"* Economic Times, September 16, 1984, p. 5.

88. Sinha, S.L.N., *"Industrial sickness and rehabilitation towards a viable approach,* Decision January 1979, p. 92.

89. Syed Amin Jafri., *Andhra Pradesh: Rapid pace of industrial development spells sickness, commerce,* annual number 1985.

90. Sinha, R. *"Role of banks in revival of sick industries,* "Economic Times, September 16, 1984, p. 5.

91. Shubhra Gar *Criteria for rehabilitating sick units,* "Through bank finance, "Southern Economist, October 1, 1981".

CHAPTER—III

DEVELOPMENT OF SMALL SCALE INDUSTRIES

The main object of this chapter is to present an outline of the Development and growth of small scale industries in the state of Andhra Pradesh with special reference to Vizianagaram, Srikakulam and Visakhapatnam districts. Along with growth, the availability of infrastructure facilities, natural resources, incentives to small scale industrial units in the state of Andhra Pradesh and Vizianagaram, Srikakulam and Visakhapatnam districts in particular also studied.

Andhra Pradesh the hub industrial activity in south India, is going all out to welcome and encourage industrial entrepreneurs. A combination of interest strengths, dynamic policies and a quick and responsible government makes Andhra Pradesh the idle location of industry, it ranks number four in investment in existing units. Andhra Pradesh stands fifth position in cumulative disbursement of assistance by central financial institutions. The state of Andhra Pradesh which is popularly known as the 'rice bowl of India' is also surging ahead on the industrial front. The state has, in fact, witnessed a faster transformation from agriculture to industrial advancement in the recent past. Andhra Pradesh has rich and abundant natural resources and cheap and peaceful labour. It has also recorded a steady growth in the number of large and medium industries. Small and tiny sectors are assuring a greater role in the further industrialisation of the state. The observation made in this regard supports this view. The state, in fact, is going towards industrialisation after green revolution through the small scale and tiny sectors.

GROWTH AND DEVELOPMENT OF SMALL AND TINY SECTORS IN ANDHRA PRADESH

There is a significant growth in small scale industries in Andhra

Pradesh in the recent past. The district industries centres set up by the government have greatly contributed to the promotion of small and tiny units in the rural areas. The number of small scale industries significantly increased to 2,01,868 units by the end of March '97 as against 27,648 units in 1980 and mostly 8090 unit in 1970. This indicates that they are increased by more than seven times in a short span of one and half decades. Their investment has also increased constantly. According to the data available, their investment has increased from Rs. 2097.98 crores in the end of March '97 and Rs.465.17 crores in 1980 and only Rs. 22.8 crores in 1970. During the years 1980 and 1997 the growth is registered by about four and half times. Similarly growth is also observed in the case of generation of employment by the small scale sector. The employment potential enormously increased to 21.24 lakh persons by the end of March 1997 as against 2.31 lakh persons in 1985, 1.80 lakh persons in 1970.

Table—3.1 The Growth No.of Small Scale Industries in the State of Andhra Pradesh During 1980-81 to 1996-97

Year	*No.of Units Established*	*Employment Generated*	*Credit Assistance (Rs. in lakhs)*
1980-81	3170	53232	3783.65
1981-82	4560	73496	4228.56
1982-83	5620	86035	5664.94
1983-84	5864	89030	6508.41
1984-85	7242	102425	8155.44
1985-86	8302	74700	9402.00
1986-87	8487	108243	8320.00
1987-88	10,483	125726	10734.00
1988-89	12,107	154162	13075.00
1989-90	13,349	167093	17612.00
1990-91	14,836	182564	16284.09
1991-92	16,625	168225	14148.66
1992-93	14,645	147702	13176.00
1993-94	16,211	182283	12749.00
1994-95	17,191	125251	13,709.15
1995-96	19869	128334	18377.06
1996-97	23,307	155980	20760.16
Total	201868	2124481	209798.57

The table 3.1 explains the growth of small and tiny units in all sectors from the year 1980-81 to 1996-97. The table explains the growth in number of units, employment generation and credit assistance by financial agencies and other. The growth of number of units are increasing continuously up to 1991-93. In 1980-81 there were only 3170 units. In the year 1990-91 the number increased to 14836 units and in 1991-92 to 16625 in the year 1992-93 number of units established reduced to 14645. Afterwards up to 1996-97 the establishment of new units increased. The employment generation in small and tiny units also increased simultaneously. The more interesting thing is the average employment generated per unit is reduced from 17 persons per unit in 1980-81 to 14 persons per unit in 1985-86, 12 persons per unit in 1990-91 and 6 persons per unit in 1996-97, may be this due to sophisticated machinery and increase of self employment units. The credit assistance to small scale industry is also increased from Rs. 3783.65 crores in 1980-81 to Rs. 20,760.16 crores in 1996-97. This increase is almost 6 folds. The above table makes it further clear that the small and tiny units have been increasing from year to year. Their employment generation and financial assistance have also been significantly increased. This gives an idea that in the recent years small and tiny units in the state are growing considerably from all sides.

LARGE AND MEDIUM INDUSTRIES

The development and growth of large and medium scale industries is also very significant in the state. There are 1277 units by the end of March 1995 with a total investment of Rs. 24369.30 crores providing employment to 6,18,480 people in the state. This number increases to 1518 unit is by end of March '96 and 1781 units by the end of March'97. The investment is also increased to Rs. 26447.36 by the end of March '96 and Rs. 30495.00 crores for the end of March '97. This shows a tremendous growth in large scale industry in the state. But compared with small scale it is very low.

The table 3.2 shows the number of large and medium industries commissioned, their investment pattern and employment generation from 1994-95 to 1996-97.

Table—3.2 The Growth of Large and Medium Scale Industries Commissioned in the State of Andhra Pradesh from 1994-95 to 1996-97

	31-3 -95	*31-3-96*	*31-3-97*
No.of large and medium units	1277.00	1518.00	1781.00
Investment (Rs. in crores)	24369.29	26447.36	30495.00
Employment	618480.00	640391.00	623975.00

The most important and interesting point to be noted here is that 1781 large and medium industrial units with an investment of Rs. 30495 crores provided employment only to 6.23 lakh persons, whereas 2,01,868 small and tiny units with only Rs. 2097.98 crores of investment are able to provide employment to 21.24 lakh persons. This indicates the two important features of small and tiny sectors, namely(a) labour intensiveness and (b) capital sparing.

INFRASTRUCTURE FACILITIES

The state offers industrial development areas, industrial estate growth centers, an export processing zone, as exim park and specialised complexes like a chemical complex, plastic complex, leather complex and a software technology park. Out of 1289 new industrial investment proposals since July 1991, 741 are already in production or in advanced stages of implementation.

The industrial map of Andhra Pradesh showing industrial estates, industrial development areas, autonagars, and industrial growth centers is given in next page.

The state government ensures the speediest clearances to enable the shortest leadtime in setting up industrial projects. To this end, a documentation and clearnance center has been set up as a unified point for both receipt and clearnance of applications. Escort officers are nominated to receive the applications, expedite processing by the departments concerned and to deliver final approvals to the industrialists.

Andhra Pradesh has 208 industrial development areas and industrial estates spread over 19,000 acres, It has 370 acres of land and ready buildings in the Visakhapatnam export processing zone, It also have 800 acres in Visakhapatnam port based exim park and 800 acres in the

M.—1 ANDHRA PRADESH INDUSTRIAL MAP

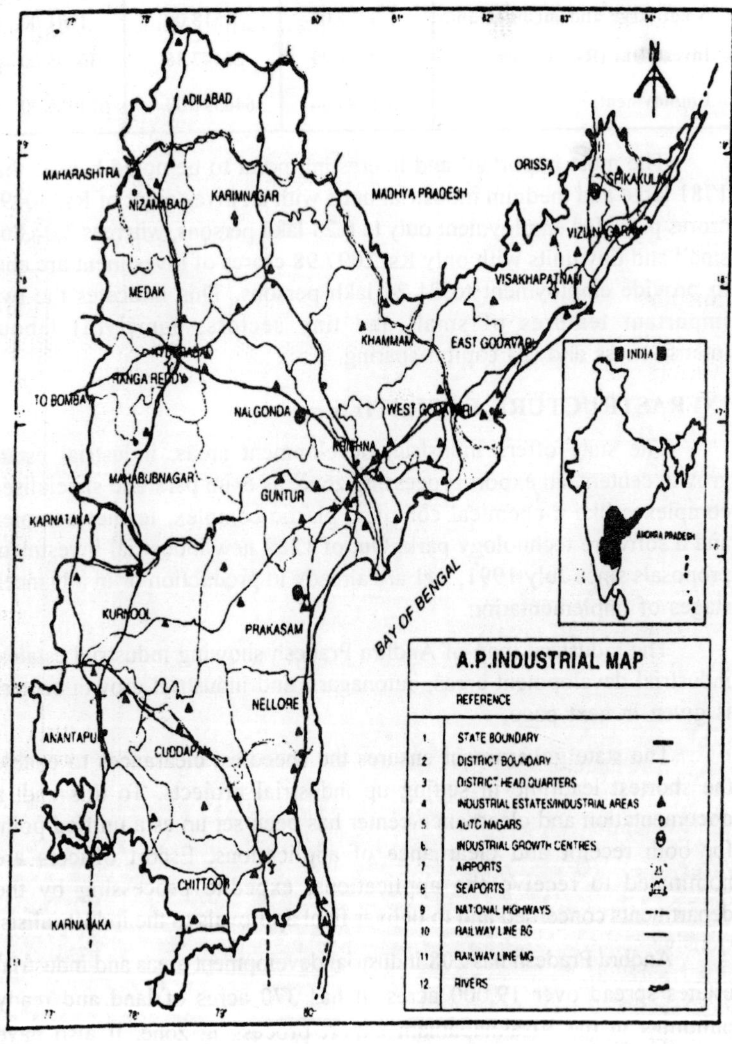

vicinity of Kakinada port, further, it has a chemical complex with a common effluent treatment plant as Pashamylaram, 50 kms from Hyderabad and a software part for the electronics industry in Hyderabad.

The state government welcomes private initiative for setting up infrastructural facilities for a hardware technology park near Hyderabad. Land is available at reasonable prices, if an industry wishes to purchase private land.

Power

Andhra Pradesh State has a strong power base with 7200mw of installed capacity. This installed capacity is going to be doubled by the year 2002 A.D. As a part of reforms, the state Government is planning to restructure the A.P.S.E.B.

Transport

Andhra Pradesh State has excellent road, rail and air connections to various parts of the country. It has 1,45,000 kms network of roads, 1400 kms of major highways being upgraded as express ways with world bank aid (US$ 350 mil.) over 5,000 kms of rail lines. One third of country's rail cargo passes through Vijayawada rail terminal. The state has eleven ports along the 960 kms of coastline deep water ports at Visakhapatnam and Kakinada with Visakhapatnam port handling the largest volume of cargo in the country. The state also have minor ports at Gangavaram, Krishnapatnam and Vodarevu being developed with private participation. Inland container freight depot and air cargo complex are available at Hyderabad, the capital city.

Telecommunications

Andhra Pradesh State has largest number of telephone exchanges in the country. Modern communication facilities like cellular and pager services are also available.

Water

The three major rivers Godavari Krishna and Penna with their extensive canal system are providing adequate water for industrial use for all parts of the state.Up to 10 mgd of water can be immediately made available to industries in and around Hyderabad. The state has one of the highest precipitation's in the country and also has substantial groundwater resources.

OPPORTUNITIES

Agro/Horticulture

Andhra Pradesh enables the potential investor to make fruitful forays into Agro based industries like fruit concentrates, fruit and vegetable pulps, pastes and powders. Frozen fruit and vegetables, snack food, dehydrated products, oleoresins etc.

Minerals

The state extends full support to its partners in progress for exploration development and export of minerals.

Port Based Industrialisation

The 960 km long coastline and abundance of ports opens opportunities for exploration and exploitation of hydro carbons, petroleum refineries, petro-chemicals, tank farms and long terminals in the state.

Software

Andhra Pradesh, with abundance of skilled manpower and latest infrastructure invites a major role in networking and data-cum software, object oriented designs and technologies, electronic design automation (DEDA), software, re-engineering, RDBMS, CAD/CAM-2d/3d graphic modeling, gist, unix internals and more.

Textiles

Andhra Pradesh is famous for its age old textile tradition, skilled artisans and latest technology spread a red-carpet welcome to manufacture cotton and silk yarn, man-made fibres, weaving, processing and knitting, non-woven fabrics, readymades etc., Thus, it provides opportunities in all these fields.

Infrastructure Development

To create a strong based for accelerating pace of growth, the state of Andhra Pradesh encouraging private participation in the areas of power, ports, airports, expressways, mega industrial infrastructure parts (centers of excellence) etc.

Telecommunications

An open door policy the State welcomes investment in the manufacture of switching systems, pagers, connectors various types of cables, transmission equipment and terminals like cordless phones, pay phones, fax machines and modems.

RESOURCES

Agro-Horticultural Sector

The State of Andhra Pradesh is a leading producer of cash crops like tobacco, groundnut, chilllies, turmeric, oil seeds, cotton, sugar cane and jute. It also produces some of the finest varieties of fruits like mangoes, citrus, grapes, guavas, sapotas, papayas and bananas. It has a large area under food grains, vegetables, fruits, flowers and plantation crops. Wide range of Agro-climatic conditions suitable for a variety crops.

This provide opportunities for establishing wide range of Agro Based and food processing units.

Mineral Sector

The Andhra Pradesh state has a vast potential for on-shore exploration of oil and natural gas. It is the leader in granite exports and has abundant deposits of limestone. It is the only state in south India with large coal deposits. It has the second largest deposits of bauxite in India. The state has endowed with extensive deposits of gold, diamonds, copper, manganese, dolomite, iron ore, lead, zinc, mica and beach sands containing atomic minerals.

As the State is rich in mineral resources, it provides good opportunities to the entrepreneurs who wish to start mineral based units.

Human Resources

The State has large pool of skilled and dedicated workforce. It has a large spread of Universities, technical colleges, it is, polytechnics for providing skilled and unskilled manpower. A special point which needs a say is that the State is going to provide 20,000 Engineering seats both Private and Government colleges from the year 1998-99. The State is the home for more than 50 prestigious central and state research and training establishments like ASCI, IICT, CCMB, DRDL, IIIT etc.

INCENTIVES TO SMALL SCALE INDUSTRIES

Target 2000 Scheme

The Government of Andhra Pradesh has introduced a new policy for industries called 'Target—2000' in order to accelerate industrial development.

All new industrial units whether large, medium or small which are located anywhere in the state of Andhra Pradesh except within municipal corporation areas of Hyderabad, Vijayawada, and Visakhapatnam are going into commercial production on or after November 15, 1995 are eligible for the following incentives.

I) An investment subsidy of 20 per cent of the fixed capital not exceeding Rs. 20.00 lakhs will be given.

II) A sales tax deferment limited to 135 per cent of fixed capital investment in a period of 14 years will be given. The deferred amount will be treated as deemed loan on making available security of fixed assets of the industry, pari-passu with financial institutions and on finalisation of assessment by the commercial tax authorities for each year or sales tax exemption for a period of 7 years limited to a ceiling of 135 per cent of fixed capital investment. This applies during the entire holiday period at the option of industry effective from the data of commencement of commercial production.

All new industries other than those setup in the municipal corporation areas will be eligible for 25 per cent rebate in power bill (both demand and energy) for a period of 3 years from the date of commencement of commercial production. The rebate shall be allowed by the Andhra Pradesh state electricity board (APSEB) in its monthly bills. The maximum total admissible rebate for the 3 years will be Rs. 50.00 lakhs in respect of large and medium industries and Rs. 30.00 lakhs in respect of small scale industries.

Expansion Project

Existing industrial units in eligible areas, setting up expansion project in products involving entracement capacity by 25 per cent for the products of the same product-line, will be eligible for sales tax deferral or sales tax exemption for the enhanced turnover above the base turnover as defined for a period of 14 years or 7 years respectively subject to a ceiling of 135% of additional fixed capital investment made, from the date of commencement of commercial production by the expansion project. Base turnover for this purpose shall be the best production achieved during three years proceeding the year of expansion of the maximum capacity expected to be achieved by the industry as per the appraisal made by the finance institution before funding the project whichever is higher.

Diversification Forward Integration Project

Existing industrial units in eligible areas making investment for a new product involving diversification or forward integration, with an enhancement at least by 25 per cent of fixed capital investment as well as enhancement of turnover by 25 per cent. In value terms will be eligible for sales tax deferral or sales tax exemption as defined in expansion project on the new product on value addition over and above the base turn over as defined above for a period of 14 years or 7 years respectively subject to a ceiling of 135 per cent of additional fixed capital investment made from the date of commencement of commercial production of the diversification/forward integration project.

Backward Integration Project

Existing industrial units in eligible areas rises investment for an intermediate product involving backward integration, with an enhancement of at least 25 per cent of fixed capital investment as well as enhancement of turnover or value addition by 25 per cent in value terms will be eligible for sales tax defferal or sales tax exemption on the intermediate product or value addition over and above the base turnover, as defined above for a period of 14 years or 7 years respectively subject to a ceiling of 135% of additional fixed capital investment made from the date of commencement of commercial production of the backward integration project. The same limits and conditions are specified above will apply.

Captive Power Plants

Captive power plants including cogeneration units are eligible for capital investment subsidy at 20 per cent on fixed capital investment subject to a maximum of Rs. 20.00 lakhs, whichever is less.

Small Industry Promoting Agencies

There are a good number of industry promoting agencies functioning in the state of Andhra Pradesh. They are established after the formation of the state (1956). They have made a mark in the development of the state industrially. Their services are appreciable in this regard. In the absence of these agencies the state would have remained industrially undeveloped. Therefore, the role played by these agencies in the industrialisation of the state in the past need not be over emphasised. However, an attempt is made in the following pages to outline their origin and objectives along with their growth and working in the industrialisation of the state.

Andhra Pradesh Industrial Development Corporation Limited (APIDC)

Andhra Pradesh Industrial Development Corporation (APIDC) was set up in 1960. It was established to monitor the expenditious and planned development of small, medium and large scale industries in the state. The mission of APIDC is enriching society through sustained industrial growth. Today it has an authorised capital of Rs. 110 crores and paid up capital of Rs. 96.23 crores. So far APIDC (31-3-98) promoted 756 units with a total investment generated Rs. 5496.20 crores and created employment for 1,39,324 persons.

Objectives

The objectives of the corporation are as follows:

to identify, promote and finance, through equity participation, the setting up of large and medium scale projects;

to function as an extended arm of the national level financial institutions IDBI, IFCI, ICICI, IRBI, and to co-ordinate all efforts for any integrated development of industries in the state; and

to achieve overall development with emphasis on backward area development and increased employment opportunities duly exploiting the potential resource endowments and technical skills in the state.

Activities

The corporation takes up the following activities.

Promotion and implementation of new project ideas through encouraging subsidiaries, joint/assisted ventures.

Obtaining letters of intent/licences from government of India for select industries. Comprehensive escort services to entrepreneurs. Equity participation extending terms loans and seed capital. Providing assistance under equipment refinance scheme extending assistance for modernisation of plant and machinery for higher productivity.

The promotional and training activities are exclusively attended by the special cell entrepreneurial development and guidance center.

Systematic monitoring of units and rehabilitation of viable sick units.

Andhra Pradesh Industrial Infrastructure Corporation Limited (APIIC)

Andhra Pradesh Industrial Infrastructure Corporation (APIIC) was set up in 1973. The corporation establishes industrial development areas equipped with all infrastructure facilities like developed land, power, water resources, sheds, roads and communications and housing for the development of large medium small scale industries at potential growth centers in the state.

Normally standard sheds measuring 30' and 50'/30 x 62.6i/144' x 33.6' duly approved by the factory authorities are made available on all the industrial estates. Plots are allotted as per the needs and requirements of the individual projects. The layouts of IDAs/IEs are approved by the town planning department/urban development authorities and factories department regarding site location and structure, with provision of roads, street lights, drainage etc. The power supply is also arranged by APSEB. In all aspects the plots developed or sheds constructed are for ready use by the allottees. Plots/sheds are allotted on outright sale basis.

The allottees shall pay 50% of the land cost 30% of the shed cost, all the case may be, within one month from the date of receipt of allotment order. He should execute a sale agreement with full stamp duty within one month from the date of receipt of allotment letters. He should also execute a promote for the balance 50% of land cost 170% of shed cost which is to be paid within one along with 16% interest per annum from the date of taking possession of a plot/shed.

Andhra Pradesh Small Scale Industrial Development Corporation (APSSIDC)

Andhra Pradsh Small Scale Industrial Development Corporation Limited (APSSIDC) was established on 1.3.1961 to aid, counsel, assist, protect and promote the interest of small scale industries in the state of Andhra Pradesh.

Activities

The main activities of the corporation are:

— promotion and development of small scale industries;

— marketing assistance to small scale industries;
— procurement and supply of raw-materials to small scale industries;
— running of production units and general engineering workshops.

For promotion of new industries APSSIDC renders service like counceling preparation of project profilies, organising seminars, participation in entrepreneurial development programmes (EDPs) in co-ordination with the concerned departments and agencies, conducing special integrated entrepreneurial development programmes for weaker sections of the society and first generation entrepreneurs, participation in intensive industrial promotion campaigns and management appreciation programmes etc.

APSSIDC has 13 raw-material servicing centers spread all over the state as supply centers to the small scale industries in the respective zones. The supply of iron and steel, pig, iron, coke, paraffin wax are effected through these centers. The corporation is also dealing with non-ferrous materials such as zinc, copper, tin, cadium etc., as agent on behalf of material servicing centers (RMSC) Santhnagar, Hyderabad.

The corporation is also acting as consignment agent of Indian Petro Chemicals Corporation Limited (IPCL) in distribution of plastic material such as keyline indotheme and PVC materials. The distribution is as per quota fixed by IPCL to the individual industries. The corporation also provides finance to small scale industries units against guarantee for procurement of essential raw-materials.

APSSIDC assists in marketing the produced of small scale industries units in the state of Andhra Pradesh.

Andhra Pradesh State Financial Corporation (APSFC)

Andhra Pradesh State Financial Corporation is a primary term lending institution financing small and medium scale industries in the state. Road information relating to the various schemes of financial assistance will be offered by the corporation for small scale/medium industries and other industry related activities is provided the fore running paras.

Industrial concerns under any form of ownership whether proprietary or partnership, registered co-operative society, private or public limited company engaged in or proposed to engage in one or more of the following activities are eligible for financial assistance:

a) Manufacture, preservation of processing of goods;

b) Mining including development of mines;

c) Generation or distribution of electricity or any other form of energy;

d) Maintenance, repair, testing or servicing machinery or any description or vehicles or motor boars or trailers or tractors;

e) Assembling, repairing, or pacing any article with the aid of machinery or power;

f) For setting up or development of as industrial area/estate;

g) The research and development of any processor product in respect of industrial activities;

h) Providing special or technical knowledge or other services for the promotion of industrial growth;

i) Marketing support to small, cottage and village industries;

Assistance for non-industrial (eg. transport, hotels, hospitals, nursing homes, fishing etc activities is also provided by the corporation.

The corporation does not extend financial assistance towards working capital except under composite loan scheme, single window scheme and self employment schemed for young entrepreneurs.

Schemes of APSFC

The following are the various schemes for the financial assistance offered by the corporation for small scale industries:

1. Composite loans

100% loan assistance up to Rs. 50,000/- for cottage, village and tiny industries sector with a repayment period of 3 to 10 years is allowed at places with population less than 5 lakhs.

2. Scheme for physically handicapped and SC & ST entrepreneurs

100% financial assistance for equipment or working capital or both with maximum amount of loan not exceeding Rs. 50,000/- projects exceeding cost of Rs. 50,000 will be financed on liberal terms including soft loans assistance to SC/ST entrepreneurs.

3. Single window scheme

New, tiny and small scale industrial units whose cost of projects excluding working capital margin) does not exceed Rs. 20.00 lakhs and the total working capital requirement at the normal level of operations is upto Rs. 10.00 lakhs, are eligible for assistance under the scheme. With over all debt equity ratio depending upon nature of activity working capital loans exceeding Rs. 1.00 lakh, should be suitably secured to the extent of 60% Repayment period will be maximum 10 years with a moratorium period of 24 months for term and 36 months for working capital loan.

4. Women entrepreneur scheme

Projects in small scale industries sector with women entrepreneur having minimum 51% share in equity are eligible for assistance. Assistance shall be given based on debit equity ratio and minimum promoters contribution which varies depending upon line of activity. Term loans are repayable over a period of not exceeding 10 years with an initial moratorium period upto 2 years.

5. Mahila udyog nidhi scheme

New industrial products with project cost not exceeding Rs. 10.0 lakhs promoted by women entrepreneurs with minimum of 51% share in equity are eligible for capital assistance as foft loan at 6% service charges upto maximum of 15% of project cost in addition to term loan to meet the gap in equity. Minimum promoters contribution shall be based on the nature of activity. Projects under single window scheme also can be extended assistance under this scheme provided the entrepreneurs satisfy the criteria under both schemes. Soft loan under mahila udyog nidhi scheme is admissible against cost of fixed assets. The soft loan repayment period will be maximum 10 years with a moratorium period upto 5 years.

6. Self employment scheme for young entrepreneurs

The scheme is applicable to unemployed youth in the age group of 20-40 (45 years in the case of SC/ST) whose parental income does not exceed Rs. 12,000 per annum having minimum educational qualifications.

A.P. State Non-Resident Indian Investment Corporation Ltd., (ANRICH)

ANRICH has been established with the express purpose of providing servicing and facilities Non-Resident Indians (NRIs) in implementing their investment plans in industrial and other projects.

The scope of services of ANRICH includes identification of feasible projects, Liaison with government departments, securing infrastructural facilities, securing various clearances in minimum time, providing services of reputed consultants, securing finance from institutions and commercial banks etc. ANRICH act as an agent on behalf of the NRIs from the conceptual stage till the projects are grounded.

Andhra Pradesh Electronics Development Corporation Limited (APEDC)

Andhra Pradesh Electronics Development Corporation Limited was established excessively for the promotion of the electronics industry in the state. It plays a catalytic role and offers (i) equity participation (ii) marketing assistance (iii) establishment of separate industrial estates, and (iv) provision of technology tie-up and product development.

Equity participation : The corporation promotes industries as assisted units, helping them right from project conception to the final implementation state which include selection of product lines and adoption of appropriate technology, quality control, after sales services and creation of proper brand image. The extent of equity participation is decided based on location, nature of the industry and related parameters and the assistance by and large covers the entire spectrum of electronics from components to computer systems.

Marketing assistance : To supplement the efforts of individual units, APEDC offers marketing assistance through institutional marketing and its own distribution channels located at Vijayawada, Visakhapatnam, Tirupati, Karimanagar and Hyderabad.

Electronics industrial estates : The corporation has set-up industrial estates at Karakambadi near Tirupati, Gannavaram near Vijayawada and at Kushaiguda near Hyderabad and offer sites ready-built space to individual industrial units. The corporation has plans for a software technology park, hardware technology park and a women entrepreneurs complex.

Andhra Pradesh State Agro Industries Development Corporation Limited (APAGROS)

Agro Industries Development Corporation which was setup in the year 1968, Its main purposes are to develop lands included in command areas of irrigation project and to drill bore wells in drought areas. It has a self employment scheme for rural youth.

Under the scheme unemployed youth in rural areas are trained in different trades like servicing and repairing of agricultural machinery, electrical equipment like pump sets etc. To establish small units with the financial assistance from commissioner special employment schemes. Unemployed youth are also assisted in setting up several agro based industries such as essential oils, apirary units, seed cleaning and processing units, agricultural implements, dehuller flour mills etc.,

Andhra Pradesh Mineral Development Corporation Limited (APMDC)

Andhra Pradesh is richly endowed with huge deposits of diverse minerals, viz limestone, coal, clay, iron ore asbestos, barrettes, dolomite manganese, graphite, quartz, mica, bauxite etc. About 35 minerals are being commercially exploited. In most cases 70% to 80% of exploited minerals/ore is sent out of state or country in their raw form. Except the cement grade lime stone which is utilised in cement factories in the state. Having realised the importance of the mineral wealth and the need for their proper explosion, Andhra Pradesh Mineral Development Corporation limited was established in 1961. The corporation is inviting NRIs to come forward for the development of mineral based industries in Andhra Pradesh. The corporation will provide all facilities, including joint venture programmes.

Andhra Pradesh Industrial and Technical Consultancy Organization (APITCO)

This organisation is sponsored by the Industrial Development Bank of India. It provides consultancy services in promotion of new industries, diversification modernization of existing industries, identifying feasible and profitable scheme in small, medium and large scale sectors and undertaking detailed studies on the techno-economic feasibility of industrial units identified as having scope. So far APITCO with professional expertise will make the project report and also follow up with the financial institutions.

Out of the a over 100 units are in production as at various stages of implementation. APITCO helps by conducting market surveys to establish whether the proposed product has market, and if so at what price and of what quality, so far, APITCO has conducted 40 market surveys which have helped entrepreneurs/organisations to take investment decision. APICTO takes up monitoring or running units and guiding the management in efficient functioning of units by APITCO will be or great help us it will give an impartial third party view of the operations and heath of the units financed by them. This will enable speedy assistance to units to ensure success.

Andhra Pradesh State Trading Corporation (APSTC)

APSTC has been set up to promote exports from state and to stimulate export entrepreneurship to import into the state various raw-materials required by industries, particularly in the small scale sector, and to undertake internal trading in selected goods identified from time to time.

Andhra Pradesh Assistance Center for Entrepreneurs (APACE)

APACE has been set up to guide industrial entrepreneurs in the formulation and implementation of projects and to solve their various problems. It acts as a one window agency and provides them a range of services. APACE guides entrepreneurs in identification of feasible industries, help them receive the necessary industrial licences by registration, secure incentives and subsidies, solve implementation and operational problems provides escort services in securing land, power, finances and solves their problems in implementation.

GROWTH AND WORKING OF INDUSTRIES IN VIZIANAGARAM DISTRICT

About the District

Vizianagaram district was formed on Ist June, 1979 with head-quarters at Vizianagaram with portions covered from Srikakulam and Visakhapatnam districts. It is situated within the geographical co-ordination of 170 00'and 19o 15' of the northern latitude and 83o 00 and 83o 45' east by Srikakulam district, on west and south by Visakhapatnam district, on the southeast by the bay of Bengal and northeast by Orissa state. It consists of 34 Mandals with 1548 villages comprised in two revenue divisions viz, Vizianagaram and Parvathipuram.

The map showing the mandal division of Vizianagaram district is given in the next page to understand its geographical structure.

Vizianagaram has got glorious past in the history in promotion art and culture and a seat for renewed educational institutions. The Government of India have sanctioned a growth center at Bobbili for accelerated growth of industries.

M.—2 VIZIANAGARAM DISTRICT INDUSTRIAL MAP

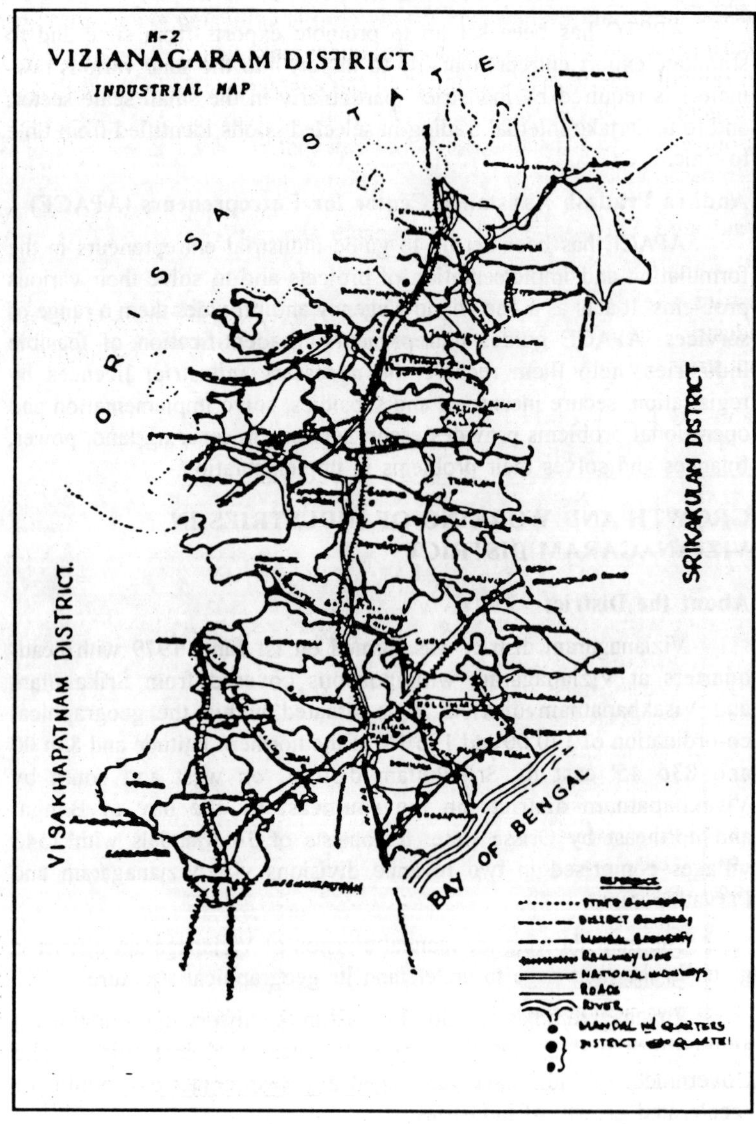

Agricultural Resources

Vizianagaram district is predominantly dependent on agriculture, about 84 per cent of the population of the district is living in rural areas. The major crop grown in the district are paddy, ragi, bajra, sugarcane, pulses, mesta and ground nuts. Paddy crop is cultivated mainly during kharif season in 80 per cent of its area under tanks which in turn depend on rainfall. Due to erratic rainfall all the average yields in the district are generally low compared to the state average. The agricultural resources of the district becomes vital raw material for a wide range of agro based industries like rice mills, oil mills, jute mills, sugar mills etc.

Small and Tiny Units in Vizianagaram District

Table 3.3 shows that industry-wise small and tiny units in the district. The table reads nearly one-third of the units relate to agro based industry. The engineering and allied based industry and forest based industries are in second and third places respectively.

Table—3.3 List of S.S.I. and Tiny Units Registered with District Industries Centre as on 31-03-1996

Sl. No.	*Category*	*No.of units*	*Investment (Rs. in lakhs)*	*Employment*
1	*2*	*3*	*4*	*5*
1.	Food products	832	1,362.99	8,424
2.	Beverages, tobacco & tobacco products	18	15.76	110
3.	Cotton textiles	6	3.77	31
4.	Wood, silk and synthetic	—	—	—
5.	Jute, hemp, mesta & coir	8	27.73	144
6.	Hoisory and garments	22	9.68	366
7.	Wooden products	453	154.92	2,488
8.	Paper products	84	45.39	464
9.	Leather products	95	53.87	567
10.	Rubber and plastic products	77	76.47	280
11.	Chemical and chemical products	60	304.32	694
12.	Non-metal mineral products	70	408.31	596
13.	Basic metal industries	176	330.05	2,569

cont.

1	*2*	*3*	*4*	*5*
14.	Metal products	245	376.77	1,491
15.	Machinery parts except electrical	40	42.53	145
16.	Electrical machinery	12	36.95	76
17.	Miscellaneous mfg. Industries	116	192.85	867
18.	Transport equipment and parts	6	9.11	180
19.	Repairing/servicing industries	719	290.63	2,621
	Total	3,039	3,742.09	22,113

Source : Records of district industries center, Vizianagaram.

Large and Medium Industries

There are only nineteen large and medium industries in the district as against 1781 industries in the state as on 31-03-1997. Among the 19 industries, 5 are agro based, 6 are jute based, 2 are mineral based, 5 are engineering and allied based, and one each belongs to extile, leather and automobile industries. These industries with an investment of Rs. 5094 lakhs are providing employment to 13,360 persons.

Infrastructure Facilities

Availability of power, water, transport and communication, training and education facilities, banking facilities, etc. are the basic necessities per industries to thrive in a region. The following are the infrastructure facilities available in the district for the growth and development of industries.

Railways

The district is served by a wide net work of railways. Vizianagaram railway junction connects Raipur, Howrah, Bhubaneshewar, Bokaro, Madras. The route length of the railways passing through the district is 215 km and this railway line covers 29 railway stations.

Roadways

The district is served by a wide net work of roadways. The total length of roads is 2,954.49 kms. Out of this, National highways constitute 125.33 kms, and state highways accounts for 717.76 kms. Zilla Parishad, municipalities and panchayat samithies roads are 211.20 kms. altogether. The Madras-Howrah, national highway goes through Vizianagaram.

Power

The 132kv power supply is being received by 2 main tenders mainly 1) 132 kv single circuit tapped from Machikand to T.B Vara and ii) 132 kv double circuit line from T.B Vara to Garividi. From Garividi substation one 33 kv feeder is covering Vizianagaram, Bhogapuram, Nellimarla taluk's. the second 33 kv feeder is covering Gajpathinagaram, S. Kota and Viyyampeta taluk's, third 33 kv feeder covering Bobbili, Salur, Parvathipuram and Kurapam taluk while fourth 33 kv feeder is covering Cheepurupalli taluk. Alternative feeder is also available from Gajuwaka substation to Vizianagaram district when break down occurs on these lines. 33/ii kv substations at Kotthavalasa, Gummalakshmipuram and Balijipeta were commissioned.

Water

There are no major irrigation projects in Vizianagaram district. The sources of irrigation are tank, ponds, and dug wells. Sources of canal irrigation are in Kurupam, Bhogapuram panchayat samithies, and significantly high in S.Kota and Bobbili panchayat samithies.

INFRASTRUCTURE FACILITIES PROVIDED BY APIIC

Besides these above facilities the district has some physical infrastructure facilities developed by APIIC which are shown in the following table:

Table—3.4 Infrastructure Facilities in Vizianagaram District as on 31-3-96

S. No.		*Entend of land developed*	*Developed plots*	*Factory sheds constructed*	*Vacancy available allotment*	
					Plots	*Sheds*
1.	Industrial estate, V.T. Agraharam, Vizianagaram	—	52	13	—	—
2	Industrial estate, Nellemarla, Vizianagaram	—	79	6	65	1
3.	Mini industrial estate, V.T. Agraharam, Vizianagaram	—	—	8	—	1
4	Growth centre, Bobbili	825 acres	—	—	—	—

Source : Records of APIIC, Vizianagaram.

The Government of India have sanctioned an industrial growth center at Bobbili, with a total investment of Rs. 30 crores for providng the required physical infrastructure to industrial units. An extent of 825 acre's of private land was taken position by the additional commissioner and handed over to the zonal manager, Andhra Pradesh industrial Infrastructure Corporation Limited., Visakhapatnam.

Banking

State Bank of India is the lead bank of the district. By the end of 31st March, 1996 there are 75 Commercial Bank branches, 61 Grameen bank branches, 17 Co-operative Central Bank Branches, 9 Co-operative Urban Banks and one Andhra Pradesh State Finance Corporation branch office working to extend financial assistance to entrepreneurs of the district.

The following Table 3.5 shows the key indicators relating to banking information published by lead bank consisting of No. of branches, deposits, advances, C.D. ratio, total P.S., DRI, 20 point programme etc., of Vizianagaram district.

Table—3.5 Key Indicators of all Banks in Vizianagaram District as on 31-03-1996

Name of the Bank	*No. of Branches*	*Deposits*	*Advances*	*C.D Ratio*	*Total P.S.*	*D.R.I.*	*20 point program*
1	*2*	*3*	*4*	*5*	*6*	*7*	*8*
State Bank of India	31	10,454	7,368	70	3,272	14	782
State Bank of Hyderabad	3	914	326	36	187	2	7
Andhra Bank	14	3,807	1,121	29	659	6	264
Bank of India	1	255	271	106	99	2	27
Bank of Baroda	1	269	164	61	95	—	—
Central Bank of India	1	129	69	53	56	—	—
Canara Bank	6	1,671	634	38	425	8	144
Corporation Bank	2	582	134	23	79	10	64
Indian Overseas Bank	6	852	709	83	474	4	210
Indian Bank	3	621	272	40	198	3	22
Syndicate Bank	1	539	138	26	32	—	4
Vijaya Bank	1	296	92	31	49	—	9
Vysya Bank Ltd.	2	1,021	374	37	116	—	—
Union Bank of India	2	562	520	93	215	4	67
S.V.G. Bank	61	4,374	4,187	96	3,827	—	—
Punjab National Bank	1	1,126	341	30	176	2	112
Total		27,472	16,720	61	9,957	46	—

Source: Lead Bank Annual Report. 1996-97.

GROWTH AND WORKING OF INDUSTRIES IN SRIKAKULAM DISTRICT

About the District

Srikakulam district came into existence in 1950. It is bounded on the north and west by Orissa State, east by the Bay of Bengal and south by Vizianagaram district. Srikakulam town, the district head-quarters is at a distance of 96 kms. from the new steel city of Visakhapatnam.

The district has a coast line of 193 kms. and has vast marine potential. A minor fishing harbour is coming up at Bhavanapadu. The earliest manganese deposits known in India were from Srikakulam district.

Srikakulam district consists of 37 revenue mandals and three revenue divisions. The map showing the division of Srikakulam district is given in the next page.

Agricultural and Horticulture Resource

The total gross irrigated area in the district is about 2 lakh hectares, which forms 55% of the total area of district. The principal food crops are paddy, jowar bajra and while commercial crops are mesta, sugarcane, groundnut.

Based on the above resources the following industrial units are established in the district. They are rice and flour mills, jute mills, sugar industry, kraft paper, jute stick powder etc.

The main horticulture resources in the district are cashew, coconut. There are 10,000 hectares of coconut and about 11,000 hectares of cashew are cultivated. Based on these resources about 130 cashew kernels processing industries, 11 coir de-fibering units, one curled coir unit, 2 two ply coir yarn units and one desiccated coconut powder units are came into existence. Minor forest produce available are ginger, tamarind, soapnuts, beedi leaves, turmeric.

Small and Tiny Units in Srikakulam District

Table 3.6 shows different category of small and tiny units in the district. The table reads that nearly one-fourth of the units relate to agro based industry. The forest based and chemical based industries are in second and third places respectively.

M.—3 ANDHRA PRADESH SRIKAKULAM DISTRICT MAP

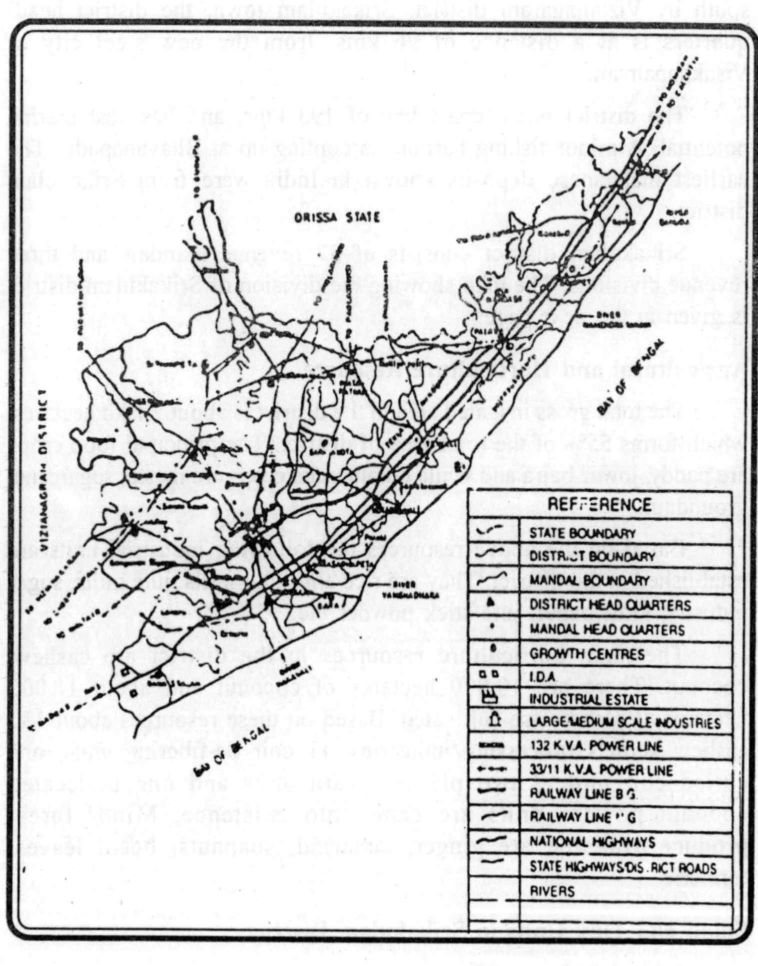

Table—3.6 Categorywise Distribution of Small and Tiny Industries of Srikakulam District as on 31-3-96

S.No.	*Category of units*	*No.of Units*	*Investment (Rs. in lakhs)*	*No.of Persons Employed*
1.	Agro Based	1,339	290.12	11,594
2	Forest Based	1,113	250.399	5,799
3	Mineral Based	135	191.12	2,268
4	Textile Based	192	126.14	1,168
5	Engineering Based	324	932.01	1,804
6	Chemical Based	475	592.86	4,468
7	Livestock Based	93	15.15	378
8	Building and Material Based	128	186.69	11,756
9	Others	1,575	1,145.61	6,603
	Total	5,374	3,730.1	35,838

Source : Records of district industries center, Srikakulam.

Large and Medium Industries

Though, the district is basically a backward one, the large and medium industries have been well developed here mainly due to the Central Government's special backward subsidies available in this district up to 1993. There are 32 large and medium industries in the district as against 1781 industries in the state. Among these 32 industries 14 belong to Agro based category viz., jute, sugar, paper and solvent extraction units, 6 units belong to chemical based category, viz., manufacturing dye stuffs, chemicals, acids etc., 9 belong to engineering & allied based category viz., pig iron unit, re-rolling mills, ferro chrome unit etc. Besides the above there is also one textile unit functioning in the district. All these industries with a total capital of Rs. 30,320.08 lakhs are providing employment to 6396 persons.

Infrastructure Facilities

Availability of power, water, transport and communication, training and education facilities, banking facilities etc., are the basic necessities for industries to thrive in a region. The following are the infrastructure facilities available in the district:

APIIC developed physical infrastructure facilities in the district which can be seen in the following table in detail.

Table—3.7 Infrastructure Facilities in Srikakulam District as on 31-3-97

Sl.	Name of the estate	Extend of land developed in acres	Plots			Sheds		
			Developed	Allotted	Vacant	Developed	Allotted	Vacant
1	Industrial estate Amadalavalsa	7,899	49	46	3	4	4	0
2	Industrial estate Kasulapuram	6,299	25	23	2	23	16	7
3	Mini industrial estate Kasulapuram for SC's.	20' *30' (sheds)						
4	Mini industrial estate Balga	0.61	6	6	0	0	0	0
5	Industrial estate Seethampeta.	2.2	49	34	15	20	14	6
6	Indl. Dev. Area Pydibeemavaram	410 (-) 60.00 for infr.dev. 35,00 acres.	350 acres	273 acres	77 Acres 10	10	0	10
7	Indl. estate, Palasa	30	99	8	91	0	0	0

Source : Records of APIIC, Srikakulam.

Railways

The Madras Howrah broad guage railway line passed through the district covering a length of 156 kms connecting important places of Ponduru, Amadalavalasa, Naupada, Palasa and Ichapuram in the district. The nearest railway station from the district headquarters is Amadalavalasa which is at a distance of 13 kms. from Srikakulam town. There is also a meter guage railway line of 37 kms. Starting from Naupada and passing through Tekkali and Pathapatnam linking up with Parlakimidi of Orissa state.

Roadways

The length of national highway (N.H.5) running in the district has 173.40 kms., and 2,119 kms., of two national highways. Besides the mandal parishad and gram panchayats are maintaining 1102 kms and 1,102 kms. lengths of roads within the district. The Andhra Pradesh State Road Transport Corporation is running a fleet of buses for providing transport facilities for the people of the district.

Power

Power is supplied to this district from Andhra Pradesh ring main through Kothagudem thermal power station, Vijaywada thermal power station and Soberu projects. The distribution is done through substations of 132 kv substation Garividi and Chilakapalem through various 33/11 kv substations.

Water Supply

The important rivers in the district are Nagavali, Vamsadhara, Suvarnamukhi , Mahendratanaya and Bahuda. The Nagavali and its tributaries provides irrigation for major parts of Palakonda, Ponduru, Rajam, Regidi, Amadalavalasa Vangara, Santhakaviti, Boorja and Veeraghattam, and Srikakulam mandals. The Vamsadhara river provides irrigation to large extent in Pathapatnam Narasannapeta, Kotabommali, Polaki, Amadalavalasa, Gara and Saravakote mandals. Bahuda river irrigates considerable extents in Ichapuram and Kaviti mandals. The district headquarters gets water supply from Nagavali river which passes through Srikakulam town.

Table—3.8 Key Indicators of all Banks in Srikakulam District as on 31-12-97

(Rs. in lakhs)

Sl. No.	*Name of the Bank*	*No.of Brs.*	*Deposits*	*Advances*	*C.D Ratio %*	*Priority Sec.Adv.*	*Dri. Adv.*	*20 Point Program*
1	Andhra Bank	31	10,400	4,198	41	2,362	19.6	1,086.02
2	State Bank of India	31	13,947	8,479	60	4,996	20.8	183.75
3	State Bank of Hyderabad	1	226.79	81.09	36	25.83	0.08	25.83
4	Sri Visakha Grameena	58	833.56	5,723.4	69	4,292.55	0	4,292.55
5	Canara Bank	1	249.18	116.01	47	71.65	0.58	29.81
6	Union Bank of India	1	722.17	236.63	33	179.76	1.17	140.28
7	Allahabad Bank	1	493.07	129.51	26	85.88	0.18	34.95
8	Bank of India	1	64.15	45.12	70	9.13	0.04	9.13
9	Dist. Co-op. Central Bank Ltd.	15	871.55	5432.64	624	5162	0	0
10	Vijaya Bank	1	456.16	64.56	14	26.14	0.07	19.47
11	Indian Overseas Bank	2	799.56	182.71	23	89.41	1.65	28.85
12	Syndicate Bank	3	687	331.62	48	214.03	0.62	120.12
13	Indian Bank	4	674	454.64	67	380.61	4.69	322.16
14	The Vysya Bank Ltd.	2	2,116.36	1,495.74	71	771.89	0.61	5.96
	Total	152	40,040.76	26,970.[illegible]	67%	19,666.88	48.97	6,298.88

Source : Annual Report of Lead bank, 1996-97, Srikakulam.

Banking

Andhra Bank is the lead bank of the district. The other important nationalised banks in the district are the State Bank of India, 79 branches of various commercial banks, 58 rural banks (Sri Visakha Grameena bank), a branch office of Andhra Pradesh State Finance Corporation Limited, 15 Co-operative Central Bank Branches, 9 Andhra Pradesh Co-operative Agricultural Development Bank Branches are functioning in the district to extent financial assistance to entrepreneurs.

The following table 3.8 shows the key indicators relating to banking information consisting of number of branches, deposits, advances, C.D. Ratio, priority sector advances, D.R.I. advances and 20 point programme etc.

GROWTH AND WORKING OF INDUSTRIES IN VISAKHAPATNAM DISTRICT

About the District

The district derived its name from Visakhapatnam, its headquarters city. It is bounded on the north by Vizianagaram district on the south by East Godavari district, on the east by the Bay of Bengal and on the west by Orissa state. The 160 kms long coast line offers scope to develop marine and salt based industries. Its mineral wealth is sizable with deposits of bauxite, clay, graphite, lime stone, manganese and mica. The district is chiefly agricultural with a variety of crops both foodgrains as well as commercial crops. Mango, jack fruit, cashew and other fruits grow in abundance in the district besides minor forest products.

Visakhapatnam district consisting of 43 revenue mandals and three revenue divisions. The map showing the division of Visakhapatnam District in Next page.

Visakhapatnam popularly known as steel city, throbbing with maritime activity, in fast developing into one of the premier industrial centers of the country. Besides the first ever port-based steel plant, Visakhapatnam also houses some of the major public sector units Hindustan Shipyard, Bharat Heavy Plates and Vessels, Hindustan Zinc and Hindustan Petroleum and in private and joint sectors are big names such Coromandal Fertilizers, Coastal Chemicals, Hindustan polimers and Andhra Pradesh Refractories. The city's location as a strategic port endows it with the establishment of a free trade zone. Visakhapatnam is the

M.—4 VISAKHAPATNAM DISTRICT SCALE : 1.32 KMS. INDUSTRIAL MAP

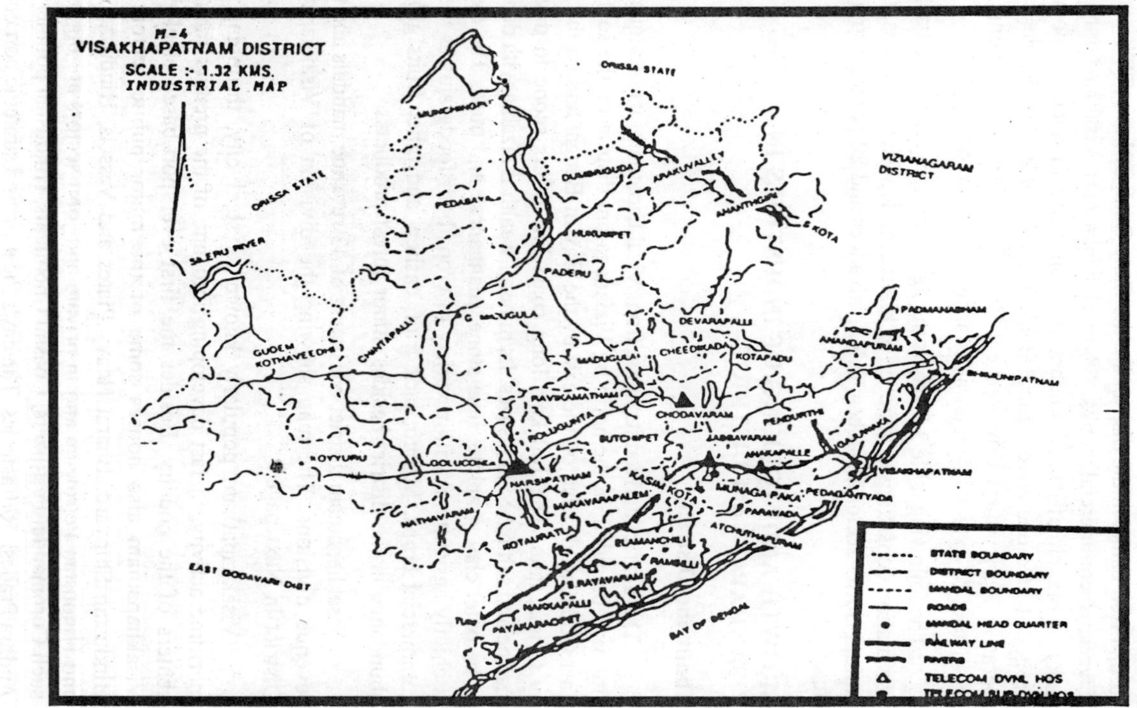

second biggest urban complex in the state, next to the capital city of Hyderabad.

Agricultural Resources

Agriculture is the main stay of around 70 per cent of the households. Though Visakhapatnam city is industrially developing, the rural areas continued to be backward due to lack of adequate irrigation facilities. Paddy is the principal food crop of the district followed by Ragi, Bajra, and Jowar. Among cash crops, sugar cane, groundnut, sesamum and chilies are important. Since there is no major irrigation system only 30% of the cropped area is irrigated under the ayacut of the medium irrigation system and minor irrigation tanks. The rest of the cultivated area is covered under dry crops depending upon the vagaries of the monsoon.

Based on the agricultural resources 4 sugar factories, a number of oil mills, cashew processing, palm fiber extraction units, flour mills have come up.

Small and Tiny Units in the District

Table 3.9 shows different categories of small and tiny units in the district. The table reads that nearly one-third of the units related to Engg. and allied based category. The forest based and agro based industries are in second and third places respectively.

Table—3.9 Categorywise Distribution of Small and Tiny Industries in Visakhapatnam District as on 31-03-96

Item	*Units*	*Investment (lakhs)*	*Employment*
Agro based	1,427	2,110.96	13,842
Forest based	3,675	850.38	30,081
Mineral based	498	1,132.42	10,414
Textile based	234	352.42	5,514
Engineering based	5,047	3,031.36	35,722
Chemical based	656	1,598.62	5,737
Livestock based	378	178.41	3,552
Building material	251	353.39	5,287
Miscellaneous	2,932	1963.56	30,444
Total	15,098	11,571.52	140,593

Source : Records of District Industries Center, Visakhapatnam

Table—3.10 Infrastructure Facilities in Visakhapatnam District as on 31-03-97

Sl. No.	Particulars of the Estates/Ida	Extent of Land Developed (Acres)	No. of Plots		No. of Sheds		Area Required for Expansion (Acres)
			Developed	Allotted	Constructed	Allotted	
1	2	3	4	5	6	7	8
1	Industrial Estate, Visakhapatnam	66.11	55	55	38	38	—
2	Industrial Developed Area						
	I) A-Block, (Site)	122.07	122.07 (Acres)	93.93 (Acres)	—	—	—
	II) B-Block, Autonagar, Vizag -12.						
	III) Assisted Pvt. Indl.Estate, Vizag-12.	156.43	216	216	42	42	—
	IV) Engineer Entrepreneurs Indl. Estate, Vizag-12.						
	V) C. Block	152.77	152.77	146.77	—	—	—
	VI) D.Block	333.46	159	152	55	54	100.00 (Exp.)
	-Do-(Expansion)	100.00	100.00		—	—	—

cont.

1	2	3	*4*	5	*6*	7	*8*
	VII) E-Block	140.00	87	20.00 12	—	—	150.45 (Exp.)
3	Ancillary Industrial Estate,	192.66	179	126	65	33	49 (Exp.)
4	Assisted Pvt. Industrial Estate, Anakapalli	30.12	72	68	4	4	11.30 (Exp.)
5	Industrial Estate Araku	7.34	13	12	2	2	—
6	Industrial Estate, Paderu	2.67	7	7	2	2	—
7	Industrial Estate, Chinthapalli	4.30	16	—	—	—	—

Large and Medium Scale Industries

53 large and Medium scale industries with an investment of Rs. 9,219 crores providing employment to 46,560 persons are functioning in the district. 14 projects with an estimated investment of Rs. 1959 crores and potential for generation of employment of about 2,162 persons are under implementations.

72 Large and Medium Scale Industries with an estimated capital investment of about 358.31 crores and having scope of employment to about 10,668 persons.

Infrastructure Facilities

APIIC developed physical infrastructure facilities in the district, which can be seen in the following table in detail.

Industrial Estates and Industrial Development Areas Proposed During the Eight Plan

S.No.	*Location*	*Extent of Area*	*Remarks*
1.	Extent of Industrial Development Area, Visakhapatnam-12 (E-Block)	50.00	Layout to be approved by VUDA
2	Industrial Development Area, Gurrampalem	253.00	Under Development
3.	Industrial Development Area, Aganampudi	230.00	Land Acquisition Alienation under Progress
4.	Autonagar, Narsipatnam	8.00	Layout approved by director of Town & Country Planning
5.	Industrial Estate, Chodavaram	50.00	Site to be identified
6.	Land for Petro-Chemical & Allied Industries	2000.00	Land under Acquisition.

Roadways

Transport facilities play a vital role in the development of industries. The total road length of Visakhapatnam district is 4,338 kms. Out of this, National Highway roads are 134 kms., R and B roads are 1,222 kms. Zilla Parishad roads are 1,666 kms. and panchayat samiti roads are 1916 kms. The National Highway (N.H.5) is passing through the district touching important places viz. Payakaraopeta, Yellamanchalli, Anakapalli, Visakhapatnam and Chittivalasa. All other places are well connected by state highways and Zilla parishad roads.

Railways

The district headquarters as well as the mandal headquarters except Bheemunipatnam Chodavaram, Chintapalli, Madugula and Paderu are well connected by railway line. To facilitate easy transportation for exporting Iron-Ore, Visakhapatnam is connected with D.B.K. Railway extending to a length of 720 kms. Visakhapatnam is one of the Divisioinal Headquarters of South Eastern Railway. Besides the above, Visakhapatnam port trust is maintaining artirial railway line connecting marshaling yards, Port area with outer harbour and all the major industries and stockyards. It serves a good transport facility for exports and imports. The fishing harbour which is one of the modern harbour is catering to need of fishing trade, industrialists and fisherman community.

Waterways

Visakhapatnam has a noted natural harbour. Visakhapatnam port on the east ranks first among the major ports on the east coast. It has 11 quarry berths, 3 jetty berths and 1 mooring berth besides it is the deepest harbour of the country backed up by way sophisticated automatic leading system.'

Airways

Visakhapatnam is connected by air with Madras, Hyderabad, Bhubaneswar, Raipur and Calcutta directly.

Marine Resources

The district has the advantage of having a long coast line of about 160 kms. which helped development of salt and marine based industries. Fishing is another important economic activity for 15,000 fishermen population, salt fields are concentrated at Bheemunipatnam, Karasa, Balachruvu, Vade Cheepurupalli, Pudimadaka and Revupolavaram villages. At present 15 salt factories are functioning in the district and still there is scope for establishment of 3 more factories utilising the salt produced in 2,250 acres of salt land near Devada and other places like Vakapadu, Revupolavaram.

Power

The power requirements of Visakhapatnam district is being met from 3 hydro power substations at upper Sileru (120.0 M.W. installed capacity), lower Sileru (460.0. M.W. installed capacity) and Machkund (joint project 80.3 M.W. installed capacity) Through a wide net work of 41 existing substations. This district is having a rural electric co-operative society with headquarters at Anakapalli (Kasimkot).

Water

The irrigation requirements of the district are being met through Thandava, Kalyanapulova and Ghambhiragedda reservoir (capacity 58.66 m.cft.) besides 5 major irrigation tanks.

The drinking water requirements of Visakhapatnam town are being met by Meghadrigedda, Tadipudi (Vizianagaram district) and Ghambiragedda reservioirs, besides supplying to large and medium scale industrial units to an extent of 30 M.G.D. the requirement of Visakhapatnam steel plant is being met from Yeluru Reservoir (East Godavari district) through canal system and partly from Raiwada canal system.

The estimated supply of water requirement of the coming large and medium scale and small scale industries is about 100 M.G.D. which is proposed to be met by tapping of the existing reservoirs through modernization to canal system and from Godavari through Yeluru canal systems, which is likely to be taken up at an estimated cost of Rs. 200 crores during 8th plan.

Banking

State Bank of India is the lead bank of the district. 206 branches of various commercial banks, a branch office of the Andhra Pradesh State Financial Corporation. One Cooperative Central Bank with 22 branches, 23 branches of Urban Banks and 49 branches of Visaka Grameena Bank (47 rural and 2 urban) are functioning in the district. All the branches of the Commercial Banks and Andhra Pradesh State Financial Corporation are extending financial assistance to entrepreneurs of the districts. Besides the regional office of APIDC and NABARD which are catering to the needs of industrialists both in Urban and Rural areas.

Export Processing Zone

With a view to boost the exports from the state, the Visakhapatnam Export Processing Zone is being set up in an area of 400 acres at Duvvada Railway Station, by the side of Madras-Calcutta Rail Line, which is proposed to be developed in two phases, first phase an extent of ac. 163.00; at a cost of Rs. 17.00 crores. Basic infrastructural facilities such as developed land/plots for construction of factory buildings, standard design factory buildings providing ready built accommodation, roads, power and water supply, drainage system etc., are being provided. In addition, customs clearance facilities are offered within the zone premises itself without any extra cost. Facilities are also provided for banking, post office, telex, telephone cleaning agents etc., in the service center located in the zone.

The state government is arranging to provide water to an extent of I.M.G.D. power to an extent of 10 MW and approach road up to the periphery of E.P.Z.

The Government of India has set up a board for the administration of E.P.Z. and the office of Development Commissioner for monitoring and implementing the programme.

In order to ensure successful functioning of two units in the zone and to generate exports, the government has offered a liberal package of incentives like approvals at one single point, import of capital goods without import licence, exemption of customs duty, Central excise duty, allowing 100% foreign ownership, exemption of income tax, C.S.T. etc., liberal sanction of foreign exchange etc., besides the state incentives and subsidies.

Atomic Minerals Complex (nuclear complex)

The Andhra Pradesh Mining Corporation, Hyderabad is contemplating to set up one Sen sand processing unit at Visakhapatnam, utilising the Sea Beach sand available between Visakha-Bheemili area, which constitutes the Atomic Minerals like Monazite, Zicron, Silicon, Illuminite etc. The unit will be set jointly with M/s National Mineral Development Corporation, M/s Indian Rare Earths Corporation, the Department of Atomic Energy and Defense Research and Development Organisation. The estimated cost of the project is about Rs. 100 crores.

Petro-chemical Complex

By making use of the chemical residues of M/s Hindustan Petroleum Corporation Limited, one Naphtha Crackers Project and Naphtha based synthetic fiber and other bye-product plants are proposed for establishment in and around Visakhapatnam with a capital investment of Rs. 500 crores and other bye-products about Rs. 1100 crores:

CHAPTER—IV

GROWTH AND ORGANISATION OF SAMPLE UNITS

The main purpose of this chapter is to present an analysis of the sample units based on the primary data collected from them on various aspects like growth, capital investment, capacity installed and utilised, causes for idle capacity, output etc., Attempts have been made to examine the working of small scale units in Vizianagaram, Srikakulam and Visakhapatnam districts. In respect of their different aspects as mentioned above. Besides, the growth of total small scale units in these 3 districts since 1980 is also studied. The growth and working of sample units and their analysis is done to ascertain working of small scale units in these districts in the mobilisation of resources of capital and their effective utilisation.

GROWTH OF TOTAL UNITS

As the study covers a period from 1980 to 1996, the small scale units established up to 31-3-1980 and units established after that date is analysed as shown in the following 4.1 table with regard to Vizianagaram, Srikakulam and Visakhapatnam districts.

Table—4.1 Growth of total Small Scale Units in Vizianagaram, Srikakulam and Visakhapatnam Districts from 1980-1996

Period	*Vizianagaram district*	*Srikakulam district*	*Visakhapatnam district*
Up to 31-03-1980	193	247	592
From 01-04-80 to 31-3-96	271	237	524
Total	464	484	1,116

Source : Permanent S.S.I. registers of district industries centres of Vizianagaram, Srikakulam and Visakhapatnam.

The above table shows that there are 464,484, and 1116 small scale industrial units in Vizianagaram, Srikakulam and Visakhapatnam districts respectively as on 31st March, 1996. With regard to Vizianagaram district as on 31st March 1980 these were a total of 193 small scale units of different strata. After April 1980, 271 small scale units of different starta started and thus a total of 464 units were seen from the permanent small scale industries register of district industries center, Vizianagaram. This shows more than an half of the units were came into existence in a short span of one and half decade.

Similarly with regard to Srikakulam district there were 247 units as on 31-3-1980, this number reached to 484 by the year ending 1996. That means nearly half of the total units that is 237 came into existence after April, 1980. In fact Srikakulam district is a backward one, the growth of small scale units is almost at par with Vizianagaram district is mainly due to benefits given by the Central Government declaring this as a backward district.

When compared to Vizianagaram and Srikakulam districts the total number of units established in Visakhapatnam district is almost double in number. By the year ending 1979-80 there were 592 small scale units in Visakhapatnam district as per district industries centers small scale industries register. Since then almost the same number of units that is 524 were started from April 1980 to 31 st March 1996, thus raising the total 1116. The researcher observed that the fasten growth of small scale units in this district is due to rapid industrial development.

A birds eye view of the table shows that total number of small scale units in Visakhapatnam district had more than what Vizianagaram and Srikakulam districts together have. Availability of infrastructure facilities in the district as a whole and in Visakhapatnam city in particular fetches a lot for establishment of more small scale units in Visakhapatnam district when compared to other 2 districts.

The researcher observed that industrially Visakhapatnam district is a developed district when compared to other 2 districts. Vizianagaram district is an industrially developing district. However, because of higher concentration of jute mills (large and medium) in the district to some extent hampers the growth of small scale units. Though the Srikakulam district is a backward one the subsidies and other facilities attracted the small entrepreneurs to start the units.

GROWTH OF SAMPLE UNITS IN VIZIANAGARAM DISTRICT

Growth of different type of small scale units in Vizianagaram district between 1991-96 is shown in table 4.2.

Table—4.2 Growth of Different Type of Small Scale Units in Vizianagaram District (1991-96)

Year	*Agro based*	*Forest based*	*Chemical based*	*Mineral and Building material based*	*Engineering and Allied based*	*Total*
1991-92	8 (57.2)	2 (14.3)	1 (-)	3 (21.4)	1 (7.1)	14 (31.8)
1992-93	13 (59.1)	3 (13.6)	1 (4.5)	3 (13.6)	2 (9.2)	22 (50.0)
1993-94	19 (63.3)	3 (10.0)	1 (3.3)	5 (16.7)	2 (6.7)	30 (68.2)
1994-95	21 (58.3)	5 (13.9)	1 (2.8)	6 (16.7)	3 (8.3)	36 (81.8)
1995-96	23 (52.3)	8 (18.2)	2 (4.5)	7 (16.0)	4 (9.0)	44 (100.00)

Note : Figures in brackets indicate percentage to the horizontal totals.

It is evident from the table that different types of small scale units could not secure the same rate of growth. The Agro based units constitute 57.2% of total sample units in the year 1991-92. Out of the total no.of 44 sample units, only 14 units were there in the year 1991-92, 22 in the year of 1992-93, 30 in the year 1993-94, 36 in the year 1994-95, 44 by the end of 1995-96. The total number of Agro based units during these 5 years period is more than other category of industrial units. During the year 1991-92 these were 8 Agro based units, 2 Forest based units, 3 Mineral and Building material based units, and one Engineering and Allied based units and thus totaling to 14 (31.8%), out of total 44 sample units existing during the year 1991-92. During the year 1992-93 5 more Agro based and 3 more forest based, units were started. During this year one unit of Chemical based were started. One more engineering based unit was also started. In that year and thus the total number of units increased from 14 to 22 consisting of 50% in the total sample units of 44. In the third year that is 1993-94 6 more Agro based units, 2 more Mineral and Building material based units were started in addition to the previous number of units and raising the number of small scale sample units to 30. The year 1994-95 Agro based and Forest based units of 2 each mineral and building material based and engineering and allied based one unit each were started making the total number 36. During 1995-96 2 units in Agro based category and 3 units in Forest based category were started. Chemical based, Mineral and Building material based, engineering and allied based units of one each are also started during this year. And thus making the total number of sample units as 44. Out of 44 sample units 23 are Agro based 8 are Forest based, 2 are Chemical based, 7 are Mineral and Building material based and 4 are Engineering and Allied based units.

The 23 Agro based units that is 52.3% in the total strata consist of 8 rice mills, 7 oil mills, 4 flour mills, units manufacturing of 2 agriculture implements 2 cold storage houses, 8 Forest based small scale units (18.2%) consist of one unit each from manufacturing of plywood, and venner sheets, bobbins, spools, mill boards, paper cones, sawing and planning of wood. And 2 Chemical based units (4.5%) preparing Organic Chemicals and dyes are included in sample units. 3 mini cement plant, 2 tiles manufacturing units, one stone crushing unit and one cement pipes manufacturing unit are taken as sample under mineral and building material based category of 7 units (16%) 2 aluminum utensils manufacturing units, one general engineering unit and one steel wire drawing unit are included in engineering and allied based unit.

GROWTH OF SAMPLE UNITS IN SRIKAKULAM DISTRICT

Table—4.3 Growth of Different Type of Small Scale Units in Srikakulam District (1991-96)

Year	*Agro based*	*Forest based*	*chemical based*	*Mineral and Building material based*	*Engineering and Allied based*	*Total*
1991-92	13	1	1	2	2	19
	(68.4)	(5.3)	(5.3)	(10.5)	(10.5)	(43.1)
1992-93	17	1	1	2	2	23
	(74.0)	(4.3)	(4.3)	(8.7)	(8.7)	(52.2)
1993-94	21	2	1	3	3	30
	(70.0)	(6.7)	(3.3)	(10.0)	(10.0)	(68.1)
1994-95	26	2	2	4	4	38
	(68.4)	(5.3)	(5.3)	(10.5)	(10.5)	(86.4)
1995-96	30	3	2	4	5	44
	(68.2)	(6.8)	(4.5)	(9.0)	(11.5)	(100.00)

Note : Figures in brackets indicate percentage to the horizontal total.

Table 4.3 shows the growth of small scale units in Srikakulam district between 1991 to 1996. It is evident from the table that different type of small units also could not secure the same rate of growth. The Agro based units constitute 68.4% of total sample units in the year 1991-92. Out of total no. of 44 sample units, only 19 units were there in the year 1991-92, 23 in the year 1992-93, 30 in the year 1993-94, 38 in the year 1994-95 and 44 at the end of 1995-96. During these 5 years the growth of Agro based units are more than other categories of small units. These were 13 Agro based, one each in Chemical and Forest based units 2 units each in Mineral and Building material and Engineering and Allied based category. In the year 1991-92 out of 19 units established. During the year 1991-93 only 4 more Agro based units were started. 4 Agro based units and one of Forest, Mineral and Building material, and Engineering and Allied based units are established in the year 1993-94. Out of 38 units in the year 1994-95, 5 Agro based, one each in Chemical, Mineral and Building material, Engineering and Allied based units were started. In the year 1995-96 4 more Agro based, one in each of Forest and Engineering and allied based units were started in addition to the previous units.

The 30 Agro based units that is 68.2% in the total strata consist of 14 rice mills, 6 flour mills, 2 dall mills, 4 cashew-kernal units, one oil mill, one coir based unit, one jute stick powder unit, and one jute based particle board unit. 3 Forest based units, that is 6.8% of the total units consist of wooden furniture manufacturing unit, and 2 sawing and planning wood units. And 2 Chemical based units i.e. 4.5% of the total sample units were engaged in manufacturing chlorinated parafinwax and oxygen and acytilin gas. 4 units that is 9% of the total strata are belong to mineral and building material based units. These are 1 mini cement plant, 2 granite slabs making units and one stone crusher. 5 Engineering & Allied based units that is 11.5 of the total sample units are in manufacturing of welding electrodes, non-ferrous castings, steel furniture, stainless steel pots and aluminum utensils.

Growth of Sample Units in Visakhapatnam District

Growth of different type of small scale units in Visakhapatnam district from 1991 to 1996 is shown in table 4.4.

The table shows that different types of units in Visakhapatnam district could not secure same rate of growth. Out of the total no.of 100 sample units only 27 units were there in the year 1991-92, these includes each 7 units in Forest and Engineering and allied based units, 5 units of Agro and Mineral and Building material based units alongwith 3 Chemical based units. The total no.of Engineering and Allied based units during these 5 years period is more than that of 25% of the total units other category of industrial units. The Forest and Mineral and Building material based units are equal in number that is 22% each next to followed by engineering and Allied based units. Out of the 100 sample units 47 units were there in year 1992-93, 58 units in the year 1993-94, 82 units in the year 1994-95. During the year 1992-93 there were 6 Agro based units, 4 Forest based units, Mineral and Building material and Engineering and Allied based units of 4 each and 2 more Chemical units were started. All these occupy 47% of the total sample units. In the third year that is 1993-94, 6 more Forest based units, one each in Agro based, Mineral and Building material based units and 3 Engineering and Allied based units were started in addition to the pervious number of units. There was considerable growth in all the categories of industries in the year 1994-95. With the 24 new units established, during year 1994-95 *viz* 6 (six) each in Mineral and Building material and Engineering and Allied based units, 5 in Chemical based, 3 units in Forest based and 2 units in Agro based and the total no. increased to 82 units. During the year 1995-96 6 units in Mineral and Building material based category, 4 units in Agro based, each 3 units in Chemical and Engineering allied based units and 2 more units in Forest based category were started.

Table—4.4 Growth of Different Type of Small Scale Units in Visakhapatnam District (1991-96)

Year	*Agro based*	*Forest based*	*Chemical based*	*Mineral and Building material based*	*Engineering and Allied based*	*Total*
1991-92	5 (18.5)	7 (26.0)	3 (11.0)	5 (18.5)	7 (26.0)	27 (27.0)
1992-93	11 (23.4)	11 (23.4)	5 (10.6)	9 (19.2)	11 (23.4)	47 (47.0)
1993-94	12 (20.7)	17 (29.3)	5 (8.6)	10 (17.2)	14 (24.2)	58 (58.0)
1994-95	14 (17.1)	20 (24.4)	10 (12.2)	16 (19.5)	22 (26.8)	82 (82.0)
1995-96	18 (18.0)	22 (22.0)	13 (13.0)	22 (22.0)	25 (25.0)	100 (100.00)

Note : Figures in brackets indicate percentage to horizontal total

18 Agro based units, 22 Forest based units, 13 Chemical based units, 22 Mineral and Building material based units and 25 Engineering and Allied based units were included in the total 100 sample units.

The 18 Agro based units that is 18% of the total units consist of 8 rice mills, 4 oil mills, and each one of cashew processing, palm fiber extraction unit, flour mill and jute based unit. Out of 22 Forest based units, that is 22% of the total, 4 are plywood manufacturing units, 8 furniture making l0 sawing and planning of wood units. The 13 units of Chemical based units involved in manufacturing of magnesium sulphate, hydrochloric acid, sulphuric acid, manufacturing of hydrochloric acid, zinc sulphuric, distilled water, of each 2 out of 22 Mineral and Building material based units 8 were mini cement plants, 6 tiles units, 2 of each fly ash brick units, spun pipes, hallow concrete bricks, stone crushers. The 25 Engineering and Allied based unit that is 25% of the total strata consist of 8 steel and aluminum fabrication units, 5 general engineering workshops, 4 ferrous and non-ferrous casting units, material handling equipment manufacturing unit, wire nails making unit, bolts and nuts, steel wire drawing, steel rolling mill, aluminum building materials, heavy earth moving equipment, and unit making aluminum utensils.

STRUCTURE OF CAPITAL

Vizianagaram District

Out of 44 small scale sample units 8 units have fallen sick, that is why the remaining 36 healthy units are taken into consideration for all analysis purposes. It is interesting to know that the capital structure of small scale units in this district witnessed a vast variances.

Table—4.5 Distribution of Small Units According to Total Capital Employed in Vizianagaram District.

(Rs. in lakhs)

Category of units	*0-25*	*25-50*	*50-75*	*75 above*	*Total*
Agro based	4	3	4	8	19
Forest based	1	3	1	1	6
Chemical based	—	1	1		2
Mineral and Building material based	—	—	—	6	6
Engg. &Allied based	1	1	1	-	3
All Industries	6	8	7	15	36

The data given in table 4.5 reveal that differences in size of total capital exist not only in different category of units, but also between different units in the same category. One important feature is observed in capital distribution of units that is out of 19 Agro based units 8 units have investment of Rs. 75 lakhs and above and all the 6 units in Mineral and Building material based category also have investment of Rs. 75 lakhs and above. 4 units in Agro based, one unit each in Forest, Engineering and Allied based category have an investment of less than 25 lakhs. 3 units each from Agro and Forest based and one unit each from Chemical and Engineering and allied based have investment range between Rs. 25 lakhs to Rs. 50 lakhs. 4 units from Agro based and one unit each from forest, Chemical, Engineering and allied based have investment between Rs. 50 lakhs and Rs. 75 lakhs. 8 units from Agro based, 1 unit from Forest based and 6 units from Mineral and Building material based category have an investment of more than Rs. 75 lakhs.

4 units from Agro based, 2 units from Forest based and one unit each Mineral and Building material and Engineering and Allied based are excluded from this table as they have fallen sick.

Srikakulam District

Out of 44 sample small scale units 6 units only have fallen sick, for that reason the remaining 38 healthy units only are taken into consideration for analysis purpose.

There is a lot of variance between different type of categories in Srikakulam district. The data given in table 4.6 explains that differences in size of total capital employed and also exhibits the difference between different units in same category.

Table—4.6 Distribution of Small Units According to Total Capital Employed in Srikakulam District

(Rs. in lakhs)

Category of units	*0-25*	*25-50*	*50-75*	*75 above*	*Total*
Agro based	8	9	5	4	26
Forest based	2	1	—	—	3
Chemical based	—	1	—	1	2
Mineral and Building material based	—	—	1	2	3
Engg. & Allied based	3	1	—	—	4
All industries	13	12	6	7	38

The most distinct feature with Vizianagaram and Visakhapatnam districts is one of 38 sample units 25 units i.e., more than 50% of the units are in below Rs. 50 lakhs category. Another important feature is out of 26 Agro based units only 4 units and out of 3 Chemical based unit 2 are above Rs, 75 lakhs category. There is no above Rs. 50 lakhs ınit in Forest and Engineering and Allied based category. Out of 38 units 7 units are above Rs. 75 lakhs category those are 4 Agro based, 2 Mineral and Building material based, and one in Chemical based. Out of 13 below Rs. 25 lakhs category 8 are Agro based and 3 are Engineering and Allied based and 2 are Forest based units. 9 units in Agro based and 1 each in Agro Chemical and Engineering and Allied based units are exist in between Rs. 25 lakhs and Rs. 50 lakhs category. Out of 6 units in Rs. 50 to 75 lakhs category 5 are Agro based and one is mineral and building material based category.

4 units from Agro based, one unit each from Mineral and Building material and Engineering and Allied based category are deleted from this table as they have fallen sick.

Visakhapatnam District

In Visakhapatnam district out of 100 selected sample units have fallen sick out of 22 sick units 4 units from Agro based, 5 units from Forest based, 2 units from Chemical based, 6 units from Mineral and Building material based and 5 units from Engineering and Allied based category. That is why the remaining 78 units are taken into consideration for all analysis purposes.

Table—4.7 Distribution of Small Units According to Total Capital Employed in Visakhapatnam District

(Rs. in lakhs)

Category of units	*0-25*	*25-50*	*50-75*	*75 above*	*Total*
Agro based	2	1	3	8	14
Forest based	7	4	3	3	17
Chemical based	—	1	1	9	11
Mineral and Building material based	2	1	8	5	16
Engg. & Allied based	5	8	3	4	20
All Industries	16	15	18	29	78

The table 4.7 shows the total capital employed by small scale units in this district witnessed vast variances. It also reveals that differences in size of total capital exist not only in different category of units, but also between different units in the same category. Out of 78 sample units 47 units i.e., more than 50% are Rs. 50 lakhs investment and above one interesting feature is observed in capital distribution of units i.e., out of 11 Chemical based units 9 units have investment of Rs. 75 lakhs and above. 7 units in Forest based, 5 units in Engineering and allied based, 2 each in Agro and Mineral and Building material based units are in below Rs. 25 lakhs category. 8 units from Engineering and Allied based category, 4 units in Forest based category and 1 each in Agro, Chemical and Mineral and Building material based category have an investment range between Rs. 25 lakhs to 50 lakhs. 8 units from Mineral and Building material based, 3 units each in Agro Forest and Engineering and Allied based and 1 unit from Chemical based are in the investment of Rs. 50 lakhs to Rs. 75 lakhs. 9 units in Chemical based, 8 units in Agro based, 5 units in Mineral & Building material based, 4 units in Engineering & Allied based, and 3 units in Forest based are in investment of above Rs. 75 lakhs.

Fixed Vs Working Capital

The total productive capital in small scale industry is broadly divided into two categories, fixed capital and working capital. Any unit to get into production requires investment in the fixed assets such as land, and building, machinery, tools and equipment's, furniture and fixture, etc. To ensure production, it needs working capital for day to day operation, such as purchase of raw-materials, payment of daily and weekly wages and other direct expenses.

For the purpose of valuation of fixed assets three different methods can be adopted.

1. Historical value, i.e., the price at which items were purchased.
2. Book value, i.e., the purchase rice less depreciation.
3. The replacement value, i.e., the value which the industrialist would have to pay to replace the existing set of assess by another of equal productive capacity.

The concept of replacement value appears to be most appropriate as it reflects the market appreciation of value of fixed assets which is not taken into account in either historical value or book value. But great practical difficulties are encountered in the calculation of replacement value of fixed assets. It depends upon the data collected from the industrialists on the value of fixed assets purchased by them. But in most of the cases the industrialists have no knowledge of the present price of their equipment. As the historical value of assets does not reflect the present value of fixed assess, it is avoided. So it is decided to assess fixed assets of different industries in terms of depreciated or book value.

Great difficulties have been experienced in collecting data on the book value of assets. Many units do not maintain any systematic record of their accounts. Provision or depreciation is not even made in some of the units. The book value of the assets, therefore, has been calculated through the following procedure. The value and year of establishment of different fixed assets are noted. The expected life of each of these items is ascertained from the entrepreneurs. The rate of depreciation is calculated by dividing the value of assets by their life period. The depreciated value of each item is therefore arrived at by deducting from the historical cost, the value of depreciation calculated by multiplying the rate of depreciation by the number of years (from the year of installation to the year of survey).

Vizianagaram District

Table 4.8 summarises the composition of productive capital employed in different small scale industrial units covered under study of Vizianagaram district.

Table—4.8 Structure of Capital of Sample Units of Vizianagaram District as on 31-3-96

(Rs. in lakhs)

Category of units	*No.of units*	*Total fixed capital*	*Total working capital*	*Total productive capital*	*Average productive capital*
Agro based	19	577.5	430	1007.50	53.02
Forest based	6	74.5	148	222.50	37.07
Chemical based	2	28.5	81.5	110.00	55
Mineral and Building material based	6	202.0	375.0	577.00	96.16
Engg. & Allied based	3	63	35	98	32.66

It is found from the table that the average amount of capital invested is different in different categories. If the amount of capital invested is taken as criteria for calculating the size of the unit variation in size is observed in different categories. The average productive capital of Mineral and Building material based units is as high as Rs. 96.16 lakhs. The Engineering and Allied based units posses the lowest average capital of Rs. 32.66 lakhs. The average capital of Chemical, Agro, and Forest based units are in the order of Rs. 55 lakhs, Rs. 53 lakhs and Rs. 37 lakhs respectively.

It will be found that investment in fixed capital constitutes greater proposition in Agro based and Engineering and Allied based units, where as the working capital is more in other categories of units.

From the table it can be said that the Mineral and Building material based units have more productive capital than other category of units. The Forest based units and Engineering and Allied based units have very limited average productive capital. The Agro based and Chemical based units are also have a moderate average productive capital. It is clear from the analysis that the small scale units of the Vizianagaram district is in need of more working capital.

Srikakulam District

The composition of productive capital employed in different small scale units in Srikakulam district covered under study are explained in table 4.9.

Table—4.9 Structure of Capital of Sample Units of Srikakulam District as on 31-3-96

(Rs. in lakhs)

Category of units	*No.of units*	*Total fixed capital*	*Total working capital*	*Total productive capital*	*Average productive capital*
Agro based	26	505	631.25	1,136.25	43.7
Forest based	3	22	57	79	26.33
Chemical based	2	30	88	118	59
Mineral and Building material based	3	93.00	192.00	285.00	95.00
Engg. & Allied based	4	42	28	70	17.5

A lot of variances are found from the table between different categories of units. If the amount of capital invested is taken as criteria for measuring the size of the unit, a wide range of variation in size is observed. The average productive capital is as high as in Mineral and Building material based units with Rs. 95 lakhs. Engineering and Allied based units have the lowest average capital of Rs. 17.50 lakhs. The average capitals of Chemical based, Agro based and Forest based category of units have Rs.59 lakhs, rs. 43 lakhs and Rs. 26.33 lakhs respectively.

Investment in fixed capital constitutes greater proportion in Engineering and Allied based units and where as working capital requirement is more than double in Forest, Chemical and Mineral and Building material based units and Agro based also have a moderate working capital.

Visakhapatnam District

Table 4.10 gives the details of productive capital employed in different small scale industrial units could under study of Visakhapatnam district.

Table—4.10 Structure of Capital of Sample Units of Visakhapatnam District as on 31-3-96

(Rs. in lakhs)

Category of units	*No.of units*	*Total fixed capital*	*Total working capital*	*Total productive capital*	*Average productive capital*
Agro based	14	399	490.5	889.50	63.53
Forest based	17	268	439.7	707.7	41.62
Chemical based	11	295	685.5	980.5	89.13
Mineral and Building material based	16	486.5	616.75	1,103.25	68.95
Engg. & Allied based	20	596.75	280.65	877.4	43.87

It is found from the table that there is a lot of variance in size among different categories of units. The Chemical based units stand in highest position with Rs. 89.13 lakhs of average productive capital when compared to other categories. The Forest based units and Engineering and Allied based units have the lowest average productive capital of Rs. 41.62 lakhs and Rs. 43.87 lakhs respectively. The average productive capitals of Mineral and Building material based and Agro based are in moderate position of Rs. 68.95 and Rs. 63.53 respectively.

It is found that investment in fixed capital constitutes a greater proposition in Engineering and Allied based units and where as the working capital is more in other categories of units. From the table it can be understood that the small scale units of Visakhapatnam district is in need of more fixed capital besides working capital.

The fixed capital in Agro based units of Vizianagaram and Srikakulam districts and Engineering and Allied based units of Visakhapatnam district is high among all the categories of industrial units in these 3 districts. The working capital in Chemical industry is more than double than that of fixed capital in all the 3 districts. The average productive capital is more in Mineral and Building material based units in Vizianagaram and Srikakulam districts and the average capital is high in Chemical based units in Visakhapatnam district.

Share of Fixed and Working Capitals in the Total Capital

The share of fixed and working capitals in the total capital in 3 districts is studied in the following pages.

Vizianagaram District

The relative shares of fixed and working capital in the total capital of the small industrial units of Vizianagaram district are portrayed in table 4.11.

Table—4.11 Analysis of Fixed and Working Capital Employed in Different Units of Vizianagaram District 1995-96

(Rs. in lakhs)

Category of units	*Average fixed capital*	*Average working capital*	*Average total capital*	*Ratio of fixed capital to total capital*	*Ratio of working capital to total capital*
Agro based	30.39	22.63	53.02	0.57	0.43
Forest based	12.41	24.66	37.07	0.33	0.67
Chemical based	14.25	40.75	55	0.25	0.75
Mineral and Building material based	33.66	62.50	96.16	0.35	0.65
Engg. & Allied based	21	11.66	32.66	0.64	0.36

It is found from the table that the fixed capital in Agro based units and Engineering and Allied based units have a large proportion in total capital when compared to Forest based, Chemical based and Mineral and Building material based units. The ratio of fixed capital to total capital in Agro based units is 0.57 and in Engineering and Allied based is 0.64. It denotes that Agro based units and Engineering and Allied based units have sufficient capital bare when compared to other categories of units. The ratio of fixed capital to total capital in regard to Mineral and Building material, Forest based and Chemical based are in the order of 0.35, 0.33 and 0.25 respectively. It can be said that these 3 categories of units require more working capital than of fixed capital.

Srikakulam District

Table 4.12 shows the ratio of fixed and working capital in the total average capital of small scale units in Srikakulam district.

Table—4.12 Analysis of Fixed and Working Capital Employed in Different Industries in Srikakulam District 1995-96.

(Rs. in lakhs)

Category of units	*Average fixed capital*	*Average working capital*	*Average total capital*	*Ratio of fixed capital to total capital*	*Ratio of working capital to total* capital
Agro based	19.42	24.27	43.7	0.44	0.56
Forest based	7.33	19.00	26.33	0.28	0.72
Chemical based	15.00	44.00	59.00	0.25	0.75
Mineral and Building material based	31.00	64.00	95.00	0.33	0.67
Engg. & Allied based	10.50	7.00	17.50	0.60	0.40

It can be understood from the table that Engineering and Allied based and Agro based units have large proportion in total capital when compared to Chemical, Forest and Mineral and Building material based units. The ratio of fixed capital to total capital in Engineering and Allied based units is 0.60 and Agro based is 0.44. It denotes that Engineering and Allied category units have sufficient capital and where as Agro based have a moderate capital. The ratio of fixed capital to total capital in regard to Mineral and Building material based, Forest based and Chemical based units are in the order of 0.33, 0.28, 0.25 respectively. It shows these 3 categories require more working capital than fixed capital. The ratio of working capital to total capital in Chemical based units is 0.75, in Forest based units is 0.72 and in Mineral and Building material based units is 0.67. In Engineering and Allied based category and Agro based category the ratios are low viz., 0.40 and 0.56 respectively.

Visakhapatnam District

The ratio of fixed capital and working capital in the total capital of the small industrial units of Visakhapatnam district are given in Table 4.13.

Table—4.13 Analysis of Fixed and Working Capital Employed in Different Categories of Units in Visakhapatnam District (1995-1996)

(Rs. in lakhs)

Category of units	*Average fixed capital*	*Average working capital*	*Average total capital*	*Ratio of fixed capital to total capital*	*Ratio of working capital to total* capital
Agro based	28.5	35.03	63.53	0.44	0.56
Forest based	15.76	25.86	41.62	0.37	0.63
Chemical based	26.81	62.31	89.13	0.3	0.7
Mineral and Building material based	30.4	38.54	68.95	0.44	0.56
Engg. & Allied based	29.83	14.03	43.86	0.68	0.32

The above table explains that the ratio of fixed capital in total capital of Engineering and Allied based units have a large portion of 0.68 when compared to other category of units. It denotes that Engineering and Allied based units have sufficient fixed capital. The ratio of working capital to total capital is high in Chemical based and Forest based units i.e., 0.70 and 0.63 respectively. The ratio of working capital to total capital is moderate in Agro based and mineral and building material based units with 0.56 each. The ratio of working capital to total capital is very low i.e., 0.32 in Engineering and Allied based category. The ratio of fixed capital to total capital in regard to Chemical based, Forest based, Mineral and Building material based, Agro based are in order of 0.30, 0.37, 0.44 and 0.44 respectively.

CAPACITY

Installed Vs Utilised

Productive efficiency of a firm depends to a greater extent on the utilisation of its capacity. The capacity of a unit is measured in terms of production. This reflets on the output potential of the firm. The capacity of the firm means the existing capacity of plant and machinery for a year. The installed capacity of an industry is, however, rarely utilised to its full extent. Under utilisation of capacity is a common feature in our Indian industries and the same applies to this small scale sector too.

Under utilisation of capacity has special significance in respect of small scale units when compared to large units. In case of the large scale units the effect of under utilisation is felt both machinery and labour. But in the case small scale units, as the extent of mechanism is not large, the burnt of under utilisation in these units affects the workers mostly.

The capacity utilisation in regard to small scale units of Vizianagaram, Srikakulam and Visakhapatnam Districts are studied in the following pages.

Vizianagaram District

The data collected from the sample industrial units of the district have been analysed to find out the trend of capacity utilisation during the period 1991-96. The analysis of data is presented in the Table 4.14. Capacity utilisation is expressed as a percentage of installed capacity.

Table—4.14 Extent of Capacity Utilisation in Different Categories of Units of Vizianagaram District 1991-96

Category of units	*1991-92 (%)*	*1992-93 (%)*	*1993-94 (%)*	*1994-95 (%)*	*1995-96 (%)*
Agro based	80	82	61	42	60
Forest based	67	70	57	41	50
Chemical based	—	65	65	60	58
Mineral and building material based	65	70	62	50	48
Engg. & Allied based	70	52	55	45	35

It is found from the table that the capacity utilisation varies from category to category as well as from year to year.

The capacity utilisation with regard to Agro based units during 1991-92 and 1992-93 was as high as 80% and 82% respectively. However, it is only 42% in the year 1994-95. During the years 1993-94, 95-96 witnessed 61% and 60% of capacity utilisation respectively.

Government leavy policy and export restrictions on rice mills and dal mills, and implementation affects of essential commodities act, etc., Are the reasons observed by the researcher for the shortfall of capacity utilisation since 1994-95 in these Agro based units. On similar lines to Agro based units the capacity utilisation in Forest based units during 1991-92 and 92-93 was 67% and 70% respectively. Government restriction on Forest based units and hike in labour prices have created problem for Forest based units since 1993-94. Thus the capacity utilisation was came down to 57%, 41%, and 50% respectively during the last 3 years.

In case of Chemical based units the capacity utilisation ranges between 58% and 65%. The capacity utilisation in Mineral and Building material based units is between 50% to 70% in the first 4 years i.e., 1991-92 to 1994-95. During the year 1995-96 the capacity utilisation came to a minimum of 40%. In case of Engineering and Allied based units during the year 1991-92 the capacity utilisation was 70%. Afterwards it declined and came to 52, 55, 45 percentages respectively during the next 3 years. In the year 1995-96 because of strikes, power shortage and other reasons the capacity utilisation came to a very minimum level of 35%. On the whole a similarly can be observed in regard to all categories of units i.e., during the years 1991-92 and 92-93 the capacity utilisation was high and it came down in the next 3 years.

The extent of capacity utilisation in different categories of small scale units during the year 1995-96 can be seen in Table. 4.15

Table—4.15 Extent of Capacity Utilisation in Different Industrial Units of Vizianagaram District During the Year 1995-96

(Rs. in lakhs)

Category of units	*Total capacity installed*	*Total capacity utilised*	*Total capacity utilised as a percentage of total installed capacity*
Agro based	1,720	1032.00	60
Forest based	598	299.00	50
Chemical based	326	189.08	58
Mineral and Building material based	1,560	748.80	48
Engg. & Allied based	105	36.75	35
Total	4,309	2305.63	53

The above table denotes the total capacity installed and total capacity utilised of various categories of industrial units in terms of rupees. The total capacity installed of these 5 categories of units was Rs. 4309 crores. Where as their capacity utilisation was Rs. 23.05 crores which is only 53% of all the categories of units put together.

Srikakulam District

Table 4.16 shows that the capacity utilisation varies from year to year and category to category.

Table—4.16 Extent of Capacity Utilisation in Different Categories of Units of Srikakulam District During 1991-96

Category of units	*1991-92 (%)*	*1992-93 (%)*	*1993-94 (%)*	*1994-95 (%)*	*1995-96 (%)*
Agro based	75	75	50	48	38
Forest based	70	72	60	62	68
Chemical based	60	58	70	65	68
Mineral and Building material based	80	68	65	60	62
Engg & Allied based	45	52	70	68	52

The capacity utilisation in Agro based industrial units during the years 1991-92 and 1992-93 was as good as 75%. From the year 1993-94 onwards the utilisation come down to very low i.e., during 1993-94 the capacity utilisation is 50% in 1994-95 it is 48% and in the year 1995-96 it is only 38%. This is the lowest utilised capacity in Agro based category between 1991-92 to 1991-96. Not only in Agro based units it is also the same in regard to other categories of units.

The capacity utilisation in Forest based units in all the years is above 60%. In the first two years i.e., 1991-92 and 1992-93 iit was as high as 70% and 72% respectively. In the year 1993-94 it come down to 60% and again it gradually increased to 62% in 1994-95 and to 62% in 1995-96. Forest based is one of the two categories which is maintaining capaçity utilisation above 60%.

70% in the Chemical based units category the capacity utilisation was as high as in the year 1993-94. In the first two years of 1991-92 and 1992-93 the capacity utilisation was only 60% and 58% respectively. The capacity utilisation was 65% and 68% in the years of 1994-95 and 1995-96 respectively.

In case of Mineral and Building material based category the capacity utilisation was as good as between 60% to 80%. In the year 1991-92 it reached to a maximum of 80%. This is the highest percentage of capacity utilised in all the years and not only in Mineral and Building material based categories but also in all the categories of units. The capacity utilisation from the year 1992-93 to 1995-96 was between 60% to 68%. In the year 1992-93 it was 68% in 1993-94 it was 65% in 1994-95 it was 60% and in the last years of 1995-96 it was 62%.

The Engineering and Allied based units show a lot of variance in the capacity utilisation. It varies from 45% in the year 1991-92 to 70% in the year 1993-94. In the year 1994-95 the capacity utilisation was 68% and in the years 1992-93 and 1995-96 were of 52%.

It is observed from the table that in 1991-92 and 1992-93 the capacity utilisation was high in Agro, Forest and Mineral and Building material based units and in the year 1993-94 it was high in Chemical and Engineering and allied based units.

Table 4.17 depicts the extent of capacity utilisation in different categories of small scale units during the year 1995-96.

Table—4.17 Extent of Capacity Utilisation in Different Industrial Units of Srikakulam District During 1995-96

(Rs. in lakhs)

Category of units	*Total capacity installed*	*Total capacity utilised*	*Total capacity utilised as a percentage of total installed capacity*
Agro based	2,520	957.60	38
Forest based	230	156.40	68
Chemical based	352	239.40	68
Mineral and Building material based	768	476.15	62
Engg. & Allied based	84	43.70	52

The above table explains the total capacity installed and total capacity utilised of various categories of industrial units in terms of rupees. The total capacity installed of these 5 categories of units was Rs. 3954 crores, where as their capacity utilisation was Rs. 1873.25 crores, which is only 57.6% of all the categories of units put together.

Visakhapatnam District

It is found from the table 4.18 that there is lot of variance in the capacity utilisation among different categories of units and in different years.

Table—4.18 Extent of Capacity Utilisation in Different Categories of Units in Visakhapatnam District During 1991-96

Category of units	*1991-92 (%)*	*1992-93 (%)*	*1993-94 (%)*	*1994-95 (%)*	*1995-96 (%)*
Agro based	60	55	47	72	84
Forest based	50	52	76	67	79
Chemical based	48	50	62	57	63
Mineral and Building material based	70	80	82	45	30
Engg. & Allied based	45	52	50	78	82

The capacity utilisation in Agro based units during the year 1995-96 was as high as 84%. This is maximum percentage of capacity utilised in all the categories of units.

In the remaining years the capacity utilisation was between 47% to 72%.

In the Forest based category in the first two years the capacity utilisation was normal with 50% and 52%. During the year 1993-94 it increased to 76% and again in 1994-95 it slightly reduced to 67% and in finally during the year 1995-96 it reduced to 79%.

In the Chemical based category the capacity utilisation was very low during the years 1991-92 and 1992-93 with 48% and 50% respectively. But later during the year 1995-96 it increased to 63%. In the last two years the capacity utilisation again came down to 62% and 57% respectively.

The Mineral & Building material based category exhibits a lot of difference in capacity utilisation from year to year. The capacity utilisation was gradually increased from 70% in the year 1991-92 to 80% in the year 1992-93 and to 82% in the year 1993-94. From the year 1993-94 onwards it reduced drastically and reduced to minimum of 45% and 30% in the years 1994-95 and 1995-96 respectively. The 30% is the lowest capacity utilisation during these five years period in all the categories of units.

In the Engineering and Allied based category the position is just opposite to that of Mineral and Building material based category. In the year 1991-92 the capacity utilisation was very low i.e., 45%. From the year 1991-92 onwards it increased continuously to 52%, (except in 1993-94) and reached to a maximum of 82%, during the year 1995-96.

The extent of capacity utilisation in different categories of small scale units in Visakhapatnam district during the year 1995-96 can be seen in table 4.19.

The table denotes the total capacity installed and total capacity utilised of various categories of industrial units in terms of rupees. The total capacity installed of these 5 categories of units was Rs. 9027 crores, where as their capacity utilisation was Rs. 5738.73 crores which was 67.6% of all the categories of units put together.

Table—4.19 Extent of Capacity Utilisation in Different Industrial Units of Visakhapatnam District During 1995-96

(Rs. in lakhs)

Category of units	*Total capacity installed*	*Total capacity utilised*	*Total capacity utilised as a percentage of total installed capacity*
Agro based	1,952	1,639.68	84
Forest based	1,760	1,390.4	79
Chemical based	2,055	1,294.65	63
Mineral and Building material based	2,420	726	30
Engg. & Allied based	840	688.8	82

After the analysis of the capacity utilisation of these three districts, it is found that during the year 1991-92 it was commendable in the units of Vizianagaram and Srikakulam districts and during the year 1995-96 of Visakhapatnam district. In these three districts the Chemical based units showed an average of 60% to 65% capacity utilised.

CAPACITY UTILISATION

Besides the differences between different categories of industrial units it is observed during the survey that with in the industry also there are wide differences existing among industrial units in the utilisation of capacity.

A district wise analysis showing different levels of capacity utilisation in percentages is given in the following pages.

Vizianagaram District

Table 4.20 gives a picture of distribution of small scale units of Vizianagaram district based on the capacity utilisation.

It is found from the table that only 6 units i.e., 16.67% of the total number of units surveyed are working with a maximum capacity i.e, more than 80%. 4 of them are from Agro based category and the remaining two are from Forest based and Mineral and Building material based category. As many as 30 units have an unutilised capacity varying from 20% to 80%. Maximum number of units i.e., 36.11% are found to be using 41% to 60% of their respective installed capactiy. The data presented in the table reveal that out of total number of 36 units as many as 13 units from all the groups have capacity utilisation of 41% to 60% as against 2 units below 20%. There are 10 units which are using capacity ranging from 61% to 80%, 5 units are working at a capactiy ranging between 21% to 40%. From the above analysis it is clear that the excess capacity exhists in all categories of units.

Table—4.20 Distribution of Units According to Utilisation of Capacity of Vizianagaram District During 1995-96

(No. of units)

Category of units	*Up to 20 per cent*	*21 to 40 per cent*	*41 to 60 per cent*	*61 to 80 per cent*	*Above 80 per cent*	*Total*
Agro based	—	2 (10.53)	7 (36.84)	6 (31.58)	4 (21.05)	19
Forest based	1 (16.67)	1 (16.67)	3 (50)	—	1 (16.67)	6
Chemical based	—	1 (50)	—	1 (50)	—	2
Mineral & Building material based	—	1 (16.67)	2 (33.33)	2 (33.33)	1 (16.67)	6
Engg. & Allied based	1 (33.33)	—	1 (33.33)	1 (33.33)	—	3
Total	2 (5.55)	5 (13.89)	13 (36.11)	10 (27.78)	6 (16.67)	36

Note : Figures in brackets indicate the percentages to total.

From the above analysis it is evident that almost all the small scale units in this district are not working to their fullest capacity.

Srikakulam District

Table 4.21 gives a picture of distribution of small scale units of Srikakulam district based on the capacity utilisation.

Table—4.21 Distribution of Units According to Utilisation of Capacity of Srikakulam District During 1995-96

Category of units	*Up to 20 per cent*	*21 to 40 per cent*	*41 to 60 per cent*	*61 to 80 per cent*	*Above 80 per cent*	*Total*
Agro Based	4 (15.38)	8 (30.77)	5 (19.23)	4 (15.38)	5 (19.23)	26
Forest based	—	—	2 (66.67)	1 (33.33)	—	3
Chemical based	—	1 (50)	1 (50)	—	—	2
Mineral & Building material based	—	1 (33.33)	1 (33.33)	1 (33.33)	—	3
Engg. & Allied based	1 (25)	—	1 (25)	1 (25)	1 (25)	4
Total	5 (13.16)	10 (26.31)	10 (26.31)	7 (18.42)	6 (15.79)	38

Note : Figures in brackets indicate percentages to total.

It is found from the table that only 6 units i.e., 15.79% of the total number of units surveyed are working at a maximum capacity of more than 80%. Out of six, 5 of them are Agro based units and one is an Engineering and Allied based units, 5 units are utilising only less than 20% of their installed capacity. Out of these 5 units 4 are Agro based units and one is Engineering and Allied based unit. There are 10 units in both 21 to 40% and 41 to 60% range of capacity utilisation. 8 Agro based units and one each of Chemical and Mineral and Building material based units are in the 21 to 40% range. 5 Agro based units, 2 Forest based units and one each of Chemical based, Mineral and Building material based and Engineering and Allied based units are in the 41 to 60%. 7 units i.e., 4 Agro based and one each of Forest based, Mineral and Building material based and Engineering and Allied based units utilised their capacity ranging from 61 to 80%. It can also be observed from the table that as many as 32 units have an unutilised capacity varying from 20% to 80%. The above analysis thus clearly says that excess capacity exists in all categories of units.

Visakhapatnam District

The distribution of capacity utilisation in small scale units of Visakhapatnam district is shown in table 4.22.

Table—4.22 Distribution of Units According to Utilisation of Capacity of Visakhapatnam District During 1995-96

Category of units	*Up to 20 per cent*	*21 to 40 per cent*	*41 to 60 per cent*	*61 to 80 per cent*	*Above 80 per cent*	*Total*
Agro based	1 (7.14)	2 (14.28)	4 (28.57)	2 (14.29)	5 (35.71)	14
Forest based	2 (11.76)	2 (11.76)	6 (35.29)	5 (29.4)	2 (11.77)	17
Chemical based	— (27.27)	3 (36.36)	4 (27.27)	3 (9.10)	1	11
Mineral & Building material based	4 (26.25)	5 (31.25)	3 (18.75)	2 (12.5)	2 (12.5)	16
Engg. & Allied based	2 (10)	1 (5)	4 (20)	8 (40)	5 (25)	20
Total	9 (11.54)	13 (16.67)	21 (26.92)	20 (25.64)	15 (19.23)	78

Note : Figures in brackets indicate percentages to total.

It is clear from the table that only 15 units i.e., 19.23% of the total units surveyed are working above 80% of the installed capacity. 5 units each of Agro based and Engineering and Allied based, 2 units each of Forest based and Mineral and Building material based and one unit of Chemical based are in this range. There are 20 units i.e., 25.64% consisting of 2 units each of Agro based and Mineral and Building material based, 5 units of Forest based, 3 units of Chemical based and 8 units of Engineering and Allied based category which are utilising 61 to 80% of their installed capacity. 21 units belong to 4 each Agro based, Chemical based and Engineering and Allied based, 6 units of Forest based and 3 units of Mineral and Building material based category have utilised 41 to 60% of their installed capacity. 13 units consisting of 2 units each from Agro based, Forest based, Chemical based, 5 units of Mineral and Building material based and one Engineering and Allied based units utilised less capacity i.e., 21 to 40% range. Only 9 units utilised less than 20% of their installed capacity. They are one Agro based unit, 2 each of Forest based unit and Engineering and Allied based units and 4 of Mineral and Building material based units.

From the above table it is evident that almost all the small scale units in this district are not working to their fullest capacity.

REASONS FOR IDLE CAPACITY

The analysis in the above pages denotes idle capacity in all categories of units. The reason of this idle capacity district-wise analysed in the following pages.

Vizianagaram District

The reason for the existing idle capacity have been ascertained from the sample units and depicted in Table 4.23.

Table—4.23 Reason for Idle Capacity in Different Industrial Units of Vizianagaram District

(No. of units)

Category of units	*No.of units giving reasons for idle capacity*	*Lack of demand*	*Shortage of finance*	*Raw-material difficulties*	*Other reasons (strikes, govt. policy. power shortage etc.)*
Agro based	19	3 (15.79)	4 (21.05)	—	14 (73.68)
Forest based	6	1 (16.67)	2 (33.33)	2 (33.33)	3 (50.0)
Chemical based	2	—	1 (50)	1 (50)	2 (100.0)
Mineral & Building material based	6	2 (33.33)	2 (33.33)	1 (16.67)	4 (66.67)
Engg. & Allied based	3	1 (33.33)	2 (66.67)	—	2 (66.67)
Total	36	7 (19.44)	11 (30.56)	4 (11.11)	25 (69.44)

Note : Figures in brackets indicate percentages to total.

The data analyses the relative importance of different factors in accounting for the presence of unutilised capacity of industrial units. The respondents have pointed out various reasons for idle capacity, but the table is formed on the basis of lack of demand, shortage of finance, raw material difficulties and other reasons for idle capacity. It is also to be noted that some units have mentioned more than one reason. It is found from the table that 19 Agro based units, have faced the problem of under utilisation. Among these rice and dall mills are facing the problem of shortage of working capital, 3 units viz one cold store house one dall mill and one dairy farm have faced the problem of lack of demand for their products. 14 units of this category have not utilised their capacity to the fullest extend due to various other reasons like government leavy policy, export restrictions on rice mills, strikes, power shortage, lockouts, machinery problems, poor quality and seasonal fluctuations etc. 2 units of this category have expressed more than one reason for their idle capacity.

Out of 6 units under Forest based category, one unit had expressed the reason for idle capacity as lack of demand for their products, one bobbins making unit faced lack of demand for its product, whenever there is a strike in jute mills. 2 saw mills of this category have poor quality based and require finance for their permanent assets, these units also facing shortage of working capital for their smooth running. 2 units of this category i.e., one saw mill and one furniture making unit are not working to the fullest capacity extent due to non-availability of quality raw-materials. Because of government restrictions, labour problems and power shortage 3 units of this category have not utilised capacity to fullest extent. The bobbin making unit besides lack of demand for its product is facing labour problem.

Shortage of finance and non-availability of raw-materials are the two reasons expressed by the 2 units under Chemical based category and also these 2 units are also facing labour problems and competition in domestic and international markets.

Under Mineral and Building material based category 2 units each have expressed the problem of demand, shortage of finance for working Capital purposes. 1 unit of this category also expressed the problem of non-availability of good quality raw-material. In this category one unit has expressed 3 problems and the one more unit has expressed 2 problems.

Under Engineering and Allied based category one unit expressed the problem of lack of demand for its products and 2 units expressed the problem of finance. 2 units of this category have also expressed the problem of shortage of power and machinery troubles along with poor quality.

Srikakulam District

Table 4.24 explains the reasons for idle capacity in small scale units of different categories of units in Srikakulam district.

Out of 26 Agro based units, 10 have faced the problem of lack of demand they are 5 rice mills, 2 cashew processing units, 2 dall mills and one coir based unit. 12 units in Agro based category have faced the problem of shortage of finance. These are 4 rice mills, two cashew nut processing plants, two flour mills, two oil mills, one in jute stick powder unit, and one particle boards making unit. 6 units of this category have faced the problem of shortage of raw-material. They are 3 cashew processing units, one coir based unit, one flour mill and one rice mill. There are 10 units in this category which have faced other problems like power shortage, labour strike, absenteeism machinery breakdowns and poor quality seasonal fluctuations etc.

Table—4.24 Reasons for Idle Capacity in Different Industrial Units of Srikakulam District

Category of units	*No.of units giving reasons for idle capacity*	*Lack of demand*	*Shortage of finance*	*Raw-material difficulties*	*Other reasons (strikes, govt. policy, power shortage etc.)*
Agro based	26	10 (38.46)	12 (46.15)	6 (23.07)	10 (38.4)
Forest based	3	—	1 (33.33)	2 (66.67)	1 (33.33)
Chemical based	2	1 (50)	1 (50)	1 (50)	1 (50.0)
Mineral & Building material based	3	2 (66.67)	1 (33.33)	1 (33.33)	2 (66.67)
Engg. & Allied based	4	2 (50)	—	—	2 (50)
Total	38	15 (39.47)	15 (39.47)	10 (26.31)	16 (42.10)

Note : Figures in brackets indicate percentages to total.

Out of 3 units in Forest based category one saw mill had expressed shortage of finance as the reason for idle capacity. In the remaining two, one furniture making unit and one saw-mill expressed the problem of availability of quality raw-material as the main reason for their idle capacity. One more unit expressed the reason for idle capacities power shortage, labour problem and availability of quality raw-material.

2 units in Chemical based category also not utilised their capacity to the fullest extent one of the Chemical unit, which is manufacturing chlorinated parafin wax expressed the reasons for idle capacity as lack of demand and non-availability of quality raw-material. Another unit of this category expressed the reason for idle capacity is lack of working capital. And one starch making unit expressed that lack of skilled labour and competition are the reasons for idle capacity.

Out of 3 units in Mineral and Building material based 2 units have expressed the problem of demand and one each have expressed the problems of finance and raw-material. One cement plant and one spun pipes manufacturing unit opined that their products are suffering with lack of demand. One mini cement plant suffered for want of working capital. One unit has expressed that problem of availability of quality raw-material. 2 units of this category have also expressed other problems like power shortage, labour problems and machinery troubles for their idle capacity. Out of 4 Engineering and Allied based units two have expressed lack of demand and 2 more have expressed power shortage and labour problems for their idle capacity.

Visakhapatnam District

The small scale industrial units of Visakhapatnam district have not utilised their capacity to the fullest extent due to many reasons. More than 50% of the units have two problems for their idle capacity. The reasons for idle capacity in Visakhapatnam district is depicted in table 4.25.

The table shows that out of 14 Agro based units 3 units are suffering from lack of demand for their products. The three units are confectionery, food processing and oil mill due to poor quality, low domestic consumption and poor packing and marketing they lack demand. Out of 14 units i.e., 14.28% are suffering from shortage of finance. They are food processing and soft drink units four units i.e., 28.50% of the total Agro based units are suffering from the problem of raw-material. Out of 14 units 12 units are suffering from reasons like government leavy policy, maintenance of standards, quality, labour problems, seasonal fluctuations, machinery problems etc.

Table—4.25 Reasons for Idle Capacity in Different Industrial Units of Visakhapatnam District

Category of units	*No.of units giving reasons for idle capacity*	*Lack of demand*	*Shortage of finance*	*Raw-material difficulties*	*Other reasons (strikes, govt. policy, power shortage etc.)*
Agro based	14	3 (21.43)	2 (14.28)	4 (28.57)	12 (85.71)
Forest based	17	4 (23.53)	6 (35.29)	9 (52.94)	8 (47.05)
Chemical based	11	3 (27.28)	4 (36.35)	4 (36.36)	7 (63.64)
Mineral & Building material based	16	8 (50)	9 (56.25)	3 (18.75)	8 (50.0)
Engg. & Allied based	20	13 (38.46)	5 (25)	—	9 (45.0)
Total	78	31 (39.74)	26 (33.33)	20 (25.64)	44 (56.41)

Note : Figures in brackets indicate percentages to total.

In Forest based category out of 17 units four units have expressed the reasons for idle capacity is lack of demand for their products. They are 2 saw mills, one furniture making unit and one plywood making unit. 6 units i.e., 35.29% of the total units informed that shortage of finance is the main reason for their under utilisation of capacity. Out of these 6, 3 are sawmills, one is wooden door frames making unit, one furniture making unit and one planning of wood unit. 9 units out of 17 i.e., 52.94% have expressed that raw material difficulties are the main reasons for the existing idle capacity in their units. 6 saw mills, 2 furniture works and one plywood unit are the units suffering from raw material problems. 8 units expressed other reasons for their idle capacity like labour problems, powercut, government environmental policy in regard to forest based units, machinery break-downs, competition etc.,

Out of 11 Chemical based units 4 units are suffering from lack of demand. These 4 units are plastic film, plastic bags, sulphuric acid, and reclamation of lubricant oil and poly film making units. units i.e., 35.29% have expressed lack of finance as the reason for idle capacity. They are LDPE and HDPE bags, colour compounds, magnesium sulfate reclamation of lubrication oil and poly film making units. 4 of Poly proline film making unit weather unit, hydrochloric acid and zinc sulphate manufacturing units have expressed their inability to utilise their capacity to the fullest extent due to non-availability of raw-material. Seven units out of 11 are suffering from other problems like machinery breakdowns, competition in domestic and international market, poor quality, power shortage, shortage of technical people etc.

In the Mineral and Building material based category 8 units out of 16 i.e. 50% are suffering from lack of demand. Out of these 8 units 3 are mini cement plants, 3 tiles units, one fly ash unit and one gypsum based brick and tiles units. 9 units in this category viz 6 mini cement plants, one tiles unit, one spun pipes unit and one hallow bricks manufacturing units are suffering from shortage of working capital. Out of 16 units 3 units are suffering from raw-material problem. These are 2 stone crushers and one tiles manufacturing unit. 8 of these units out of 16 i.e., 50% have explained some other reasons for their idle capacity like competition, quality, labour unrest, machinery troubles, government policy etc.

Out of 20 units in Engineering and Allied based category 13 units have expressed the reason for their idle capacity as lack of demand. 4 steel fabrication units, 3 general engineering works, 4 casting works and one unit each of iron re-rolling and aluminum fabrication are the 13 units facing lack of the demand for their products. The reason for idle capacity in 5 units is shortage of finance. 9 units i.e 45% have expressed other reasons like power-cut, competition, labour problems, quality, machinery troubles etc for their idle capacity.

Total Production

There is a great deal of variation from one category of industrial units to another. In respect of total production as well. Not only the quantum of production varies but also the trend of production differs from one unit to another.

Vizianagaram District

Table 4.26 presented below gives a consolidated picture of total production in different categories of small scale units of Vizianagarm district during 1991-92 and 1995-96.

From the table it can be said that the greatest contribution is made by the Agro based units and the production of these units to the total production in 1992-93, 1991-92, 1993-94, 1995-96 and 1994-95 constituted 51.75%, 46.6%, 45%, 44.75%, 41.8% respectively. The lowest contribution is made by the Engineering and Allied based units whose production in 1995-96 is only 1.59% of the total production. Coming to year wise analysis, during 1991-92 Mineral and Building material based units contributed 40.8% i.e., next to Agro based of the total production. Forest based and Engineering and Allied based units have contributed 10.6% and 2% respectively to the total production during the year. During the year 1992-93 the contribution of Mineral and Building material based units reduced to 29.4% whereas the share of Agro based units increased to 51.7%. Forest based units, Chemical based units and Engineering and Allied based unit have contributed 11.2%, 5.8% and 1.9% respectively to the total production.

Table—4.26 Trend of Total Production in Different Categories of Industrial Units of Vizianagaram District (1991-96)

(Rs. in lakhs)

Category of units	*1991-92*	*1992-93*	*1993-94*	*1994-95*	*1995-96*
Agro based	579 (46.6)	959 (51.7)	928 (45.0)	718 (41.8)	1032 (44.75)
Forest based	132 (10.6)	207 (11.2)	169 (8.3)	203 (11.8)	299 (12.96)
Chemical based	—	106 (5.8)	105 (5.2)	98 (5.7)	189 (8.20)
Mineral & Building material based	507 (40.8)	546 (29.4)	806 (39.6)	650 (38.0)	748.80 (32.47)
Engg. & Allied based	24 (2.0)	36 (1.9)	38 (1.9)	47 (2.7)	36.75 (1.59)
Total	1242 (100.0)	1854 (100)	2036 (100)	1716 (100.0)	2305.63 (100.0)

Note : figures in brackets indicate percentage to total.

During the year 1993-94 the production of Mineral and Building material based units increased to 39.6% whereas the production of Agro based units reduced to 45%. The other category of units i.e., Forest based, Chemical based and Engineering and Allied based have contributed to the production at 8.2%, 12.3% and 1.9%. During the year 1994-95 the Mineral and Building material based units have contributed 38% of the total production of that year. Forest based and Chemical based and Engineering and Allied based units occupied 3rd, 4th, 5th places contributing 11.8%, 5.7%, and 2.7% respectively to the total production. In the year 1995-96 mineral and building material based units have contributed 32.47% of the total production. Forest based, Chemical based, Engineering and Allied based units have contributed in the order of 12.96, 8.2% and 1.59%.

From the above table it is clear that Agro based units and Mineral and Building material based units have contributed more than 3/4 of the total production during the year 1991-92 to 1995-96. This share in the total production for these 5 years i.e., from 1991-92 to 1995-96 came to 87.4%, 81.1%, 84.6% 79.8% and 77.2% respectively.

When the total production in rupees is considered, except during the year 1994-95 the trend of the production showed a continuous improvement. During the year 1991-92 it was 12.42 crores which increased to Rs. 18.54 crores in 1992-93. It further increased to 23.36 crores in 1993-94. However, during the year 1994-95 because of reduction of production in Agro based units, the total production came down to 17.16 crores. But in the year 1995-96 the production in Agro based units improved significantly and thus the total production reached to a maximum of Rs. 23.05 crores.

Srikakulam District

The total production in different categories of small scale units of Srikakulam district from 1991-92 to 1995-96 is depicted in table 4.27.

From the table it can be said that the greatest contribution i.e., more than 50% of total production in all the years is made by the Agro based units and the production of these units in 1995-96 1993-94, 1994-95, 1991-92 and 1992-93. constituted 51.1%, 57.3%, 59%, 61.7% and 70.1% respectively. The lowest contribution is made by the Engineering and Allied based units whose production was 2.8%, 2.5%, 2.3%, 1.3% and 1.3% in the years 1994-95, 1993-94, 1995-96, 1992-93 and 1991-92 respectively of the total production of all the small scale units. In the year 1991-92 Mineral and Building material based units occupy second position with 26.7% next to Agro based units. The percentage in total production of Chemical, Forest, and Engineering and Allied based units are below 10%, i.e., 6.8%, 3.5% and 1.3% respectively. In the next year 1991-93 the Mineral and Building material based units share is reduced to 19.7%.

Table—4.27 Trend of Total Production in Different Categories of Industrial Units of Srikakulam District (1991-96)

(Rs. in lakhs)

Category of units	*1991-92*	*1992-93*	*1993-94*	*1994-95*	*1995-96*
Agro based	946 (61.7)	1237 (70.1)	1018 (57.3)	1210 (59.0)	957.60 (51.1)
Forest based	54 (3.5)	55 (3.1)	92 (5.2)	95 (4.6)	156.40 (8.4)
Chemical based	105 (6.8)	102 (5.8)	123 (6.9)	229 (11.2)	239.40 (12.8)
Mineral & Building material based	409 (26.7)	348 (19.7)	499 (28.1)	460 (22.4)	476.16 (25.4)
Engg. & Allied based	19 (1.3)	22 (1.3)	44 (2.5)	57 (2.8)	43.68 (2.3)
Total	1533 (100.0)	1764 (100.0)	1776 (100.0)	2051 (100.0)	1874 (100.0)

Note : Figures in brackets indicate percentage to total.

In the year 1993-94 the Agro based units share in the total production is reduced to 57.3%, where as in all the remaining categories it increased to 28.1% in Mineral and Building material based, to 6.9% in Chemical based to 5.2% in Forest based, and to 2.5% in Engineering and Allied based category units. In the year 1994-95 the Agro, Chemical and Engineering and Allied based units have increased their share to 59%, 11.2% and 2.8% respectively. The percentage in total production of Forest based Mineral and Building material based units reduced to 4.6% and 22.4% respectively.

Visakhapatnam District

Table 4.28 explains the trend of total production in different categories of small scale units in Visakhapatnam district from the year 1991-92 to 1995-96.

From the table it can be said that the greatest contribution is made by the Mineral and Building material based units during the years 1991-92 and 1992-93 with 31% and 33.75% respectively. In the year 1993-94 Forest based category units constitute highest contribution to the total production is made by Agro based units followed by Forest based Chemical based and Mineral and Building material based units.

Table—4.28 Trend of Total Production in Different Categories of Industrial Units of Visakhapatnam District (1991-96)

(Rs. in lakhs)

Category of units	*1991-92*	*1992-93*	*1993-94*	*1994-95*	*1995-96*
Agro based	417 (24.5)	841 (26.10)	783 (18.55)	1200 (24.37)	1639.68 (28.57)
Forest based	360 (21.1)	589 (18.29)	1330 (31.52)	1173 (23.83)	1390.40 (24.23)
Chemical based	268 (15.7)	465 (14.43)	576 (13.64)	1060 (21.53)	1294.65 (22.55)
Mineral & Building material based	528 (31.0)	1087 (33.73)	1238 (29.32)	1087 (22.08)	726.00 (12.65)
Engg. & Allied based	132 (7.7)	240 (7.45)	294 (6.97)	403 (8.19)	688.80 (12.00)
Total	1705 (100.0)	3222 (100.0)	4221 (100.0)	4923 (100.0)	5739.53 (100.00)

Note : Figures in brackets indicate percentages to total.

On the year wise analysis shows that in the year 1991-92 Mineral and Building material based units acquire major share with 31% in the total production followed by Agro based with 24.5%, Forest based with 21.2% Chemical based with 15.7% and Engineering and Allied based with 7.7%.

During the year 1992-93 also Mineral and Building material based units took first position with 33.73% followed by Agro based units with 26.10% in the total production. The Forest based, Chemical based and Engineering allied based category of units contribution is reduced in this year with 18.29%, 14.43% and 7.45% respectively.

In the year of 1993-94 the Forest based category contributes highest of 31.52% of the total production. The Mineral and Building material based category units occupy second place contributing 29.32% followed by Agro based, Chemical based and Engineering and Allied based category of units with 18.55%, 13.64% and 6.97% respectively.

In the year 1994-95 except Engineering and Allied based category units the share of remaining category units is more or less same. Among the remaining 4 categories Agro based stood first contributing 24.37% followed by Forest based with 23.83%, Mineral and Building material based with 22.08%, and next to the lowest is Chemical based with 21.53%.

In the year of 1995-96 Agro based category units contributed a maximum of 28.57% of the total production followed by Forest based with 24.23%, Chemical based with 22.55%, Mineral and Building material based with 12.63% and Engineering and Allied based with 12%.

Average Production

Inter-unit variations in respect of average production are also observed in small scale industrial units.

Vizianagaram District

Table 4.29 depicts the average production in different categories of units in Vizianagaram district over the period 1991-92 and 1995-96.

Table—4.29 Trend of Average Production in Different Categories of Industrial Units of Vizianagaram District (1991-96)

(Rs. in lakhs)

Category of units	*1991-92*	*1992-93*	*1993-94*	*1994-95*	*1995-96*
Agro based	72.37 (21.83)	73.76 (16.43)	54.00 (13.74)	37.78 (12.57)	54.31 (16.18)
Forest based	66.0 (19.93)	69.00 (15.37)	56.33 (14.31)	40.6 (13.53)	49.83 (14.84)
Chemical based	-	106.00 (23.62)	105.00 (26.68)	98.0 (32.62)	94.54 (28.15)
Mineral & Building material based	169.0 (51.00)	182.00 (40.55)	161.20 (40.96)	108.33 (36.06)	124.80 (37.17)
Engg. & Allied based	24.0 (7.24)	18.0 (4.03)	17.00 (4.31)	15.66 (5.22)	12.25 (3.6)
Total	331.37 (100)	448.76 (100)	393.53 (100)	300.37 (100)	335.73 (100)

Note : Figures in brackets indicate percentages to total.

It is found from the table that wide variations exist among units in respect of their average size of production. For example, during the year

1991-92 the average production in the case of Mineral and Building material based units has as high as Rs. 169 lakhs as against only Rs. 24 lakhs in Engineering and Allied based units. The average production is found to be the highest in Mineral and Building material based units during all the years covered under study. While the lowest size of average production is in the case of Engineering and Allied based units. The average production in all categories except in the case of Engineering and Allied category, reveals that there are upward and downward trends over the period of 5 years of the study. In the case of Engineering and Allied based units the average production declined from year to year and thus from Rs. 24 lakhs in 1991-92 reached to Rs. 1225 lakhs in 1995-96.

Srikakulam District

Table 4.30 explains the trend of average production of different categories of units in Srikakulam district from 1991-92 to 1995-96.

Table—4.30 Trend of Average Production in Different Categories of Industrial Units of Srikakulam District (1991-96)

(Rs. in lakhs)

Category of units	*1991-92*	*1992-93*	*1993-94*	*1994-95*	*1995-96*
Agro based	72.76 (16.32)	72.76 (17.54)	48.47 (12.16)	46.53 (12.37)	36.83 (9.74)
Forest based	54.00 (12.13)	55.00 (13.26)	46.00 (11.54)	47. (12.64)	52.13 (13.78)
Chemical based	105.00 (23.55)	102.00 (24.60)	123.00 (30.86)	114.50 (30.44)	119.70 (31.64)
Mineral & Building material based	204.50 (45.88)	174.00 (41.95)	166.33 (41.75)	153.33 (40.76)	158.72 (41.96)
Engg. & Allied based	9.50 (2.2)	11.00 (2.5)	14.66 (3.67)	14.25 (3.79)	10.92 (2.88)
Total	445.76 (100)	414.76 (100)	398.46 (100)	376.11 (100)	378.30 (100)

Note : Figures in brackets indicate percentages to total.

The table shows that there are lot of variations among different categories of units with in a category and also lot of differences among the categories from year to year. The average production of Mineral and Building material based category units is as high as 40% in all the five years. But in Engineering and Allied based category it is below 5% in all the 5 years from 1991-92 to 1995-96. The Forest based category average production is between 11.54% and 13.78%. There are lot of variations in average production from year to year and lot of ups and downs are seen in Chemical based and Agro based units. In chemical based units the average production in the 5 years varies from 23.55% to 31.64% i.e. Rs 36.83 lakhs to 72.76 lakhs and in Agro based category it varies from Rs. 36.83 lakhs i.e., 9.74% to 72.76 lakhs i.e., 17.54%.

Visakhapatnam District

The average production of different categories of units in Visakhapatnam district is explained in table 4.31.

Table—4.31 Trend of Average Production in Different Categories of Industrial Units of Visakhapatnam District (1991-96)

(Rs. in lakhs)

Category of units	*1991-92*	*1992-93*	*1993-94*	*1994-95*	*1995-96*
Agro based	83.4 (23.92)	76.45 (20.91)	65.25 (16.17)	85.71 (24.58)	117.12 (29.55)
Forest based	51.42 (14.75)	53.54 (14.64)	78.23 (19.39)	69.00 (19.78)	81.78 (20.65)
Chemical based	89.33 (25.62)	93.00 (25.43)	115.20 (28.55)	106.00 (30.39)	117.69 (29.66)
Mineral & Building material based	105.60 (30.29)	120.77 (33.03)	123.80 (30.68)	67.93 (19.47)	45.37 (11.44)
Engg. & Allied based	18.85 (5.40)	21.81 (5.9)	21.00 (5.1)	20.15 (5.78)	34.44 (8.7)
Total	348.60 (100)	365.57	403.48 (100)	348.79 (100)	396.4

Note : Figures in brackets indicate percentage to total.

The average production is high in Mineral and Building material based category in the year 1993-94 with Rs. 123.80 lakhs and low with Rs. 21 lakhs in Engineering and Allied based category.

The average production in Mineral and Building material based category units is high in the years 1992-93, 1993-94 and 1991-92 with Rs. 123.80 lakhs, Rs. 120.77, and Rs. 105.60 lakhs (i;e., 30.68%, 33.03%, and 30.29%) respectively. In the year 1994-95 and 1995-96 it come down to Rs. 67.93 lakhs and Rs. 4.37 lakhs respectively. 19.47% and 11.44% respectively which is the next to the lowest in these two years. The average production of Chemical based units in all the 5 years is between Rs. 93 lakhs and Rs. 117.69 lakhs i.e., from 25.43% to 29.69%. The average production in Forest based category units and Agro based category units for all the 5 years is between Rs. 51.42 lakhs and Rs. 81.78 lakhs and between Rs. 65.25 lakhs and Rs. 117.12 lakhs respectively.

TREND OF TOTAL AND AVERAGE PRODUCTION

Vizianagaram District

The trend of total and average production in different categories of units in Vizianagaram district during 1995-96 can be seen in table 4.32.

Table—4.32 Trend of Total and Average Production in Different Categories of Industrial Units of Vizianagaram District During 1995-96.

(Rs. in lakhs)

Category of units	*No. of units*	*Total production*	*Average production*
Agro based	19	1032.00 (44.77)	54.31 (16.2)
Forest based	6	299.00 (12.96)	49.83 (14.8)
Chemical based	2	189.08 (8.20)	94.54 (28.2)
Mineral & Building material based	6	748.80 (32.48)	124.80 (37.2)
Engg. & Allied based	3	36.75 (1.59)	12.25 (3.6)
Total	36	2305.63 (100)	335.73 (100)

Note : Figures in brackets indicate percentages to total.

From the table it is interesting to know that though the Agro based units contribute 44.77% of the total production, their share in average production is only to the extent of 16.2%, contrary to this, the contribution of Chemical based units to the total production is only 8.2% where as their share in average production is 28.2%.

Srikakulam District

Table 4.33 explains the trend of total production and average production of different categories of units in Srikakulam district during the year 1995-96.

Table—4.33 Trend of Total and Average Production in Different Categories of Industrial Units of Srikakulam District During 1995-96

(Rs. in lakhs)

Category of units	*No.of units*	*Total production*	*Average production*
Agro based	26	957.60 (51.1)	36.83 (9.7)
Forest based	3	156.40 (8.4)	52.13 (13.8)
Chemical based	2	239.40 (12.9)	119.70 (31.7)
Mineral & Building material for based	3	476.16 (25.4)	158.72 (42.0)
Engg. & Allied based	4	43.68 (2.2)	10.92 (2.8)
Total	38	1873.24 (100)	378.31 (100)

Note : Figures in brackets indicate percentages to total.

The table shows more interesting figures relating to total production and average production. The total production in Agro based categories is highest with 51.1% and at the same time the average production shows only 9.7%, contrary to this the contribution of Chemical based units is only 12.9% in the total production and it is 31.7% in the contribution of average production.

Visakhapatnam District

The total production and average production of different categories of units are given in table 4.34.

Table—4.34 Trend of Total and Average Production of Different Categories of Industrial Units of Visakhapatnam District During 1995-96

(Rs. in lakhs)

Category of units	*No.of units*	*Total production*	*Average production*
Agro based	14	1639.68 (28.6)	117.12 (29.6)
Forest based	17	1390.40 (24.2)	81.78 (20.7)
Chemical based	11	1294.65 (22.6)	117.69 (29.6)
Mineral & Building material based	16	726.00 (12.6)	45.37 (11.5)
Engg. & Allied based	20	668.80 (12.0)	34.44 (8.6)
Total	78	5739.53 (100)	396.4 (100)

Note : Figures in brackets indicate percentages to total.

From the table much differences can be observed in the percentages of total production and average production in the case of Engineering and Allied based category of units. There percentage in total production is 12 where as there percentage in average production is only 8.6. Similarly, in case of Agro based and Chemical based units the percentage of average production is more than the percentage of total production. Contrary to it, in case of Forest based and Mineral & Building material based units the percentage of average production is less than the percentage of total production.

CHAPTER—V

AN ANALYSIS OF THE PROBLEMS OF SAMPLE UNITS

The main objective of this chapter is to analysis various problems faced by small industrial units in Vizianagaram, Srikakulam and Visakhapatnam districts. Attempts have made to highlight the problem based on the data collected by the researcher. Further, efforts are also made to analyse the reasons for the problems that are identified so as to suggest appropriate measures to resolve the same.

During the survey it is observed that the small scale units in these 3 districts are suffering from several problems which hamper their spontaneous growth. The unit are small but the problems faced by them seem to be big. In general, it is observed that almost every unit is hit by some problem or the other depending upon its size and structure. It is identified that production, labour, marketing and financial problems are the major problems. Further, sickness is also became one among the major problems in recent years. This is why the problem of sickness and its analysis is dealt with separately in the following chapter. The problems of production, labour marketing and financial are discussed in the following pages in this chapter.

PRODUCTION PROBLEMS

Vizianagaram District

For smooth running of any industrial unit the problem of production shall be minimum. If a unit faces production problems it may not work to fullest capacity and may not achieve its target. The production problems to some extent are responsible for idle capacity in any industrial unit. In Vizianagaram district out of 36 healthy small scale units except

12 all the remaining units are facing production problems. The detailed information can be seen in the following table.

Table—5.1 No of Units Facing Production Problems of Different Categories of Industries in Vizianagaram District

Category of units	*Total no of units*	*Shortage of raw materials*	*Shortage of power*	*Machinery problems*	*Without problems*
Agro based	19	—	6 (31.58)	4 (21.05)	9 (47.37)
Forest based	6	2 (33.33)	3 (50)	1 (16.67)	—
Chemical based	2	1 (50)	—	—	1 (50)
Mineral & Building material based	6	1 (16.67)	2 (33.33)	1 (16.67)	2 (33.33)
Engg. & Allied based	3	—	2 (66.67)	1 (33.33)	—
Total	36 (100)	4 (11.11)	13 (36.11)	7 (19.44)	12 (38.46)

Note : Figures in brackets indicate percentages total.

From the above table it can be noted that 2/3rd of the sample units in Vizianagaram district suffer from several production problems. It is clear from the table that 4 out of 36 i.e. 11.11% of total small scale units suffer from shortage of raw materials. Category wise, 2 units from Forest based and one unit each from Chemical and Mineral and Building material based have expressed the problem of raw material shortages. One saw mill and one mill board units in Forest based category are facing the problem of regular supply of quality wood from the nearby forest. The entrepreneurs of these 2 units opined that the shortage is due to non-availability of quality wood in the nearby forest at reasonable rates and government restrictions on auctions.

The dyes unit under Chemical based category is facing the problem of raw-material i.e., Chemicals. This unit has to get the required chemicals from outside the state. It is facing the non-availability of chemicals in right time at reasonable rate from outside the state i.e., from Maharastra state. One unit engaging stone crushing expressed the problem of delay in allotment of stone quarries to the units. Agro based and Engineering and Allied based units have expressed that their units are not facing any severe production problem.

24 units out of 36 which are facing production problems, 13 i.e. 36.16% are facing the problem of shortage of power. 6 Agro based units, 3 Forest based units and 2 units each of Mineral and Building material and Engineering and Allied based units are facing this problem.

The power supply in the state of Andhra Pradesh for the last 10 to 15 years is not sufficient. Further, the government of Andhra Pradesh gives first priority to agriculture and domestic consumption. The drought situations in the state some times hampers the regular supply of required power to industrial sector of the state whenever there is a shortage in supply of power. The state government imposes powercut first on industrial units. Because of this the production in both large and small scale units suffer.

Because of shortage of power supply one unit of rice mill, one unit of flour mill, one unit of oil mill, dairy products, agriculture implements, cold storage are facing the problem of low production mainly the power based Agro units like cold storage house, dairy products unit are severely suffering due to power cut.

To encourage alternative power supply the state government has been giving 20% subsidy on the cost of diesel generators and captive power plants. The small industrial development and Bank of India also finances to these projects. But in practice all the small scale entrepreneurs are not in a position to bear this additional investment.

2 saw mills and one paper cone manufacturing unit under Forest based category also have the problem of power shortage. One mini cement plant and one stone crushing unit under Mineral and Building material based category have also experienced this problem. Two Engineering and Allied based units which require continuous power supply face this problem.

Seven i.e., 19.44% units out of 24 small scale units are suffering from production problems and other machinery troubles in their production process. One flour mill, one oil mill, one agriculture implements manufacturing unit and one dall mill, under Agro based category are suffering from breakdowns in machinery. The machinery used in these units are very old and second hand one.

Because of old machinery used in one of the bobbins unit in

Forest based category is often faced the machinery trouble. Due to poor maintenance and erection problems one cement plant under Mineral and Building material based category is facing the production problems due to machinery breakdowns. One unit of Engineering and Allied category has also experienced the same problems of machinery breakdown due to poor handling by unskilled labour.

The researcher found that one third of the total units that is 12 units have not faced any production problems in recent years. Out of these 12 units 9 are under Agro based, one is under Chemical based and the remaining 2 are in Mineral and Building material based.

Srikakulam District

Table 5.2 explains the various production problems faced by the small scale units in different categories in Srikakulam district.

Table—5.2 No. of Units Facing Production Problems of Different Categories of Industries in Srikakulam District

Category of units	*Total no of units*	*Shortage of raw materials*	*Shortage of power*	*Machinery problems*	*Without problems*
Agro based	26	6 (23.8)	8 (30.77)	2 (7.69)	10 (38.46)
Forest based	3	2 (66.67)	1 (33.33)	—	—
Chemical based	2	1 (50)	—	—	1 (50)
Mineral & Building material sbased	3	1 (33.33)	1 (33.33)	1 (33.33)	—
Engg. & Allied based	4	—	2 (50)	1 (25)	1 (25)
Total	38 (100)	10 (26.31)	12 (31.58)	4 (10.53)	12 (31.58)

Note : Figures in brackets indicate percentages to total.

The above table exhibits that 68% of the small scale units in Srikakulam district are suffering from several production problems. It is evident from the table that out of 38 sample units 10 units i.e., 26.31% are suffering from shortage of raw-material. Out of 10 units, 6 units from Agro based, 2 units from Forest based and one each from Chemical and Mineral and Building material based units have expressed the same reason of shortage of raw-material. Out of 6 Agro based units 3 units are cashewnut processing unit which are facing the shortage of quality cashewnut. In the off-season the oil mill is also facing the same raw material shortage problem in off-seasons. The jute based praticle board unit is facing the problem of lack of godowns for storing the raw jute (raw-material) which is not available thorughout the year.

The two Forest based units, ie., one saw mill and one furniture making unit are suffering from raw-material problems. The furniture unit is suffering from non-availability of quality wood in the nearby market. The saw mills also facing the same quality raw-material problem and government restrictions.

One wax manufacturing unit in Chemical based category is suffering from raw-material shortage. The available raw-material in the nearby market is very costly. This is why the entrepreneurs are purchasing from other states. It affects the timely production.

In the Mineral and Building material based category one granite slabs making unit is suffering from the problem of high cost of production because of high rates of quality raw-material and high processing costs. The Engineering and Allied based units are not suffering from any raw-material problem.

12 units out of 38 units i.e., 31.58% in Srikakulam district are facing the problem of power shortage. 8 Agro based units, 2 Engineering and Allied based and one each in Mineral and Building material based and Forest based units are included here. 3 rice mills, 2 coir units, one oil mill, one flour mill, one jute stick powder unit, one particle board unit are affected with this problem of power shortage. The rice and oil mill owners expressed that the powercut problem is serious draw back in the busy season and it affects their profitability. The flour mill and coir based unit manufacturers have expressed that the powercut affect their business in all aspects. Due to powercut sometimes the production comes down and they are not in a position to supply the products to their customers in time. This affects their profitability and reputation in the market. The entrepreneurs of the jute stick powder unit expressed that this power problem of shortage is not only affects the production but also affects the labour relations. The researcher observed that powercut timings re frequently changing in that area and the workers are not adjusted to work in the powercut timings.

A saw mill under the Forest based category is also facing the problem of shortage of power. The entrepreneur expressed that he is not in a position to supply the wood to the customers in the busy summer season due to powercuts.

In the Mineral and Building material based category one mini cement plant is suffering from shortage of power problem. 2 Engineering and Allied based units i.e., 1 aluminum utensils manufacturing unit and one welding electrodes manufacturing unit are also facing the powercut problem. For these two units power is highest required for manufacturing the product. Due to frequent and long hours powercut, the wastage increases and it also affects the quality of the product.

Four units out of 38 units i.e., 10.53 per cent only are suffering from machinery troubles. They are 2 Agro based units, one unit each of Mineral and Building material and Engineering and Allied based category unit. One jute stick powder unit is suffering from machinery problems due to poor maintenance. An Agro based unit i.e., cashewnut is suffering with production problem due to poor quality machinery. One Chemical based unit i.e., starch making unit is suffering from production problem due in experienced machine operator.

12 units out of 38 i.e., 31.58% are free from production problems. The most interesting thing is that out of 12 units, 10 are Agro based and the remaining 2 belong to Chemical based and Engineering and Allied based category respectively.

Visakhapatnam District

Table 5.3 depicts the production problem of different categories of small scale units in Visakhapatnam district.

From this table it can be noted that 25% of the units i.e., 20 units out of 78 units in Visakhapatnam district are suffering from shortage of raw materials. Out of these 20 units 9 units are Forest based, 4 units are Agro based, 4 units are Chemical based and 3 units are Mineral and Building material based.

Out of 4 Agro based units, 2 are food processing units and one is rice mill and one is soft drink manufacturing unit. The food processing unit expressed lack of availability of high quality fruit pulp and other ingredients the soft drink manufacturer also expressed high transport costs and the delay in getting concentrates from outside the state.

Table—5.3 No. of Units Facing Production Problems of Different Categories of Industries in Visakhapatnam District.

Category of units	*Total no of units*	*Shortage of raw materials*	*Shortage of power*	*Machinery problems*	*Without problems*
Agro based	14	4 (28.57)	6 (42.86)	3 (21.43)	1 (07.14)
Forest based	17	9 (52.94)	5 (29.41)	3 (17.65)	—
Chemical based	11	4 (36.36)	2 (18.18)	3 (27.28)	2 (18.18)
Mineral & Building material based	16	3 (18.75)	4 (25)	2 (12.50)	7 (43.75)
Engg. & Allied based	20	—	8 (40)	5 (25)	7 (35.00)
Total	78 (100)	20 (25.65)	25 (32.05)	16 (20.51)	17 (21.79)

Note : Figures in brackets indicate percentage to total.

In the Forest based category 6 saw mills, 2 furniture making units and one plywood manufacturing unit are suffering from raw-material problem. The entrepreneur feel that the procurement of cheap and best raw-materials has become a problem. They opine that the conditions and restrictions imposed by Forest department is also one of the causes for scarcity of raw-material. The entrepreneurs of the furniture making unit also expresses the difficulty in obtaining quality wood at reasonable rates.

Out of 11 units in Chemical based category 4 units are suffering from shortage of raw-material. These four units are zinc sulphate manufacturing unit, hydrochloric acid manufacturing unit, leather unit and polyproflin film manufacturing unit. The hydrochloric acid and zinc sulphate manufacturing unit directors expressed that shortage of raw-material and high transporting costs are the problems for these units. As the chemicals are to be purchased from long distances and that too they are highly inflammable in nature and dangerous transporting and storing is a difficult task. This also increases their cost of production. 2 stone crushers and one red tiles manufacturing unit are suffering from shortage of raw-material in Mineral and Building material category. The stone crusher entrepreneurs expressed the quarry lease is high and the restrictions and conditions of the mines department are also unbearable. The redtiles manufacturing unit at Kottavalasa also suffering from non-availability of red clay in the nearby areas. The Engineering and Allied based units are not facing any serious raw material problem.

61 out of 78 units which are facing production problems, 25 i.e., 32.05% are facing the problem of shortage of power. 6 Agro based units, 5 Forest based units, 2 Chemical based units, 4 Mineral and Building material based units and 8 Engineering and Allied based units are suffering from shortage of power.

Out of 14 Agro based units 6 units are suffering from shortage of power. These six are 2 rice mills, 2 oil mills and 2 soft drinks manufacturing units. The rice mill entrepreneurs expressed that the government is supplying power to their industries only 9 hours a day, that too six hours in the early morning and 3 hours in the midnight as the unit belongs to rural feeder power supply. The entrepreneurs of soft drink units also expressed that the power cuts are very high in their busy season and that affects their production targets.

In the Forest based category 4 saw mills and one plywood manufacturing unit are suffering from shortage of power. 2 Chemical based units and 4 Mineral and Building material based units also suffering from this problem. Out of all 25 units suffering from power problem the Engineering and Allied based is the main category which is severely, affected by this power problem. All the 3 re-rolling mills, 2 ferrous and non-ferrous casting units, 2 general engineering units and one wire rope manufacturing unit is among the 8 units suffering from shortage of power.

16 outs are suffering from machinery troubles. Due to machinery breakdowns the production quantity reduces and it also affects the quality and timely supply.

One confectionery and one rice mill is suffering from production problems due to old machinery. One food processing unit is also suffering from production problem due to poor maintenance under Agro based category.

Due to old machinery and their poor maintenance 2 saw mills and one planning units are also suffering from machinery troubles. Lack of knowledge about maintenance non-availability lack of availability of skilled operators and erection faults are the main technical problems in Chemical based category units. These three units are manufacturing zinc sulphate, hydrochloric acid, reclamation of lubricant oil.

In the Mineral and Building material based category also one spun pipes manufacturing unit and one gypsum making based unit are suffering from machinery problem due to poor handling and usage of second hand machinery.

Out of 16, 5 units i.e., 31.25% in Engineering and Allied based category are suffering from machinery problems, due to continuous work, poor maintenance and machinery breakdowns.

The researcher observed that out of 78 units 17 i.e. 21.79% are not facing any serious production problem in the recent past. 7 units each in Mineral and Building material and Engineering and Allied based category, 2 units in Chemical based and one unit in Agro based.

These are one Agro based units, 2 Chemical based units and 7 each of Mineral and Building material based and Engineering and Allied based units.

Labour Problems

The small scale units are mostly labour intensive and they provide employment opportunities to the large number of people. The role of labour is mainly sided and is inevitable for the overall growth of small scale units. The small industrial units under sample survey indicated that they have labour problems like shortage of skilled and unskilled labour, labour turnover, absenteeism and strikes. The following table 5.4 depicts the small scale units facing different types of labour problems.

From the table it can be seen that 25 units out of 36 i.e., 69.44% of small scale units have labour problems. 10 units have faced 2 types of labour problems.

Out of 25 units suffering from labour problems 18 units have experienced the problem of shortage of labour, 7 units have the problem of labour turnover, 8 units suffer from absenteeism and only 2 units experienced the problem of strikes. As many as 11 units i..e., 30.56% have no labour problems.

Table—5.4 No. of Units Facing Labour Problems of Different Categories of Units in Vizianagaram District

Category of units	*Total no.of units*	*Shortage of labour*			*Labour turn over*	*Absent-eeism*	*Strikes*	*Without problems*
		Skilled	*Unskilled*	*Total*				
Agro based*	19	3 (30.0)	7 (70.0)	10 (52.63)	—	3 (15.8)	— —	9 (31.57)
Forest based*	6	—	—	—	3 (50)	1 (16.67)	—	2 (33.33)
Chemical based*	2	2 (100.0)	—	2 (100.0)	1 (50)	2 (100)	—	—
Mineral & s Material based*	6	2 (50.0)	2 (50.0)	4 (66.64)	2 (33.33)	1 (16.67)	2 (33.33)	—
Engineering & Allied based*	3	2 (100.)	—	2 (66.67)	1 (33.33)	1 (33.33)	—	—
Total	36	9 (50.0)	9 (50.0)	18 (50.0)	7 (19.44)	8 (22.22)	2 (5.56)	11 (30.56)

Note : Figures in brackets indicate percentage to total

* Units with more than one problem.

10 units from Agro based category have the problem of shortage of labour supply. Out of these 10 units seven units experienced non-availability of required skilled labour, where as 3 units face the problem of availability of unskilled labour. 2 rice mills and dairy products plant experienced the shortage of machine operators for their units. Other seven Agro based units mainly the rice mills and flour mills are facing the shortage of unskilled labour.

Two units under Chemical based category are facing the problem of skilled labour. Under Mineral and Building material based category 2 units. One cement plant and tiles factory are facing the problem of non-availability of skilled labour. These units are also in need of unskilled labour. One general engineering unit and one aluminum utensils manufacturing unit under Engineering and Allied based category are facing the problem of non-availability of skilled labour to work as fitters, turners, welders and machine operators etc. Thus 18 units out of 36 i.e. 50% are facing the shortage of both skilled and unskilled labour.

Two saw mill units and one plywood manufacturing unit entrepreneurs have expressed the problem of labour turnover under Forest category. The researcher has further, observed that the entrepreneurs have not taken care to provide safety measures to the workers which has caused the problem. One Chemical unit has also faced the problem of labour turnover. Poor working conditions and low price rate system of payment caused this trouble. One General Engineering unit has also faced the same problem. Thus a total of 7 out of 36 i.e. 19.44% small scale units have experienced the problem of labour turnover.

Three Agro based units (one jute based unit, one oil mill and one rice mill) experienced the problem of labour absenteeism, as the workers are migrated from the surrounding villages and in sowing and harvesting seasons, they go homes and to attend their agriculture activities.

One Forest based unit, 2 Chemical based units and one unit each in Mineral and Building material based and Engineering and Allied based category have also experienced the problem of absenteeism. Thus, 8 units in the total of 36 i.e., 22.22% have faced the problem of absenteeism.

Vizianagaram district is a place for concentration of medium and large scale jute mills engaging large number of workers. The researcher observed that due to the indirect effect of workers working in these units creating labour turnover and absenteeism in small scale units to some extent.

An interesting point to be noted here is that through there is an effect of workers of large scale units on the workers of small scale units, the units have not faced the problem of strikes. Only 2 units under Mineral and Building material based category have experienced the problem of strikes out of 36 small scale units. 9 units under Agro based category and 2 units under the Forest based category are free from labour problems.

Labour Problems in Srikakulam District

Table 5.5 (next page) shares the labour problems faced by different categories of small scale units in Srikakulm district.

The table shows that out of 38 units in Srikakulam district 32 units i.e. 84.21% are suffering from labour problems like shortage of skilled and unskilled labour, labour turnover, absenteeism and strikes.

Out of 32 units each in Forest based and Chemical based category, 2 units each in Mineral and Building material based category and Engineering and Allied based category and all the 26 units in Agro based category are suffering from the labour problems in one way the or the other.

Out of 32 units suffering from labour problems 12 units i.e. 31.58% are facing the problem of labour shortage. One unit in Chemical based category and one unit in Engineering and Allied based category are facing 2 types of labour problems. In Mineral and Building material based category 2 units are suffering from 3 types of labour problems. There are 6 units out of 38 i.e. 15.79% are not facing any chronicle labour problem.

8 units in Agro based category have the problem of shortage of labour supply. Out of 8 units are suffering from non-availability of unskilled labour, whereas 3 units are suffering from the problem of lack of skilled labour. 4 rice mills and one oil mill is suffering with lack of unskilled labour available in that area. The entrepreneurs expressed that in the paddy season it is very difficult to run the unit due to non-availability of labour and also with their terms and conditions. The cashewnut processing unit, jute based and coir based units in Agro based category are suffering from shortage of skilled labour for their units.

Table—5.5 No. of Units Facing Labour Problems of Different Categories of Industries in Srikakulam District

Category of units	*Total no. of units*	*Shortage of labour*			*Labour turn over*	*Absent-eeism*	*Strikes*	*Without problems*
		Skilled	*Unskilled*	*Total*				
Agro based*	26	5 (62.5)	3 (37.50)	8 (30.77)	4 (15.38)	5 (19.23)	9 (34.61)	—
Forest based*	3	—	—	—	—	1 (33.33)	— —	2 (66.67)
Chemical based*	2	1 (100)	—	1 (50)	1 (50)	—	—	1 (50)
Mineral & building material based*	3	1 (50)	1 (50)	2 (66.67)	1 (33.33)	1 (33.33)	2 (66.67)	1 (33.33)
Engineering & Allied based*	4	1 (100)	—	1 (25)	—	1 (25)	1 (25)	2 (50)
Total	38	8 (66.67)	4 (33.33)	12 (31.58)	6 (15.79)	8 (21.05)	12 (31.58)	6 (15.79)

Note : Figures in brackets indicate percentage to total.

* Units with more than one problem

One unit under Chemical based category and one unit in Engineering and Allied based category are suffering from shortage of skilled labour. They are one saw mill and one starch manufacturing unit. In the Mineral and Building material based category one spun pipes manufacturing unit is suffering with non-availability of cheap unskilled labour and one granite cutting and polishing plant experienced the shortage of skilled labour.

4 Agro based units i.e. 3 rice mills and one oil mill have expressed the problem of labour turnover. The researcher observed that the reason for high labour turnover in Chemical based unit is the non-provision of safety measures. Because of low payment, the turnover is high in Mineral and Building material based units.

Regarding absenteeism, 5 units in Agro based category are suffering from this problem. As the majority of Agro based units are situated near villages the absenteeism is more in sowing and harvesting season of paddy.

One unit each in Forest based, Mineral and Building material based and Engineering and Allied based category have also expressed the problem of absenteeism.

The most unfortunate situation in Srikakulam district is 31.58% of the units have expressed the problems of strikes. Out of 12 units which have experiences the problem, 9 are from Agro based category, 2 are from Mineral and Building material category and one is from Engineering and Allied based category. It is observed that the main reason for the strikes in rice mills, and oil mills is for higher wages.

2 units each in Forest based and Engineering and Allied based category and one unit each in Chemical and Mineral and Building material based category are free from labour problems.

LABOUR PROBLEMS IN VISAKHAPATNAM DISTRICT

Table 5.6 depicts the different problems faced by the small scale industrial units of Visakhapatnam district.

From the table it can be said that 49 units out of 78 units i.e, 62.82% of small scale units have labour problems. In these 33 units have faced 2 types of labour problems. 5 units have faced 3 types of labour problems.

Table—5.6 No. of Units Facing Labour Problems of Different Categories of Industries in Visakhapatnam District

Category of units	*Total no. of units*	*Shortage of labour*			*Labour turn over*	*Absent-eeism*	*Strikes*	*Without problems*
		Skilled	*Unskilled*	*Total*				
Agro based*	14	4 (50.00)	4 (50.00)	8 (57.14)	3 ((21.43)	2 (14.28)	3 (21.43)	6 (42.86)
Forest based*	17	2 (40.00)	3 (60.00)	5 (29.40)	2 (11.76)	2 (11.76)	2 (11.76)	6 (35.29)
Chemical based*	11	4 (57.14)	3 (42.86)	7 (63.64)	3 (27.27)	2 (18.18)	4 (36.36)	4 (36.36)
Mineral & building material based*	16	3 (37.50)	5 (62.50)	8 (50.00)	4 (25.00)	3 (18.75)	8 (50.00)	6 (37.50)
Engineering & Allied based*	20	6 (66.67)	3 (33.33)	9 (45.00)	4 (20.00)	4 (20.00)	4 (20.00)	7 (35.00)
Total	78	19 (51.35)	18 (48.65)	37 (47.43)	16 (20.51)	13 (16.67)	21 (26.92)	29 (37.18)

Note : Figures in brackets indicate percentage to total

* Units with more than one problem.

Out of 49 units suffering from labour problems 37 units have experienced the problem of shortage of labour, 16 units have the problem of labour turnover, 13 units suffer from absenteeism and 21 units experienced the problem of strikes. As many as 29 units i.e., 37.18% have no labour problems.

8 units from Agro based category have the problem of shortage of labour supply. Out of these 8 units, 4 units have experienced non-availability of required unskilled labour, whereas 4 units face the problem of skilled labour. 2 confectionery item making units and 2 food processing plants experienced the shortage of skilled labour for their units. Other 4 Agro based units mainly dall mills and oil mills have faced the problem of shortage of unskilled labour.

Out of 5 Forest based units have faced facing the problem of labour shortage, 2 furniture making units have faced the problem of non-availability of skilled carpenters and 3 saw mills are suffering from lack of unskilled labour supply to work as helpers.

In Chemical based category 4 units have experienced the problem of non-availability of experienced chemists and 3 units suffer from shortage of unskilled labour. Out of 8 units suffering from shortage of labour, 3 cement plants are suffering from skilled labour problem and 3 stone crusher and one spun pipes manufacturing units are facing the problem of unskilled labour. Out of 9 units in Engineering and Allied based category, 6 units are suffering from non-availability of experienced and skilled workers like moulders, turners, fitters, milling machine operators and welders. 3 units in this category are suffering from non-availability of unskilled labour.

16 units out of 78 units i.e. 20.51% of units in this district have experienced the problem of labour turnover. 2 rice mills and one oil mill in Agro based category, 2 saw mills in Forest based category, 3 Chemical based units, 2 cement plants, one spun pipes manufacturing unit and one stone crusher and in Mineral and Building material based category and 2 general engineering units and 2 iron re-rolling mills in Engineering and Allied based category units have experienced the problem of labour turnover. The researcher identified that the high labour turnover is due to lack of safety measures, lack of other financial and non-financial benefits to the workers. In this developed district, many new units are taking birth every week and offer alternative wages to their workers. This directly leads to labour turnover in already existed units.

13 units i.e. 16.67% of units in Visakhapatnam district are suffering from high rate of absenteeism. Out of 13 units 4 units belong to Engineering and Allied based category, 3 units belongs to Mineral and Building material based category and 2 units each from Agro, Forest and Chemical based category respectively.

21 i.e. 26.92% of units have experienced the problem of strikes. It shows the industrial unrest in alarming proportions. Under Mineral and Building material based category 8 units i.e. 6 tiles manufacturing units and 2 mini cement plants have experienced the problem of strikes. Similarly 4 units each in Engineering and Allied based category have suffered this problem. Besides these, 3 Agro based units and 2 Forest based units also suffered from this problems.

29 i.e., 37.18% of units are free from labour problems. They are 7 units in Engineering and Allied based category, 6 units each in Agro, Forest and Mineral and Building material based category units and 4 units in Chemical based category.

MARKETING PROBLEMS

Small scale industrial units in the country today are facing many difficulties in marketing their products, due to growing competition from their sister concerns. Besides competition among small scale units they are also facing competition from large and medium scale units producing the same type of product. The irregular supply of raw-material and their raising prices create difficulties in maintaining a continuous flow of production and meeting growing cost. Ultimately the small scale units face serious problems of marketing. The attitude of entrepreneur towards marketing his own product is a crucial factor in the success and growth of any enterprise. No doubt, the ability to produce is a necessary condition for success, but the ability to market the products produced is also another necessary condition for success.

Vizianagaram District

Lack of demand with regard to all categories of units and government policy with regard to Agro based units appear to be the most important impediments in marketing the products of small scale units of Vizianagaram district. For the sake of deep study, lack of demand in studies in 3 heads viz., Vizianagaram competition, seasonal fluctuation poor quality. The following table 5.7 analyses the marketing problems faced by the small scale units.

Table—5.7 No. of Units Facing Marketing Problems of Different Categories of Industries in Vizianagaram District

Category of units	*Total no. of units*	*Lack of Demand*				*Govt. policy*	*Without problems*
		Compe-tition	*Seasonal Function*	*Poor quality*	*Total*		
Agro based	19	2 (50.00)	2 (50.00)	—	4 (21.05)	13 (68.42)	2 (2.00)
Forest based	6	—	1 (33.33)	2 (66.70)	3 (50.00)	—	3 (50.00)
Chemical based	2	2 (100.00)	—	—	2 (100.00)	—	—
Mineral & Building material based	6	4 (66.70)	—	2 (33.00)	6 (100.00)	—	—
Engineering & Allied based	3	—	—	2 (100.00)	2 (66.70)	—	1 (33.30)
Total	36	8 (47.05)	3 (30.00)	6 (35.29)	17 (47.22)	13 (41.66)	6 (16.66)

Note : Figures in brackets indicate percentage to total.

It is clear from the table that 17 out of 36 units i.e., 47.22% are facing the problem of lack of sufficient demand for their products.

The lack of demand happens to be due to competition in 8 units i.e., 47.05%, Seasonal fluctuation in 3 units i.e., 17.64% and poor quality of products in 6 units i.e., 35.29%, 13 Agro based units out of total 36 units i.e. 36.11% have affected badly due to government policy in marketing their products. There are only 6 units i.e., 16.66% without any marketing problems. One dairy product manufacturing unit and one agricultural implements manufacturing unit have experienced the problem of competition with similar type of units. 2 units under Chemical based category and 4 units in Mineral and Building material based category have also experienced the same problems. Out of 4 Mineral and Building material based units facing the problem of competition, 2 mini cement plants are facing severe competition from large scale cement plants. 2 rice mills and one saw mill have experienced the problems of seasonal fluctuation, leading to lack of demand 2 units each from Forest based, Mineral and Building material based and Engineering and Allied based category are suffering from lack of demand for their poor quality products. Thus these 17 units of different categories are facing problem in marketing their product, due to lack of demand.

An interesting and specific point to be noted here in this table is that 13 Agro based units out of 19 have bitter experience and affected badly due to policy changes of the government in marketing their products.

Among these 5 rice mills have faced the marketing problem due to leavy fixation and export restrictions imposed by government. 3 flour mills experienced the same problem due to involvement of the government in fixing the price of the product. 2 dall mills and 3 oil mills have experienced the problem of marketing of their products due to high quality standards fixed by the government. In this context the researcher observed that the entrepreneurs of these Agro category have over exposed their problems.

From the above table it can be understood that 2 units of Agro based, 3 units of Forest based and one unit of Engineering and Allied based category are free from marketing problems.

Srikakulam District

Lack of demand consisting of competition, seasonal fluctuation and poor quality and government policy appear to be most important problems in marketing of the products of small scale units of Srikakulam district. Table 5.8 analyses the marketing problems faced by the small scale units.

Table—5.8 No. of Units Facing Marketing Problems of Different Categories of Industries in Srikakulam District

Category of units	*Total no. of units*	*Lack of Demand*				*Govt. policy*	*Without problems*
		Compe-tition	*Seasonal Function*	*Poor quality*	*Total*		
Agro based	26	5 (50.00)	3 (30.00)	2 (20.00)	10 (38.46)	10 (38.46)	6 (23.07)
Forest based	3	—	—	1 (50.00)	1 (33.33)	1 (33.33)	1 (33.34)
Chemical based	2	1 (100.00)	—	—	1 (100.00)	—	1 (.)
Mineral & Building material based	3	1 (50.00)	—	1 (50.00)	2 (66.7C)	1 (33.33)	
Engineering & Allied based	4	2 (100.00)	—	—	2 (50.00)	—	2 (50.00)
Total	38	9 (56.25)	3 (18.75)	4 (25.00)	16 (42.10)	12 (31.59)	10 (26.31)

Note : Figures in brackets indicate percentage to total

It is clear from the table that 16 units out of 38 units i.e. 42.10% are facing the problem of lack of sufficient demand for their products. The lack of demand happens to be due to competition in 9 units i.e. 56.25%, seasonal fluctuations in 3 units i.e 18.75% and poor quality in 4 units i.e., 25%. 10 Agro based units and one unit each in Forest and Mineral and Building material based category i.e. 31.59% of units (12 units) have affected badly due to government policy in marketing their products. 2 rice mills, 2 cashewnut processing plants and one coir based unit have experienced the problem of competition with similar types of units. One unit each in Chemical based category and Mineral and Building material based category have experienced the problem of competition from large scale units. 2 Engineering and Allied based units faced the problem with similar type units in the district. One rice mill and 2 dall mills respectively have experienced the problem of seasonal fluctuations due to non-availability of paddy and dalls. 2 units in Agro based category and one unit each in Forest and Mineral and Building material based category are suffering from lack of demand due to poor quality of their products. Thus these 4 units of different categories are facing problems in marketing their products due to lack of demand.

An interesting point to be noted here in this table is that 10 units out of 26 units in Agro based category and one unit each in Forest and Mineral and Building material based category have bitter experience and affected badly due to policy changes of the government in marketing their products. Among these 10 Agro based units 6 rice mills have faced the marketing problem due to leavy fixation and export restrictions imposed by government. 2 dall mills and 2 oil mills have experienced the problem of marketing their products due to high quality standards fixed by the government. One saw mill also badly affected due to environmental policy and Forest policy of government in marketing their products. One granite polishing unit also affected due to delay in allotting granite mines. The researcher observed that some of the entrepreneurs of these units have over exposed their problems.

Out of 10 units i.e. 26.31%, 6 Agro based units, 2 Engineering and Allied based units, one unit each of Forest and Chemical based units are free from marketing problems.

Visakhapatnam District

Table 5.9 explains the various problems faced by small scale units in Visakhapatnam district. The main problems are categorized as lack of demand consisting of competition, poor quality and seasonal fluctuation and government policy.

Table—5.9 No. of Units Facing Marketing Problems of Different Categories of Industries in Visakhapatnam District

Category of Units	*Total no. of units*	*Lack of Demand*				*Govt. policy*	*Without problems*
		Compe-tition	*Seasonal Function*	*Poor quality*	*Total*		
Agro based	14	6 (46.15)	3 (23.07)	4 (30.76)	13 (92.85)	—	1 (7.15)
Forest based	17	9 (75.00)	—	3 (25.00)	12 (70.58)	5 (29.42)	—
Chemical based	11	4 (44.50)	—	5 (55.50)	9 (81.81)	—	2 (18.19)
Mineral & Building material based	16	6 (37.50)	4 (25.00)	6 (37.50)	16 (100.00)	—	—
Engineering & Allied based	20	9 (69.23)	—	4 (30.76)	13 (65.00)	—	7 (35.00)
Total	78	34 (53.97)	7 (11.11)	22 (34.92)	63 (80.76)	5 (6.41)	10 (12.82)

Note : Figures in brackets indicate percentages to total

It is clear from the table that 63 units out of 78 units i.e. 80.76% are facing the problem of lack of sufficient demand for their products. This lack of demand happens to be due to competition in 34 units i.e. 53.79%, seasonal fluctuations in 7 units i.e. 11.11%, and poor quality of products in 22 units i.e, 34.92%. 5 Forest based units out of total 78 units i.e. 6.41% have affected badly due to government policy in marketing their products. 2 soft drinks manufacturing units and 4 confectionery items manufacturing units have experienced the problem of severe competition with similar type of units. 4 units under Chemical based category and 9 units in Forest based category have also expressed the same problem. Out 6 of Mineral and Building material and 9 Engineering and Allied based units facing the problem of competition, 2 mini cement plants are facing severe competition from large scale cement plants and 4 ferrous and non-ferrous casting works are facing severe competition from Coimbatore based casting units. Soft drink manufacturing units in Agro based category, mini cement plant in Mineral and Building material based category have experienced the problem of seasonal fluctuation in rainy season and it leads poor sales.

6 units in Mineral and Building material based category mainly tiles manufacturing units and mini cement plants, and food processing units and confectionery item manufacturing units in Agro based are facing the problem in marketing their products due to poor quality.

Only 5 Forest based units out of 78 i.e. 6.41% are only suffering from government environmental policy and procedure followed by the Forest department for cutting and transportation of wood.

From the above table it can be understood that 7 units in Engineering and Allied based category 2 units of Chemical based and one unit of Agro based category are free from marketing problems.

FINANCIAL PROBLEMS

Shortage of finance or capital is considered to be the most important factor responsible for a host of problems faced by small scale units. Most of the units in Vizianagaram, Srikakulam and Visakhapatnam districts have experienced this problem. Generally the small scale industrial units of any district depend on both equity or own capital and borrowed capital. Borrowed capital may be long term in nature i.e., for investment in equipment and other capital assets or short term in nature i.e., to meet the current needs of the unit.

Equity capital is usually provided by the entrepreneurs themselves. It is sometimes supplemented by the resources raised from friends and relatives either as partners or as share holders. Some small entrepreneurs do not encourage equity capital from outside agencies as it involves sharing of management and control. Much of this initial capital is required for the purchase of fixed assets, and the balance for working capital.

Owned capital may not be sifficient to meet the long-term needs. In such a case, besides the own capital long-term capital is needed for expansion and renovation of plants and modernisation of machinery short term credit is needed for working capital to buy raw-material and stores, to paywages, to hold stocks of finished goods etc.

The sources of finance, the problems faced by the entrepreneurs in acquiring the required finance, etc., of the sample units relating to the 3 districts is dealt with in the following pages:

Vizianagaram District

Source of Finance

The total capital particulars of small healthy industrial units of Vizianagaram district are presented in the following table 5.10

Table—5.10 Capital Particulars of Healthy Sample Units in Vizianagaram District

Category of units	*Own capital*	*Borrowed capital*	*Total capital*
Agro based	650.60 (64.57)	356.90 (35.43)	1,007.5
Forest based	150.00 (67.41)	72.50 (32.59)	2,222.5
Chemical based	68.00 (61.82)	42.00 (38.18)	110.0
Mineral & Building material based	297.00 (51.47)	280.00 (48.53)	577.0
Engineering & Allied based	50.00 (51.02)	48.00 (48.98)	98.0
Total	1215.60 (60.33)	799.40 (39.67)	2015.0

Note : Figures in brackets indicate percentage to total.

From the above table it can be observed that out of the total capital of sample units as much as 60.33% has been raised through owned capital and the remaining 39.67% is borrowed capital. Further, the table depicts that the Forest based units have a maximum investment of owned capital i.e., 67.41% as against the lowest of 51.02% of Engineering and Allied based units. Mineral and Building material based units and Engineering and Allied based units have nearly 50% of their total capital as borrowed capital. The other 3 categories of units i.e Agro, Forest and Chemical based units have less than 40% of total capital as borrowed capital.

Small entrepreneurs in general cannot depend upon on their own resources alone to meet their needs and they need to resort to some external resources on their part is pretty obvious. During the survey it is observed that Mineral and Building material based and Engineering and Allied based units have mostly depend on borrowed capital as nearly 50% of their total capital consists of borrowed capital.

In the total capital investment of Rs. 20.15 crores relating to different categories of small scale industrial units Rs. 7.99 crores i.e., 39.67% is of borrowed capital. This shows that nearly 40% of the investment of in the small scale units is said to be the outside money.

Coming to category wise, Agro based units, Forest based units, Chemical based units, Mineral and Building material based units, Engineering and Allied based units have owned capital in the percentage order of 64.57, 67.41, 61.82, 51.47 and 51.02.

From this analysis it is clear that the borrowed capital plays an important role in the development of small scale industrial units in Vizianagaram district.

The capital required by the small scale units has been acquired by them from various external sources for both fixed capital and working capital purposes. The importance of borrowings of the sample units can be seen in the following Table 5.11.

From the table it can be said that out of 36 small industrial units only 8 i.e. 22.22% have their own source of finance and all he remaining units borrowed capital from external agencies. 3 Agro based units, 2 Forest based units, 2 Mineral and Building material based units and one Engineering and Allied based units have not borrowed any finance from external sources.

Table—5.11 Importance of Borrowings in Vizianagaram District

Category of Units	Self financed units	Units that have borrowed from external agencies				Total
		Borrowed for fixed capital	Borrowed for w/c	Borrowed for fixed or w/c	Sub total	
Agro based	3 (15.79)	6 (37.5)	7 (43.75)	3 (18.75)	16 (84.21)	19
Forest based	2 (33.33)	2 (50)	—	2 (50)	4 (66.67)	6
Chemical based	—	1 (50)	—	1 (50)	2 (100)	2
Mineral & Building material based	2 (33.33)	2 (50)	—	2 (50)	4 (66.67)	6
Engineering & Allied based	1 (33.33)	1 (50)	1 (50)	—	2 (66.67)	3
Total	8 (22.22)	12 (42.86)	8 (28.57)	8 (28.57)	28 (77.78)	36

Note : Figures in brackets indicate percentage to total

The borrowed finance may be used for fixed purposes, or working capital purposes or for both. In the table, 12 units i.e. 42.86% of different categories have used their borrowed finance for fixed capital purposes only. Whereas 7 units of Agro based category, and one Engineering and Allied based category, totaling 8 units i.e., 23.57% have used borrowed finance only for working capital purposes. But 8 more units i.e., 28.57% which have borrowed finance have utilized the source for both fixed capital and working capital purposes.

Under Agro based category 6 units have utilized borrowed finance only for fixed capital purposes and 7 units utilized the borrowed capital only for working capital purposes. But 3 units have utilized the finance for both fixed and working capital purposes. . Out of the 19 units of this category 3 units have not borrowed any finance.

Under Forest based category out of 6 units 2 units have not approached for external finance. The remaining 4 units have borrowed finance and 2 of them used it for fixed capital purposes and the remaining 2 have utilized for both fixed and working capital purposes.

Under chemical based category the two sample units have gone for external finance and one of them used it for fixed capital purpose and the other used for both fixed and working capital purposes.

Under Mineral and Building material based category 2 units out of 6 have not approached any agency for financial help. In the remaining 4 units 2 of them used borrowed finance for fixed capital purposes and the remaining 2 units utilized borrowed funds for both fixed and working capital purposes.

Under Engineering and Allied based category, it seems that unit one is financially self sufficient and not approached any agency. The remaining 2 units borrowed finance and used for fixed and working capital purposes respectively.

Financing

The small scale industrial units in Vizianagaram district borrowed finance from various external sources (both organized and unorganized) viz., Commercial Banks, Andhra Pradesh State Finance Corporation, friends and relatives, moneylenders, APSSIDC and SIDBI. The following table 5.12 shows the financial assistance rendered by these agencies to the sample units.

From the table it is clear that Commercial Banks have played a dominant role in financing small scale units. Out of the total 28 units 10 units i.e., 35.71% are assisted by only Commercial Banks. APSFC and Commercial Banks' have jointly assisted 5 units, i.e., 17.86% of the total units. Commercial Banks along with moneylenders and friends and relatives have assisted 4 units, i.e., 14.28% of the total. Friends and relatives, moneylenders along with friends and relatives have assisted 3 and 2 units respectively i.e., 10.71% and 7.14%.

Among the 28 units assisted by various financial agencies 16 units are Agro based. In these 16 units 6 units are totally assisted by Commercial Banks based on their strong equity base. Commercial Banks have also assisted 2 Forest based units and 2 more Mineral and Building material based units.

Commercial Banks along with APSFC have assisted 2 units under Agro based category, one unit in Chemical based category and 2 units in Mineral and Building material based category. Similarly Commercial Banks also assisted one more Agro based unit, 2 more Forest based units and one more Engineering and Allied based category unit. Where moneylenders have also extended their financial support.

Table—5.12 No. of Units of Different Strata Financially Assisted by Commercial Banks and Other Agencies in Vizianagaram District

Category of units	*Commercial Banks*	*A.P.S.F.C.*	*Commercial Banks & A.P.S.F.C.*	*Friends & Relatives*	*Money-lenders and Friends & Relatives*	*Commercial Banks, Money-lenders, Friends & Relatives*	*Total*
Agro based	6 (37.5)	2 (12.5)	2 (12.5)	3 (18.75)	2 (12.5)	1 (6.25)	16
Forest based	2 (50)	—	—	—	—	2 (50)	4
Chemical based	—	1 (50)	1 (50)	—	—	—	2
Mineral & Building material based	2 (50)	—	2 (50)	—	—	—	4
Engineering & Allied based	— (50)	1	—	—	— (50)	1	2
Total	10 (35.71)	4 (14.28)	5 (17.86)	3 (10.71)	2 (7.14)	4 (14.28)	28

Note : Figures in brackets indicate percentage to total

The APSFC alone assisted 2 Agro based units 1 Chemical based unit and one Engineering and Allied based unit. The friends and relatives have assisted 3 units of Agro based category. They also gave some assistance to one unit in Agro based category. 2 Forest based and one Engineering and Allied based category along with Commercial Banks and moneylenders, friends and relatives along with moneylenders have also assisted 2 more units under Agro based category.

Financial Problems

The small scale units of Vizianagaram district suffer a lot for want of required financial assistance for various financial agencies. Though 28 units out of 36 units i.e., 77.78% have received assistance from various sources, it is not sufficient for their smooth running. These units fail to attract other sources of finance except from Commercial Banks and APSFC. Both Commercial Banks and APSFC have assisted 19 units out of 28 units i.e. 67.86%. The main reasons for these units for not approaching other sources of finance is higher rate of interest levied by moneylenders, friends and relatives and lack of information about other sources when compared to organized agency such as Commercial Banks', APSFC, SIDBI, APSSIDC, the moneylenders, friends and relatives charge exorbitant rate of interest. Further, the moneylenders' crucify the entrepreneurs who delay the repayment.

The following table clearly tells the interest rates in force that are being charged by Commercial Banks, moneylenders, friends and relatives and APSFC.

Table—5.13 Rate of Lending of the Commercial Banks and Money-lenders, Friends & Relatives and APSFC

Sl. No.	*Lending agencies*	*Rate of interest charged @ 5%*
1.	**Commercial Banks:**	
	COMPOSITE LOAN UP TO RS. 25,000/-	
	(a) Backward areas (12% to 0.75% interest tax)	
	(b) Other areas	12.24
	SHORT TERM ADVANCES, UNIT OF	
	(a) upto end including Rs. Two lakhs	13.5%
	(b) over Rs. 2 lakhs and upto 2.5 lakhs	18
	(c) above Rs. 25 lakhs (not excluding)	19%
2.	**Moneylenders & friends and relatives**	24% to 36%
3.	**A.P.S.F.C.**	17%

The major source of long and medium term finance to small scale industries has been the APSFC, SIDBI, APSSIDC, while the Commercial Banks cater to the needs of short term loans. In getting finance from the organized sources, several problems are reported to have been faced by small scale units of Vizianagaram district.

Various problems are encountered by small entrepreneur's of Vizianagaram district in dealing with the financial agencies in raising funds. The important among them are security, delay in sanction, insufficient financing high rate of interest and cumbersome procedures. The details about the problems experienced by the sample units can be seen from the following table 5.14.

It can be observed from the table 5.14 that out of the total 36 units 28 units only have approached financial agencies for financial help. Category wise 16 units of Agro based, 4 units of Forest based, 2 units of Chemical based 4 units of Mineral and Building material based and 2 units of Engineering and Allied based units have expressed different problems in dealing with financial agencies.

The problem of security is faced by 6 units, i.e., 21.42%. Category wise 2 units each from Forest and Chemical based units and one unit each from Mineral and Building material and Engineering and Allied based categories have expressed the problem of security.

The researcher observed that the Commercial Banks while sanctioning term loans and short term loans insist on collateral security. As small entrepreneurs are not in a position to show the required collateral security, they face this problem. Previously APSFC used to sanction term loans without collateral security, but recently it is also insisting upon this security.

8 units viz., 6 Agro based and one each from Chemical based and Mineral and Building material based units have faced the problem of delay in sanction of loans the researcher observed the delay in sanction of loans from financial agencies mainly Commercial Banks and APSFC is due to different reasons. The financial agencies argue that the delay in sanction of loans is inevitable in cases where the entrepreneurs are not produced the required project report, security documents, various permissions from State and Central Government, financial statements etc., And where permission is required from regional and zonal offices. In view of the entrepreneurs the delay in sanction of loans by the financial agencies is mainly due to unnecessary administrative delay.

Table—5.14 Financial Problems Experienced by Sample Units in Vizianagaram District

(No. of Units)

Category of Units	*No. of units approached the Financial Agencies*	*Problems*					*Without Problem*
		Security	*Relay in sanction*	*Insufficient financing*	*High rate of interest*	*Cumbersome procedure*	
Agro based	16	—	6 (37.5)	3 (18.75)	2 (12.5)	3 (18.75)	2 (12.5)
Forest based	4	2 (50.00)	—	—	1 (25.0)	—	1 (25.0)
Chemical based	2	2 (100.00)	1 (50.00)	1 (50.00)	—	—	—
Mineral & Building Material based	4	1 (25.0)	1 (25.0)	—	2 (50.0)	1 (25.0)	—
Engineering & Allied based	2	1 (50.0)	—	1 (50.0)	1 (50.0)	—	1 (50.0)
Total	28	6 (21.42)	8 (28.57)	15 (17.886)	6 (21.42)	4 (14.28)	4 (14.28)

Note : Figures in brackets indicate percentages to total.

3 units under Agro based category, one unit each from Chemical based and Engineering and Allied based category have expressed that the financial assistance received by them are not sufficient. The entrepreneurs were opined that the financial agencies allow strict rules and rigid procedures while calculating the loan to be sanctioned and ignore their practical requirements.

2 units each from Agro based category and Mineral and Building material based category and one unit each from Forest based and Engineering and Allied based category have felt that the rate of interest charged by the financial agencies particularly the unorganized agencies is exorbitant. The researcher observed that the rate of interest charged by moneylender sometimes ranges between 24 to 36% or even more. Even the organized agencies like APSFC and Commercial Banks charge heavy penalties in case of delay in repaying the instalments, which in turn indirectly causes high rate of interest to the entrepreneur.

Three Agro based units and one Mineral and Building material based units felt that while getting loans the procedure to be followed is cumbersome and ambiguous. An ordinary entrepreneur with poor education background cannot directly fill the required documents supplied by the financial agencies.

The researcher observed that even an ordinarily educated entrepreneur cannot fill up the loan application form and submit the required document on his own. He has to get the help of a chartered accountant which directly increase the cost of acquiring the loan.

However, 4 units 2 from Agro based category and one each from Forest based and Engineering and Allied based category have not expressed any problem while dealing with the financial agencies.

FINANCIAL PROBLEMS OF SAMPLE UNITS IN SRIKAKULAM DISTRICT

Sources of Finance

Table 5.15 explains the total capital composition particulars of small healthy industrial units of Srikakulam district.

Table—5.15 Capital Particulars of Healthy Sample Units in Srikakulam District

(Rs. in lakhs)

Category of units	*Own capital*	*Borrowed capital*	*Total capital*
Agro based	850.00 (74.81)	286.25 (25.19)	1,136.25
Forest based	54.00 (68.35)	25.00 (25.19)	79.00
Chemical based	70.00 (59.32)	48.00 (40.67)	118.00
Mineral & Building material based	162.00 (56.84)	123.00 (43.16)	285.00
Engineering & Allied based	45 (64.28)	25.00 (35.72)	70.00
Total	1181.00 (69.95)	507.25 (30.05)	1688.00

Note : Figures in brackets indicate percentages to total

From the above table it can be said that out of the total capital of the sample units, as much as 69.95% has been raised through owned capital and the remaining 30.05% is borrowed capital. Further, the table shows that Agro based units have a maximum investment of owned capital i.e. 974.81% as against the lowest of 56.84% of Mineral and Building material based category units. Mineral and Building material based units have nearly 45% of their total capital as borrowed capital. In the Agro based units the borrowed capital share is nearly 25% of the total borrowed capital. Whereas the remaining 3 categories of units i.e. Forest, Chemical and Engineering and Allied units have less than 40% of the total capital as borrowed capital.

Srikakulam district is a very peculiar one in borrowing funds from banks and other agencies. On an average the borrowed capital percentage is very less i.e. 30% though banks and financial agencies are offering nearly 40% to 60% of the project cost as loan. Many of the entrepreneurs expressed the reason as getting finance from banks and financial agencies is very difficult and time taking procedure. Generally they are starting the unit according to the available funds with them and with their friends and relatives. Generally they approach banks for working capital purposes.

In the total capital investment of Rs. 16.88 crores relating to different categories of small scale industrial units, Rs. 5.07 crores i.e. 30.05% is of borrowed capital. This shows that nearly 30% of the investment of small scale units is said to be the outside money.

Owned capital in Agro based units, Forest based units, Engineering and Allied based units, Chemical based and Mineral and Building material based units is in the order of 74.81%, 68.35%. 64.28%, 59.32% and 56.84% in their respective total capitals.

From the above analysis it is clear that the borrowed capital plays an important role mainly for the working capital purposes for smooth running of the units in Srikakulam district.

The importance of borrowings of the sample units can be seen in the following table 5.16.

From the table 5.16, it can be said that out of 38 units only 10 units i.e 26.31% have their own source of finance, and all the remaining have borrowed capital from external agencies. Out of 10 non-borrowed capital units, 8 belong to Agro based category and one each belong to Engineering and Allied based category and Forest based category.

Generally the borrowed finance may be used for fixed capital purposes of working capital purposes or both. In the table, 10 units i.e, 35.71% of different categories have used their borrowed finance for fixed capital purposes only. Where as only 4 units i.e. 14.28% of the units belonging to Agro based category have used borrowed finance only for working capital purposes. But 14 units i.e. 50% have borrowed funds and utilized for both the fixed capital and working capital purposes.

Out of 26 units in Agro based category 8 units i.e. 30.77% have not borrowed any capital. Out of the remaining 18 units, 6 units borrowed funds for fixed capital purposes, 4 units borrowed funds for working capital purposes and 8 units in this category have utilized the finance for both fixed capital and working capital purposes.

In the Forest based category out of 3 units one has not approached any financial agency for financial help out of the remaining 2 units one has approached for fixed capital purpose and the other has approached for both fixed and working capital purposes.

Table—5.16 Importance of Borrowings in Srikakulam District

(No. of units)

Category of units	*Self financed units*	*Units that have borrowed from external agencies*				*Total*
		Borrowed for fixed capital	*Borrowed for w/c*	*Borrowed for fixed or w/c*	*Sub total*	
Agro based	8 (30.77)	6 (33.33)	4 (22.22)	8 (44.44)	18 (69.23)	26
Forest based	1 (33.33)	1 (50)	—	1 (50)	2 (66.67)	3
Chemical based	—	—	— (100)	2 (100)	2	2
Mineral & Building material based	—	1 (33.33)	—	2 (66.67)	3 (100)	2
Engineering & Allied based	1 (25)	2 (66.67)	—	1 (33.33)	3 (75)	4
Total	10 (26.31)	10 (35.71)	4 (14.28)	14 (50)	28 (73.69)	38

Note : Figures in brackets indicate percentages to total.

Under the Chemical based category the 2 sample units have gone for external finance for both working capital and term loan purposes.

In the Mineral and Building material based category all the 3 units approached the financial agencies. One unit approached for fixed capital purpose and 2 units approached for both term loan and working capital loan purposes.

Under the Engineering and Allied based category one unit has not approached any financial agency. 2 units approached for term loan purposes and one unit has approached the agency for both fixed and working capital purposes.

Financing

The small scale industrial units in Srikakulam district borrowed finance from various organized and unorganized source *viz* Commercial Banks, Andhra Pradesh State Finance Corporation (APSFC), friends and relatives, moneylenders, APSSIDC and SIDBI. The following table 5.17 explains the sources of financial assistance rendered by these agencies to the sample units.

Table—5.17 No. of Units of Different Categories Financially Assisted by Commercial Banks and Other Agencies in Srikakulam District

Category of units	*Commercial Banks*	*A.P.S.F.C.*	*Commercial Banks & A.P.S.F.C.*	*Friends & Relatives*	*Moneylenders and Friends & Relatives*	*APSSIDC SIDBI*	*Commercial Banks, Money-lenders, Friends & Relatives*	*Total*
Agro based	1 (06.25)	4 (25.00)	5 (31.25)	2 (12.5)	2 (12.5)	—	2 (12.5)	16
Forest based	—	—	—	—	1 (50.00)	—	1 (50.00)	2
Chemical based	—	—	1 (50.0)	—	—	1 (50.0)	—	2
Mineral & Building material based	1 (33.33)	—	1 (33.33)	—	—	—	1 (33.34)	3
Engineering & Allied based	1 (33.33)	1 (33.33)	—	—	1 (33.33)	—	—	3
Total	3 (11.54)	5 (19.23)	7 (26.92)	2 (7.69)	4 (15.38)	1 (3.85)	4 (15.38)	26

Note : Figures in brackets indicate percentages to total.

From the above table it is clear that Andhra Pradesh State Finance Corporation and Commercial Banks equally played important role in financing small scale units in Srikakulam district. 5 units i.e. 19.23% out of 26 units are assisted by Andhra Pradesh State Finance Corporation and along with Commercial Banks have jointly assisted 7 units i.e. 26.92% of the total units. Commercial Banks alone financed 3 units i.e 11.54% of the total units and along with moneylenders and friends and relatives also financed another 4 units i.e. 15.38%. Friends and relatives have assisted 2 units i.e. 7.69% of the total, moneylenders and friends and relatives jointly financed 4 units i.e. 15.38% of the total capital. One unit is financed by SIDBI i.e. 3.85% of the total units financed by organized and unorganized financial agencies.

Among the 26 units assisted by various financial agencies, 16 units are Agro based, 3 units each are Mineral and Building material based and Engineering and Allied based and 2 units each are Forest and Chemical based category. Commercial Banks directly assisted only 3 units belonging to Agro based, Mineral and Building material based and Engineering and Allied based units. Along with Andhra Pradesh State Finance Corporation, Commercial Banks financed for working capital purposes to 5 Agro based units, one Chemical unit and one Mineral and Building material based unit. Commercial Bank also financed 4 units along with moneylenders and friends and relatives. Out of these, 2 are Agro based units and one each of Forest based and Mineral and Building material based units.

The Andhra Pradesh State Finance Corporation directly assisted 4 units in Agro based category and one unit in Engineering and Allied based category with a share of 19.23% in total assistance, to small scale industries in Srikakulam district alongwith Commercial Banks and Andhra Pradesh State Finance Corporation financed 7 units i.e. 26.92%.

Financial problems

The small scale units of Srikakulam district are suffering from several financial problems for want of required financial assistance from various financial agencies. Though 26 units out of 38 units (i.e. 68.42%) have received assistance from various sources, it is not sufficient for their smooth running. These units failed to attract other sources of finance except Commercial Banks and Andhra Pradesh State Finance Corporation Both the Commercial Banks and Andhra Pradesh State Finance Corporation have assisted 15 units out of 26 units i.e. 57.69%. The main reason of the units for not approaching other sources of finance is higher rates of interest levied by moneylenders, friends and relatives and lack of information about other sources.

The main source of medium and long term finance to small scale industry has been the Andhra Pradesh State Finance Corporation, SIDBI, NSISI, and APSSIDC, while the Commercial Banks cater to the needs of short term i.e., working capital purposes. In getting finance from the organized sources, several problems are reported to have been faced by small entrepreneurs of Srikakulam district.

The small entrepreneurs of Srikakulam district have experienced several problems while obtaining funds from various financial agencies. The important among them are security, delay in sanction, insufficient financing, high rate of interest and cumbersome procedures. The details about the problems experienced by the sample units can be seen from the table 5.18.

It can be seen from the table that out of 38 sample units only 26 units i.e. 68.42% have approached financial agencies for financial help. Category wise, 16 units of Agro based, 2 units each of Forest based and Chemical based and 3 units each of Mineral and Building material based and Engineering and Allied based category have expressed different problems in dealing with financial agencies.

The problem of security is being faced by 9 units i.e., 34.61% while they approached the financial agencies. Out of these 9 units 7 units belongs to Agro based category, and one unit each from Forest based and Engineering and Allied based category. The Commercial Banks and other term lending institutions insist on collateral security on sanctioning loans. The entrepreneurs are not in a position to show the required collateral security. The researcher also observed that the cost of legal opinion, engineers valuation on the secured property is also very high and time consuming.

4 units i.e., 15.38% units of Srikakulam district consisting of 2 Mineral and Building material based category and one each from Agro and Forest based category have faced the problem of delay in sanction of loans. Delay is inevitable in cases where the entrepreneurs are not in a position to submit the required licences, permissions, no objection certificate, feasibility reports from various departments. Generally in banks the reasons for delay is lack of knowledge about processing the application by the entrepreneurs.

Table—5.18 Financial Problems Experienced by Sample Units in Srikakulam District.

(No. of units)

Category of units	*No. of units approached the Financial Agencies*	*Security*	*Delay in sanction*	*Insufficient financing*	*High rate of interest*	*Cumbersome procedure*	*Without Problems*
Agro based	16	7 (43.75)	1 (6.25)	4 (25.0)	3 (18.75)	2 (12.5)	5 (31.25)
Forest based	2	1 (50.0)	1 (50.0)	—	—	2 (100.0)	—
Chemical based	2	—	—	1 (50.0)	1 (50.0)	—	1 (50.0)
Mineral & Building material based	3	—	2 (66.66)	—	—	1 (33.33)	1 (33.33)
Engineering & Allied based	3	1 (33.33)	—	1 (33.33)	1 (33.33)	1 (33.33)	1 (33.33)
Total	26	9 (34.61)	4 (15.38)	6 (23.07)	5 (19.23)	6 (23.07)	8 (30.76)

Note : Figures in brackets indicate percentage to total.

Out of 6 units suffering from insufficient finance 4 of them are Agro based and one each from Chemical based and Engineering and Allied based category.

5 units felt that the rate of interest charged by the financial agencies particularly the unorganized agencies is exorbitant. Out of the 5 units 3 units are from Agro based category, one unit each from Chemical based category and Engineering and Allied based category. The researcher observed that the rate of interest calculated by moneylenders, viz., private finance companies, chit fund companies, sometimes ranges between 24 to 36% are even more.

Due to cumbersome and length procedure, and redtapism two units each of Agro based category and Forest based category and one unit each of Mineral and Building material based category and Engineering and Allied based category suffered a lot. The main reason of entrepreneurs approaching unorganized and non-banking financial agencies is the cumbersome procedure followed by Commercial Banks and Andhra Pradesh State Finance Corporation.

Some of the entrepreneurs are in the opinion that even Commercial Banks and Andhra Pradesh State Financial Corporation charges more interest which comes to 23 to 24% after adding the interest tax, processing charges, registration expenses, inspection formalities, traveling expense the financial agencies regional and head offices etc.

However, 5 Agro based units and one unit of each in Chemical based category, Mineral and Building material based category and Engineering and Allied based category have not expressed any problem while dealing with the financial agencies.

FINANCIAL PROBLEMS OF SAMPLE UNITS IN VISAKHAPATNAM DISTRICT

Source of Finance

The total capital composition particulars of healthy industrial units of Visakhapatnam district are presented in the following table 5.19.

It is observed from the table that out of the total capital of sample units 51.17% of funds have been raised through borrowed capital. Further, the table shows that the Forest based units have a maximum investment of owned capital i.e. 79.13% as against lowest of 39.52%of Mineral and Building material based units. Agro based units have nearly 50% of their total capital as borrowed capital. Whereas the other 3 units i.e.

Chemical based, Mineral and Building material based, Engineering and Allied based units have nearly 60% of their total capital as borrowed capital.

Table—5.19 Capital Particulars of Healthy Sample Units in Visakhapatnam District.

(Rs. in lakhs)

Category of units	*Own capital*	*Borrowed capital*	*Total capital*
Agro based	464.00 (52.16)	42.50 (47.84)	889.50
Forest based	560.00 (79.13)	14.70 (20.87)	707.70
Chemical based	406.00 (41.41)	574.50 (58.59)	980.50
Mineral & Building material based	436.00 (39.52)	667.25 (60.48)	1103.25
Engineering & Allied based	360.00 (41.03)	517.40 (58.97)	877.40
Total	2226 (48.83)	2332.35 (51.17)	4558.35

Note : Figures in brackets indicate percentages to total.

The entrepreneurs of Visakhapatnam district are different from that of Vizianagaram and Srikakulam in getting finance from organised agencies. Except Forest based, all the units in the district borrowed capital from the financial agencies ranging from 50 to 60%.

In the total capital investment of Rs. 45.58 crores relating to different categories of small scale industrial units, 23.22 crores i.e. 51.17% is of borrowed capital. This shows that nearly 50% of the investment in the small scale units is said to be the outside money.

Categories wise, Agro based units, Forest based units Chemical based units, Mineral and Building material based units and Engineering and Allied based units have own capital in the percentage order of 52.16, 79.13, 41.41, 39.52 and 41.02.

Based on the above analysis it is clear that the borrowed capital plays an important role in development of small scale industrial units of Visakhapatnam district.

The importance of borrowings of the sample units can be seen in the table 5:20

Table—5.20 Importance of Borrowings in Visakhapatnam District.

(No. of units)

Category of units	*Self financed units*	*Units that have borrowed from external agencies*				*Total*
		Borrowed for fixed capital	*Borrowed for w/c*	*Borrowed for fixed or w/c*	*Sub total*	
Agro based	2 (14.28)	—	3 (25)	9 (75)	12 (85.71)	14
Forest based	6 (35.29)	3 (27.27)	1 (9.09)	7 (63.64)	11 (64.70)	17
Chemical based	2 (11.76)	2 (22.22)	2 (22.22)	5 (55.55)	9 (88.24)	11
Mineral & Building material based	4 (25)	4 (33.33)	3 (25)	5 (41.67)	12 (75)	16
Engineering & Allied based	5 (25)	7 (46.67)	3 (20)	5 (33.33)	15 (75)	20
Total	19 (24.36)	16 (227.12)	12 (20.34)	31 (52.54)	59 (75.64)	78

Note : Figures in brackets indicate percentages to total

From the above table it can be said that out of 78 healthy units only 19 units i.e. 24.36% have their own source of finance, and all the remaining capital is borrowed capital from external agencies. 6 Forest based units, 5 Engineering and Allied based units 4 Mineral and Building material based units and 2 units each from Chemical and Agro based category have not borrowed any finance from external sources.

The borrowed funds may be used for fixed capital purposes, or working capital purposes or for both. As per the 16 i.e. 27.12% units of different categories have used their borrowed finance for fixed capital purposes only. 12 units i.e. 20.34% belonging to 3 units from each from Agro, Mineral and Building material and Engineering and Allied based category, 2 units from Chemical based and one unit from Forest based category borrowed funds only for working capital purposes. But 31 units i.e. 52.54% which have borrowed finance have utilized for both fixed capital and working capital purposes.

In the Agro based category 3 units utilized the borrowed funds for working capital purpose only. 9 units of this category have utilized the borrowed capital for both fixed capital and working capital purposes. No unit has borrowed funds only for fixed capital purpose in this category.

Out of 14 units of this category only 2 units i.e. 14.28% have not borrowed any finance.

Under the Forest based category out of 17 units 6 units i.e. 35.29% have not approached for any external finance. In remaining 11 units 3 units approached and utilized borrowed funds for fixed capital purposes. One unit used the borrowed funds for working capital purpose and 7 unit utilized the borrowed funds for both the fixed and working capital purposes.

In the Chemical based category 2 units utilized the borrowed finance for fixed capital purpose and 2 units utilized for working capital purpose 5 units in this category borrowed funds for both fixed capital and working capital purposes. 2 i.e. 11.76% of units have not approached any financial agency for financial help.

Under the Mineral and Building material based category out of 16 units 4 units have not approached any external agency for finance. Out of the remaining 12 units, 4 units, borrowed capital for fixed assets, 3 units borrowed this funds for working capital purpose and 5 units borrowed funds for both working capital and borrowed capital purposes.

In the Engineering & Allied based category out of 20 units 5 units have not approached any financial agency as they are self sufficient. 7 units in this category borrowed funds for fixed capital purpose. 3 units in this category borrowed funds for working capital purpose and 5 units borrowed funds for both fixed capital and working capital purposes.

Financing

The small scale industrial units in Visakhapatnam district borrowed funds from various external sources (both organized and unorganized) such as Commercial Banks, Andhra Pradesh State Finance Corporation, APSSIDC, SIDBI, Moneylenders, and Friends and Relatives. The following table 5.21 shows the financial assistance rendered by these agencies to the sample units.

From the table it is clear that Commercial Banks have played an important role in financing small scale units. Out of the total 59 units 16 units i.e. 27.12% are assisted by only Commercial Banks. Andhra Pradesh State Finance Corporation and Commercial Banks have jointly assisted 12 units i.e., 20.34% of the total units Commercial Banks along with moneylenders, friends and relatives, moneylenders along with friends and relatives have assisted 5 i.e. 8.47% and 2 i.e., 3.39% units respectively.

Table—5.21 No. of Units of Different Strata Financially Assisted by Commercial Banks and Other Agencies in Visakhapatnam District

Category of units	*Commercial Banks*	*A.P.S.F.C.*	*Commercial Banks & A.P.S.F.C.*	*Friends & Relatives*	*Moneylenders and Friends & Relatives*	*APSSIDC & SIDBI*	*Commercial Banks, Money-lenders, Friends & Relatives*	*Total*
Agro based	3 (25.00)	1 (08.33)	3 (25.00)	—	—	2 (16.67)	3 (25)	12
Forest based	2 (18.18)	3 (27.27)	2 (18.18)	2 (18.18)	1 (9.09)	—	1 (9.09)	11
Chemical based	3 (33.33)	1 (11.11)	2 (22.22)	—	—	2 (22.22)	1 (11.11)	9
Mineral & Building material based	4 (33.33)	—	3 (25.00)	2 (16.67)	—	2 (16.67)	1 (8.33)	12
Engineering & Allied based	4 (26.67)	2 (13.33)	2 (13.33)	1 (6.67)	1 (6.67)	2 (13.33)	3 (20.00)	15
Total	16 (27.12)	7 (11.86)	12 (20.34)	5 (8.47)	2 (3.39)	8 (13.59)	9 (15.25)	59

Note : Figures in brackets indicate percentages to total.

Among the 59 units assisted by various financial agencies, 12 units are Agro based, 11 units are Forest based, 9 units are Chemical based, 12 units are Mineral and Building material based and 15 units are Engineering and Allied based. 16 units financed by Commercial Banks are 4 units each of Mineral and Building material based and Engineering and Allied based category , 3 units each of Agro based and Chemical based category and 2 units of Forest based category. Commercial Banks along with State Finance Corporation have assisted 3 units each of Agro based and Mineral and Building material based category and 2 units each of Forest, Chemical and Engineering and Allied category units. Andhra Pradesh State Finance Corporation alone financed 7 units i.e. 11.86% of the total financial assistance. Out of these 7 units belongs to forest based category, 2 units belong to Engineering and Allied based category and one unit each of Agro based and Chemical based category. SIDBI and APSSIDC with their hire purchase of machinery scheme financed 8 units i.e. 13.59%. These 8 units consist of each of 2 units Agro, Chemical, Mineral and Building material and Engineering and Allied based category.

Financial Problems

The small scale units of Visakhapatnam district suffer a lot for want of required financial assistance from various financial agencies, though 59 units out of 78 units (i.e. 75.64%) have received assistance from various sources, as it is not sufficient for their smooth running. Both State Finance Corporation and Commercial Banks have assisted 35 units out of 59 units i.e. 59.32%. These units have not approached other sources of finance because higher rate of interest levied by money lenders, friends and relatives and lack of information about other sources of finance. When compared to organized agencies such as commercial banks, Andhra Pradesh State Finance Corporation, SIDBI, the money lenders friends and relatives charge exorbitant rates of interest.

Similar to Vizianagaram and Srikakulam districts the small entrepreneurs of Visakhapatnam district also faced various problems in dealing with the financial agencies is raising funds. The important among them are security delay in sanction, insufficient finance, high rates of interest and cumbersome procedures. The details about the problems experienced by the sample units can be seen from the following table 5.22.

Table—5.22 Financial Problems Experienced by Sample Units in Visakhapatnam District

(No. of units)

Category of units	*No. of units approached the Financial Agencies*	*Security*	*Delay in sanction*	*Insufficient financing*	*High rate of interest*	*Cumbersome procedure*	*Without Problems*
Agro based	12	4 (33.33)	5 (31.25)	3 (25.0)	—	—	—
Forest based	11	3 (27.27)	5 (45.45)	3 (27.27)	—	—	—
Chemical based	9	3 (33.33)	2 (22.22)	4 (44.4)	—	—	2 (22.22)
Mineral & Building material based	12	2 (16.66)	4 (33.33)	2 (16.66)	1 (8.33)	3 (25)	—
Engineering & Allied based	15	2 (13.33)	3 (13.33)	2 (13.33)	—	4 (26.66)	4 (26.66)
Total	59	14 (23.72)	19 (32.20)	14 (23.72)	1 (1.69)	7 (11.86)	6 (10.17)

Note : Figures in brackets indicate percentages to total.

The table explains that out of 78 units, 59 units have approached financial agencies for financial help. Category wise 12 units of Agro based, 11 units of Forest based, 9 units of Chemical based, 12 units of Mineral and Building material based and 15 units of Engineering & Allied based units have expressed different problems in dealing with financial agencies.

Security is one of the main problems faced by 14 units i.e 23.72% when they approached the financial agencies. Category wise 4 units of Agro based, 3 units each Forest based and Chemical based and 2 units each Mineral and Building material and Engineering and Allied based units have experienced the problem of security.

19 units i.e. 32.20% have faced the problem of delay in sanction. These 19 units are 5 units each of Agro and Forest based category. 4 units from Mineral and Building material based category, 3 units of Engineering and Allied based category and 2 units of Chemical based category. The researcher observed that the entrepreneurs as well as the financial agencies try to blame each other for delay in sanction of loans.

4 units of Chemical based category, 3 units each of Agro and Forest based category and 2 units each of Mineral and Building material and Engineering and Allied based category have expressed that the financial assistance received by them are not sifficient. The entrepreneurs opined that the financial agencies adhere to strict valuation methods in valuing the securities and follow rigid procedures.

Only one unit in Mineral and Building material based category felt that the rate of interest charged by the financial agencies particularly the unorganized agencies is exorbitant. The researcher observed that the interest fixed by the moneylender and non-banking finance companies sometimes is unbearable or even unbelievable.

4 Mineral and Building material based units and 3 Engineering and Allied based units felt that the procedure adopted by financial agencies in sanctioning loans in cumbersome.

However, 6 units i.e., 4 from Engineering and Allied based category and 2 from Chemical based category are free from financial problems while dealing with the financial agencies.

CHAPTER—VI

SICKNESS IN SMALL SCALE SECTOR

The main purpose of this chapter is to focus special attention on the problem of sickness in Small Scale sector. An attempt is made to ascertain the extent of sickness both at national and state levels along with the examination of reasons for sickness in small scale sector. Besides these, attempts are made to focus attention on the sickness in Vizianagaram, Visakhapatnam, and Srikakulam districts and to find out the specific causes for sickness in this sector with the help of the data obtained from the respondent units which have fallen sick.

Industrial sickness is not something peculiar to our country. All over the world, some industries go down the drain. Even in Japan, about 18,000 small business houses went bankrupt (in 1977). There are many large scale industries which would have closed down but for the fact that financial institutions and other authorities bailed them out for they know that if they were not saved the very foundation of these large financial institutions would be affected. Industrial sickness is a serious malady afflicting mostly the under developed countries with low capital base and low level of technological and managerial know-how. In such countries many industrial units may die before they bear fruits, while many others never come up even after being connective and a few other fall sick due to basic constraints. India is no exception to industrial sickness.

Industrial sickness has grave socio-economic consequences. It leads to loss of employment, loss of production and blockage of scarce resources of the country. The increasing trend of sickness affects the investment climate in the country and causes loss of revenue to the exchequer. It also effects the profitability of banks and financial institutions through loss of interest on these advances, depletion of earning potential due to blockade of funds and increase in administrative expenses, on the other hand "a country where resources are so minimal and so scarce cannot afford to waste them. This is the major reason, why inspite of the fact that when it is a marginal case and its revival is doubtful, we decided in favour of rehabilitation." Because of all there adverse effects of sickness, it is in the interest of all parties, i.e. Government, banks, financial institutions and entrepreneurs that the magnitude of sickness should be minimised as quickly as possible.

The following table shows the loss incurred due to sickness in India from 1900-91 to 1995-96

Table—6.1 Loss Incurred Due to Sickness

Year	*No.of Sick units (in lakhs)*	*Output (Rs. in crores)*	*Employment (in lakhs)*	*Export (Rs. in crores)*	*Revenue (Rs. in crores)*
1990-91	2.21	16,309	13.90	950	2,772
1991-92	2.46	18,154	15.97	1,058	3,086
1992-93	2.38	17,564	14.97	1,023	2,986
1993-94	2.54	18,745	15.98	1,092	3,187
1994-95	2.69	19,852	16.92	1,157	3,375
1995-96	2.62	19,336	16.48	1,127	3,287

Source : R.B.I Bulleten & I.C.S.I. Herald - Page No. 18.

SICKNESS IN THE SMALL SCALE SECTOR IN THE STATE OF ANDHRA PRADESH

According to information supplied by Commissioner of Industries, Hyderabad there were 13,740 sick units in small scale sector and 215 sick units in large and medium scale sector in Andhra Pradesh by the end of March '95. Table 6.2 gives the number of sick units in small scale sector and the amount outstanding.

Table—6.2 No. of Sick Units and the Amount Outstanding in Small Scale Sector of Andhra Pradesh

Year	*No. of sick units (lakhs)*	*Amount outstanding (Rs. in crores)*
1994	12,218	164.66
1995	13,740	279.5
1996	14,794	298.46

Source : Commissioner of industries, Hyderabad.

From the above table that it can be said that the sickness in small scale sector of Andhra Pradesh is significant and cannot be neglected. As per the information obtained from the department of Industries, Hyderabad the sickness in small scale sector is 11% in the country where 2,68,815 units are found to be sick as on 31st March, 1995. At par with the country the percentage of sickness in the state of Andhra Pradesh is also 11. Where 14,794 units are found to be sick as on the above said date. The share of Andhra Pradesh in the sickness of the country is estimated as 5.5%[1].

The state level inter institutional committee (SLICE) organised by the Secretary, Industries, under the convenorship of RBI, has been functioning in Andhra Pradesh for the last 18 years to discuss and suggest to the financial institutions above the nursing programmme for the rehabilitation of sick units.

During March '95 the SLICE gathered information from the banks on sick units and found that there were 12,573 small sick units and out of which 10842 units are non-viable, 1370 units are potentially viable, 168 units validity to be decided and 193 units under nursing [2].

Meaning of Sick Unit

There is no single definition to distinguish a sick from a healthy unit as different agencies like the Reserve Bank of India, the Small Industry Development Organisation—have highlighted different symptoms to identify a sick unit. The Reserve Bank of India identified a sick unit as one "which has incurred cash losses for one year and in the judgement of the bank, it is likely to continue to incur cash losses for current year as well as the following year and which has an in balance in its financial structure, such as current ratio".

In this definition, profitability is emphasized to identify a sick unit. The sick industries act, 1985 recognised to employs the definition, to identify sick units. The State Bank of India defined a sick unit as one, "which fails to generate internal surplus on a continuing basis to meet its obligations and depends for its survival on frequent infusion of external funds". Thus emphasis has been laid on excessive dependence on external funds to identify a sick unit.

By combining both the definition, the symptoms of cash losses for three consecutive years, in balance in the current ratio, deterioration in the debt/equity ratio and dependence on external funds for survival may be taken to identify sick units. An industrial unit may become sick owing to either of the above symptoms or both.

Thus, profitability, ability of the industrial unit to meet short-term prepayment commitments, and long-term solvency may be used to distinguish a sick from a healthy unit. For the purpose of the present study sick units include loss making units, the unit defaulting on loan repayment and the units whose affairs are in the state of closure.

Magnitude of Industrial Sickness

The problem of industrial sickness has grown over the years and a large number of industrial units in the small scale sector and non-small scale sector are effected by it. As shown in table 6.3, the total number of sick units in December, 1980 were 24,550 with outstanding back credit of Rs. 1, 809 crores. By September, 1992, the total number of sick units had risen to 2,35,868 with an outstanding bank credit of Rs. 12,586 crores of these, sick units as many as 2,33,441 units belonged to the small-scale sector with outstanding bank credit of Rs. 3,346 crores. The number of large and medium sick units were only 2,427 but outstanding bank credit in their case was as high as Rs. 9,241 crores. The total number of sick units at the end of March, 1995 were 2,70,730 with an outstanding bank credit of Rs. 12,287 crores.

Table—6.3 Magnitude of Industrial Sickness

Number of units at the end of	*Sick/Weak Units*		
	Large and Medium	*Small*	*Total*
December 1980	1,401	23,149	24,550
September 1992	2,427	2,33,441	2,35,868
March 1995	1,915	2,68,815	2,70,730
	Outstanding Bank Credit (Rs. in Crores)		
December 1980	1,502	306	1,809
September 1992	9,241	3,346	12,586
March 1995	8,740	3,547	12,287

Source : Statistical Outline of India, Tata Services Limited., 1996-97 Table 91, Page 89. Indian Economy' By S.K. Mishra and V.K. Puri, Himalaya Publishing House, New Delhi, Page - 556.

In addition to the sharp increase in the number of sick industrial units, another serious problem is that a large number of them are non-viable. For instance the commercial banks conducted viability studies in respect of 2,58,952 sick units by the end-march, 1994 and found 2,35,327 of these units (i.e. 91 per cent) were found non-viable.

Causes of Sickness

The causes of sickness like wrong location, improper estimation of capital cost, delays and cost escalations, in adequacy of finance, delayed payments, deficiency in the management, non-availability of raw-materials, poor maintenance of plant and machinery, low labour productivity, hardship in marketing outlets, labour troubles etc., have been much responsible for sickness.

The research studies have revealed that sickness in small scale industries is broadly caused by two sets of factors—Internal and external.

External Factors

Delay in sanction and disbursement of loans, credit restraints, erratic supply of inputs, sudden change in the government policy relating to imports, exports, industrial licensing, taxation etc., Market recession, non-availability of skilled manpower, inter union rivalry, low productivity of labour, general labour unrest, demand and credit restraints, power cuts, import restriction on essential inputs, wage disparities among similar industries, change in international marketing scene etc. are some of the important external factors.

Internal Factors

Faults at the planning and constructive stage, defective plant and machinery, in appropriate financial structure, poor utilisation of assets, inefficient working capital management, absence of costing and pricing, location problems, poor maintenance of machinery, lack of quality control, absence of product planning, lack of market research, in appropriate sales promotion, bad labour relations, absence of manpower planning, lack of co-ordination in various functional areas and absence of control, lack of integrity in management, entrepreneurial incompetence are some of the important internal factors. The summary of main internal causes for sickness in a small scale unit is also shown in the following chart which is taken from Desai Vasant, Problems and Prospects of Small-Scale Industries in India.

SUMMARY OF THE MAIN INTERNAL CAUSES OF SICKNESS IN SMALL-SCALE INDUSTRIES

SMALL-SCALE SICK UNIT

LACK OF PROPER MANAGEMENT

LACK OF WORKING FUNDS

DROP IN INTERNAL CASH GENERATION

	DROP IN PRODUCTION		INCREASED COST OF PRODUCTION		
Problem in production	*Lack of orders*	*Lack of materials*	*Increased cost of raw-materials*	*Increased overhead cost*	*Increase taxes*
1. Machine break-downs and poor maintenance	1. Competition	1. National or Regional shortage	1. Increased costs not recovered in selling prices due faulty costing	1. Inefficient production	1. Octroi
2. Poor quality of raw-materials	2. Recession	2. High cost	2. Larger orders booked at fixed prices in an inflationary market.	2. Unutilised capacity.	2. Sales tax.
3. Poor labour productivity	3. Low quality technical incompetence	3. Over due payments	3. High material cos	3. Heavy borrowing high interest. charges.	3. Excise. etc.
4. Power shortage	4. Irregular deliveries	4. Poor quality	4. High inventory cost.	4. Increased administration	
5. Lack of Production	5. Poor marketing efforts	5. Uncertain.		5. Unplanned capital expenditure.	

Source : 1) Desai Vasant, Problems & Prospects of Small-scale Industries in India, Himalaya Publishing House, Bombay, 1983, No. 34.

SYMPTOMS OF SICKNESS

There are certain symptoms of sickness, but no one symptom by itself would be an indicator of sickness and it is only when several of these factors appear simultaneously, there is cause for anxiety. Further, it can also be said that symptoms of sickness are many. The important non-financial and financial symptoms of sickness are as follows:

1. During the short period, the units running of irregular accounts with the bank continually;
2. Continuous drop in production and the utilisation of installed capacity being less than 20%;
3. Increased customer complaints;
4. Delay in payment to credit;
5. Delay in capital expenditure authorisations;
6. Decline in market share;
7. Low employee morale and high labour turnover;
8. A unit having negative capital;
9. Decline in quality and service;
10. Delay in capital expenditure authorisations.

Sickness in Small Scale Units of Vizianagaram District

It is observed in the study pertaining to Vizianagaram district that sickness is existing in alarming proportion in different category of small scale units. One of the total 44 sample units of the study, 8 units have fallen sick as depicted in table 6.4.

Table—6.4 Sickness in Small Scale Industrial Units in Vizianagaram District

Category of units	*Total no.of units*	*Total no.of sick units*	*Sick percentage of total units*
Agro based	23	4	17.93
Forest based	8	2	25.00
Chemical based	2	—	—
Mineral & Building material based	7	1	14.28
Engg. & Allied based	4	1	25.00
Total	44	8	18.18

From the above table it can be said that the sickness in small scale sectors of the district is very high when compared to sickness at national level and state level.

The 8 sick units out of 44 sample units account for as high as 18.18%. 4 of Agro based category, 2 of Forest based category and one each from Mineral and Building material based category and Engineering and Allied based category are in the list.

Out of 23 Agro based units taken as sample 4 of them i.e., 17.39% have fallen sick.1 dall mill, 1 oil mill and 2 rice mills have fallen sick in Agro based category due various reasons. The researcher observed that the poor quality of dall product produced the unit and misunderstandings between the partners made this unit to become sick. The oil mill has been closed down because of the case filed by the food adulteration and essential commodities act (civil supplies) department for not following the standards in maintaining the fat contents in the product. In this case the entrepreneur tries to blame the policy of the government. The 2 rice mills which have fallen sick are due to insufficient finance and problems with the local labour.

Out of 8 Forest based units 2 saw mills i.e. 25% have fallen sick. One saw mill is closed down due to non-availability of working capital and the other saw mill also closed down because of non-availability of working capital and also non-availability of quality wood from the nearby forest.

A mini cement plant out of 7 Mineral and Building material based units i.e., 14.25% have fallen sick mainly due to not coping it with competition with larger industrial units producing popular brands of cement. Poor quality of the product and often labour strikes also aggravated the situation and caused for closing down of this mini cement plant at Kottavalasa.

One general engineering unit out of 4 Engineering and Allied based units has fallen sick mainly due to usage of primitive machinery and machinery breakdowns. Labour problems have also stand as one among the reasons for becoming the unit as a sick unit.

The researcher faced difficulties in identifying the addressees of the entrepreneurs, whose units fallen sick. However, he made several visits and collected the required data from them.

CAPITAL STRUCTURE

The researcher collected the capital structure of sick units. The particulars of owned capital borrowed capital and total capital of 8 sick units are inserted in table 6.5.

Table—6.5 Capital Particulars of Sick Units in Vizianagaram District

(Rs. in lakhs)

Category of units	*Total no.of sick units*	*Owned capital*	*Borrowed capital*	*Total capital*
Agro based	4	136.84 (66.57)	67.70 (33.43)	204.54
Forest based	2	82.91 (74.75)	28.00 (25.25)	110.91
Mineral & Building material based	1	40.55 (38.51)	64.73 (61.49)	105.28
Engg & Allied based	1	14.50 (51.45)	13.68 (48.55)	28.18
Total	8	274.80 (61.21)	174.11 (38.79)	448.91

Note : Figures in brackets indicate percentage to total.

The table reveals that owned capital of sick units accounts for 61.21%. The owned capital ratio in the total capital of the sick units in Agro based, Forest based, Mineral and Building material and Engineering and Allied based categories of units are in the order of 66.57%, 74.75%, 38.51%, and 51.45%. The table also reveals that the four Agro based sick units have a total capital investment of 2.04 crores, 2 Forest based sick units have 1.10 crore, one Mineral and Building material based unit has Rs. 1.05 crores and one Engineering and Allied based units has 0.28 crores investment. 4 Agro based units, 2 Forest based units, 1 Mineral and Building material based unit and 1 Engineering and Allied based unit have total capitals in the order of Rs. 2.04 crore, Rs. 1.10 crore, Rs. 1.05 crores and 0.28 crores. Thus these 8 sick units out of 44 sample units have a total capital investment of Rs. 4.48 crores. In this total capital the owned capital amounts to Rs. 2.74 crore that is 61.21% and borrowed capital accounts to Rs. 1.74 crore that is 38.79%. This clearly indicates that the dependents of sick units on borrowed capital significant.

The sick units of the district borrowed funds from Commercial Banks, Andhra Pradesh State Finance Corporation, moneylenders, friends and relatives. The details of sick units and their borrowed capital from various organised and unorganised agencies are showed in table 6.6.

Table—6.6 Details of Sick Units and their Borrowed Capital from Various Organised and Unorganised Agencies in Vizianagaram District

(Rs. in lakhs)

Category of units	*Total sick units*	*Commercial Banks*		*APSFC*		*Money Lender*		*Friends & Relatives*		*Total Borrowed Capital*
		No.of units	*Amount*	*No.of units*	*Amount*	*No.of units*	*Amount*	*No.of units*	*Amount*	
Agro based	4	2	32	1	23	1	—	1	12.7	67.70
Forest based	2	1	19.5	—	—	—	8.5	—	—	28.00
Mineral & Building material based*	1	1	24.73	1	40	—	—	—	—	64.73
Engg. & Allied based*	1	1	4.62	1	9	1	—	—	—	13.68
Total	8	5	80.91 (48.47)	3	72.00 (41.35)	1	8.50 (4.88)	1	12.70 (7.29)	174.11

Note : Figures in brackets indicate percentages to total

* Units taken loans from more than one agency

From the above table it can be said that out of 8 sick units 5 got assistance from Commercial Banks, 3 got assistance from Andhra Pradesh State Finance Corporation and one each from moneylenders, friends and relatives. One unit of Mineral and Building material based and one unit of Engineering and Allied based got assistance both from Commercial Banks and Andhra Pradesh State Finance Corporation. The Commercial Banks assisted 2 Agro based units with an amount of Rs. 32 lakhs. They also assisted one unit each under Forest based, Mineral and Building material based and Engineering and Allied based by giving them Rs. 19.50 lakhs, 24.73 lakh and Rs. 4.68 lakhs respectively. Thus Commercial Banks, assisted 5 sick units out of 8 for Rs. 80.9 lakhs that is 46.47% of the total borrowed funds from various organised and unorganised agencies. It means nearly 50% of the borrowed money of sick units come from Commercial Banks only.

The Andhra Pradesh State Finance Corporation assisted 3 units viz one each from Agro based, Mineral and Building material based category and Engineering and Allied based units. These 3 units have already got assistance from Commercial Banks. The State Finance Corporation assisted to 3 units i.e., 41.35% for term loan purposes. One unit from Forest based category and one unit from Agro based category are assisted by moneyenders and friends and relatives respectively.

These 8 units which have fallen sick took financial help from the above mentioned organised and unorganised agencies and failed to repay the loans because of this sickness. And thus, an amount of Rs. 1.74 crores is blocked in the hands of these 8 units.

Table 6.7 given hereunder shows the reasons for sickness in sample units in terms of no.of units.

The table gives a picture that out of 8 sick units 4 units i.e., 50%, 2 from Agro based and 2 from Forest based, have fallen sick mainly due to financial crisis.

3 units that is 37.5%, 1 unit each from Agro based, Forest based, Mineral and Building material based have fallen sick due to marketing their products. 3 units, one unit each from Agro based, Mineral and Building material based, and Engineering and Allied based have fallen sick due to labour problems.

2 Agro based units one Forest based unit and one Engineering and Allied based unit have fallen sick having 2 problems. The Mineral and Building material based unit has fallen sick having 3 problems. Different

Table—6.7 Statement Showing the Reasons for Sickness in Sample Units of Different Strata in Vizianagaram District

Category of units	*Managerial problems*	*Financial problems*	*Marketing problem*	*Production problem*	*Labour problem*	*Govt. Policy*	*Total no.of sick units*
Agro based	1	2	1	-	1	1	4
Forest based	-	2	1		-	-	2
Mineral & Building material based	-	-	1	1	1	-	1
Engineering & Allied based	-	-	-	1	1	-	1
Total	1 (12.5)	4 (50.0)	3 (37.5)	2 (25.0)	3 (37.5)	1 (12.5)	8

Note : Figures in brackets indicate percentage to total.

categories of units which have fallen sick and their specific reasons for sickness have already been discussed in table 6.1.

SICKNESS IN SMALL SCALE UNITS OF SRIKAKULAM DISTRICT

It is found from the study relatives to Srikakulam district that sickness is high psroportion in different categories of small scale units. Out of total 44 sample units of the study, 6 units have fallen sick as depicted in table 6.8.

Table—6.8 Sickness in Small Scale Industrial Units in Srikakulam District

Category of units	*Total no.of units*	*Total no.of sick units*	*Sickness percentage of total units*
Agro based	30	4	13.33
Forest based	3	—	—
Chemical based	2	—	—
Mineral & Building material based	4	1	25
Engg. & Allied based	5	1	20
Total	44	6	13.63

The above table shows the sickness position in small scale sector of the Srikakulam district is very high when compared to sickness at national level and state level. But compared with Vizianagaram and Visakhapatnam districts the sickness in Srikakulam district is less.

The 6 sick units out of 44 sample units account for as high as 13.63%. The 6 sick units belong to Agro based category (4), one Mineral and Building material category (1) and Engineering and Allied based category (1).

Out of 30 Agro based units taken as sample 4 of them i.e. 13.33% have fallen sick. 2 rice mills, 1 cashew kernal products manufacturing unit and one oil mill have fallen sick in Agro based category due to various reasons.

The researcher observed that out of 4 units, one oil mill, one rice mill and one cashew kernal products units are facing the high working capital problem. Besides these one rice mill is facing labour problem with trade unions. The researcher observed the reasons for closure of one rice mill is due to disputes between partners and continuous machinery problems. One cashew kernal product unit is closed down due to marketing problems of their product. The entrepreneur of the unit expressed that quality and lack of knowledge about exports and costly raw-material are main reasons for closer of their unit besides working capital problem. One oil mill have fallen sick due to government policy relating to maintenance of records, fat percentage in oils and diversification of funds to other businesses.

One unit out of 4 Mineral and Building material based category i.e. Unit manufacturing granite slabs has fallen sick due to high cost of production and poor quality and competition. The main reason for high cost of production is high labour wages as per mines act, allotment of mines from the government is also a costly affair, and competition with big granite companies is also play a crucial role for closure of the unit.

One general engineering unit out of 5 units i.e. 20% in Engineering and Allied based category have fallen sick due to heavy competition and lack of working capital problem.

The researcher faced several problems in identifying the addresses of the entrepreneurs and whose units fallen sick and many of them are not interested to discuss about their sick unit. However, he made several visits and collected required data from them.

Capital Structure

The researcher collected the capital structure of sick units. The particulars of owned capital, borrowed capital and total capital of 6 sick units are inserted in table 6.9.

Table—6.9 Capital Structure Particulars of Sick Units in Srikakulam District

(Rs. in lakhs)

Category of units	*Total no.of sick units*	*Owned capital*	*Borrowed capital*	*Total capital*
Agro based	4	98.30 (62.09)	60.00 (37.91)	158.3
Mineral & Building Material based	1	65.00 (61.32)	41.00 (38.68)	106
Engg. & Allied based	1	12.00 (62.17)	7.30 (37.83)	19.3
Total	6	175.30 (61.81)	108.30 (38.19)	283.6

Note : Figures in brackets indicate percentages to total.

The above table exhibits that owned capital of sick units accounts for 61.81%. The owned capital ratio's in the total capital of the sick units in Agro based, Mineral and Building material based and Engineering and Allied based categories of units are in the order of 62.09%, 62.32%, and 62.17%. The table also reveals that the four Agro-based units have a total capital investment of Rs. 1.58 crores, one Mineral and Building material based unit have Rs. 1.06 crores and one Engineering and Allied based unit has Rs. 0.19 crores investment. Thus these 6 sick units out of 44 sample units have a total capital investment of Rs. 2.83 crores out of the total capital of Rs. 2.83 crores, Rs. 1.75 crores i.e. 61.81% is owned capital and Rs. 1.08 crores i.e. 38.19% is borrowed capital. This reveals that the dependence of sick units on borrowed capital is significant.

The sick units of the district borrowed funds from Commercial Banks, Andhra Pradesh State Finance Corporation, moneylenders, friends and relatives. The details of sick units and their borrowed capital from various organised and unorganised agencies are seen in table 6.10.

From the table 6.10 it can be said that out of 6 sick units 3 of them got assistance from Commercial Banks, 2 of them got assistance from Andhra Pradesh State Finance Corporation and one each from money lenders and friends and relatives. One unit out of 6 units got assistance both from Andhra Pradesh State Finance Corporation and friends and relatives. The Commercial Banks assisted 2 Agro based units with an amount of Rs. 28 lakhs and also they assisted one Mineral and Building material based unit with an amount of Rs. 41 lakhs. The Commercial Banks assisted 3 sick units out of 6 sick units for Rs. 69 lakhs i.e. 63.71% of the total borrowed funds from various organised and unorganised agencies. It means that more than 60% of the borrowed capital of sick units come from Commercial Banks only.

The Andhra Pradesh State Finance Corporation assisted 2 units out of 6 units. Out of these two, one belongs to Agro based category and other belongs to Engineering and Allied based category. The Engineering and Allied based unit got assistance from Andhra Pradesh State Finance Corporation for term loan purpose and also got assistance

Table—6.10 Details of Sick Units and their Borrowed Capital from Various Organised and Unorganised Agencies in Srikakulam District

(Rs. in lakhs)

Category of units	*Total sick units*	*Commercial Banks*		*APSFC*		*Money Lender*		*Friends & Relations*		*Total Borrowed Capital*
		No.of units	*Amount*	*No.of units*	*Amount*	*No.of units*	*Amount*	*No.of units*	*Amount*	
Agro based	4	2	28	1	24	1	8	—	—	60
Mineral & Building material based*	1	1	41	—	—	—	—	—	—	41
Engg. & Allied based*	1	—	—	1	5	—	—	1	2.3	7.3
Total	6	3	69.00 (63.71)	2	29.00 (26.77)	1	8.00 (7.38)		2.30 (2.12)	108.3

Note : Figures in brackets indicate percentage to total.

* Units taken loan from more than one agency.

from friends and relatives for working capital purpose. One unit in Agro based category is financed by moneylenders and one unit in Engineering and allied based category is finance by friends and relatives for working capital purpose.

Because of these 6 units which have fallen sick took financial help from the above noted organised and unorganised agencies and failed to repay the loan due to sickness and an amount of Rs. 1.08 crores is blocked in the hands of these 6 units.

The reasons for sickness in sample units in terms of no.of units are shown in table 6.11. The table gives a picture that out of 6 sick units 4 units i.e. 66.66% three from Agro based and one from Engineering and Allied based have fallen sick due to financial crisis.

3 units i.e. 50% that includes each one Agro based, Mineral and Building material and Engineering and Allied based units have fallen sick due to marketing of their products. One Agro based and one Mineral and Building material based unit are facing labour problems. Out of 2 units facing problems with government policy one belongs to Agro based and the other is Mineral and Building material based unit, are facing labour problems. And 2 Agro based units expressed that managerial problem is one of the main reason for the sickness of their units.

3 units in Agro based category out and one in Engineering and Allied based category also have fallen sick due to more than 2 reasons, one Agro based unit and one Mineral and Building material based unit have fallen sick due to more than 3 reasons. The specific reasons for each unit sickness in different categories of units have already discussed in Table 6.8

Table—6.11 Statement Showing the Reasons for Sickness in Sample Units of Different Strata in Srikakulam District

Category of units	*Managerial problems*	*Financial problems*	*Marketing problem*	*Production problem*	*Labour problem*	*Govt. Policy*	*Total no. of sick units*
Agro based	2	3	1	1	1	1	4
Mineral & Building material based	—	—	1	—	1	1	1
Engineering & Allied based	—	1	1	—	—	—	1
Total	2 (33.33)	4 (66.66)	3 (50.0)	1 (16.66)	2 (33.33)	2 (33.33)	6

Note : Figures in brackets indicate percentages to total.

SICKNESS IN SMALL SCALE UNITS OF VISAKHAPATNAM DISTRICT

It is observed in the study pertaining to Visakhapatnam that sickness is existing in alarming proportions in different categories of small scale units. Out of total 100 sample units 22 units have fallen sick as shown in Table 6.12

Table—6.12 Sickness in Small Scale Industrial Units in Visakhapatnam District

Category of units	*Total no.of units*	*Total no.of sick units*	*Sickness percentage of total units*
Agro based	18	4	22.22
Forest based	22	5	22.72
Chemical based	13	2	15.38
Mineral and Building material based	22	6	27.27
Engg. & Allied based	25	5	20
Total	100	22	22

The sickness in small scale sector of Visakhapatnam district is very high. The sickness in state level and national level is 11% but the sickness in Visakhapatnam district is 22% i.e. Out of 100 units 22 units are fallen sick. The 22 sick units belong to Agro based category (4), Forest based category (5), Chemical based category (2), Mineral and Building material based category(6) and Engineering and Allied based category (5).

Out of 18 Agro based units taken as sample 4 of them i.e., 22.22% have fallen sick. One confectionery, one rice mill, one food processing unit and one flour mill have fallen sick in Agro based category due to various reasons. The researcher observed that the poor quality and high price of confectionery products are the main reason for sickness of unit besides lack of finance. One rice mill have fallen sick due to lack of working capital. The food processing unit is failed in maintaining quality standards as per the importer specifications and also with competition with giant companies in domestic market and international market are the main reasons for closer of the unit. One flour mill have fallen sick due to requirement of high working capital requirement. The big companies like Godrej, Hindustan Lever are also marketing similar products. There small companies are not in a position to complete with these big companies and to stand in the market they have to give long term credit to the dealers.

In the Forest based category out of 22 units 5 units have fallen sick. Out of 5 units 4 are sawmills. One saw mill is closed due to disputes between partners and lack of finance. One saw mill is closed due to labour problem as it is established in interior place and also the restrictions imposed by Forest department. Non-availability of quality wood in the near forest and problems in participation in Forest auctions for procuring the wood is the main reason for closure of one saw mill. One saw mill have fallen sick due to insufficient working capital, high powercut in the busy summer reason and high wages, rent and other expenses as it is situated in the main market. One plywood manufacturing unit have fallen sick due to competition with big companies.

Out of 13 Chemical based units 2 units have fallen sick i.e. 15.38%. One plastic bags manufacturing unit has fallen sick due to insufficient finance and competition with neighbouring state units in quality and price.

One hydrochloric acid manufacturing unit is closed due to competition and quality. It also facing the problem in maintaining the strict implementation of pollution control rules imposed by the state government.

In the Mineral and Building material based category 6 units out of 22.27% i.e. highest percentage of sickness in all categories of units which have fallen sick. In the total 6 Mineral and Building material based category there are 3 mini cement plants, one hallow brick unit, one tiles making unit and one stone crusher. All the 3 cement units are closed due to various reasons and one common reason for all the 3 units is shortage of working capital. Besides this one unit in Kottavalasa mandal is closed due to labour strike also. One unit is closed due to competition in the market with big companies and one more unit is closed due to poor quality of the product due to installation of second hand machinery and poor maintenance.

One hallow brick unit had fallen sick due to high competition in the market for quality, long time credit and lack of finance.

Another unit in Kottavalasa town is closed down due to seasonal demand and labour unrest in busy season. One stone crusher unit is also fallen sick due to seasonal demand, high production cost and poor quality.

Capital structure

Table 6.13 explains the capital particulars of sick units collected by the researcher.

Table—6.13 Capital Particulars of Sick Units in Visakhapatnam District

Category of units	*Own capital*	*Borrowed capital*	*Total capital (Rs. lakhs)*
Agro based	140.00 (54.09)	118.82 (45.91)	258.82
Forest based	154.73 (73.96)	53.48 (26.04)	208.21
Chemical based	83.81 (40.26)	124.36 (59.74)	208.17
Mineral and Building material based	213.50 (50.38)	210.21 (49.62)	423.71
Engg. & Allied based	96.50 (41.00)	138.85 (59.00)	235.35
Total	688.54 (51.60)	645.72 (48.40)	1,334.26

Note : Figures in brackets indicate percentages to total.

The table explains the particulars of owned capital, borrowed capital, and total capital of 22 sick units. The table shows that owned capital of sick units accounts for 51.60%. The owned capital ratio in the total capital of the sick units in Forest based is very high as 73.96% and further it followed by Agro, Mineral and Building material, Engineering and Allied and Chemical based categories with 54.09%, 50.38%, 41% and 40.26% respectively. The table also reveals that the four Agro based sick units have a total capital investment of Rs. 2.58 crores, 5 Forest based sick units have Rs. 2.08 crores, 2 Chemical based units have Rs. 2.08 crores, 6 Mineral and Building material based units has Rs. 4.23 crores and 5 units has Rs. 2.35 units investment. These 22 sick units out of 100 units have a total capital investment of Rs. 133.42 crores out of this Rs. 68.85 crores is owned capital i.e. 51.60% and Rs. 64.57 crores i.e. 48.40% is borrowed capital.

The sick units of the district borrowed funds from Commercial Banks, Andhra Pradesh State Finance Corporation, moneylenders, friends and relatives. The details of sick units and their borrowed capital from various organised and unorganized agencies are shown in table 6.14.

Table—6.14 The Details of Sick Units and their Borrowed Capital from Various Organised and Unorganized Agencies in Visakhapatnam District

Category of units	*Total sick units*	*Commercial Banks*		*APSFC*		*Money Lender*		*Friends & Relatives*		*NSISI*		*Total Borrowed*
		No.of units	*Amount*	*No.of units*	*Amount*	*No.of units*	*Amount*	*No.of units*	*Amount*	*No.of units*	*Amount*	
Agro based	4	1	24	2	66	—	—	1	28.82	—	—	118.82
Forest based	5	3	32	1	14	1	7.48	—	—	—	—	53.48
Chemical based*	2	2	89.36	1	35	—	—	—	—	—	—	124.36
Mineral & Building material based *	6	3	58.71	4	132	—	—	1	19.5	—	—	210.21
Engg. & Allied based *	5	3	60	2	41.35	1	16.5	—	—	1	21	138.85
Total	22	12	264.07 (940.89)	10	288.35 (44.65)	2	23.98 (3.71)	2	48.32 (7.48)	1	21 (3.25)	645.72

Note : Figures in brackets indicate percentages to total.

* Units taken loans from more than one agency.

From the above table it can be said that out of 22 units 12 of them got assistance from Commercial Banks, 10 of them got assistance from Andhra Pradesh State Finance Corporation and two each from moneylenders and friends and relatives and one unit is assisted by small industry service institute under hire purchase scheme. Two units each in Engineering and Allied based and Mineral and Building material based category, and one Chemical based unit got assistance both from Commercial Banks and Andhra Pradesh State Finance Corporation.

The Commercial Banks assisted one Agro based unit which has an investment of Rs. 24 lakhs and 3 Forest based units which have an investment of Rs. 89.36 lakhs and 3 Mineral and Building material based category units which have an investment of Rs. 58.71 lakh and under Engineering and Allied category which have an investment of Rs. 60 lakhs. The Commercial Banks assisted 12 sick units out of 22 units for Rs. 264.07 lakhs i.e. 40.89% of the total borrowed funds from various organised and unorganised agencies. It means that the Commercial Banks stands second position after the Andhra Pradesh State Finance Corporation with 44.65% in total borrowed funds for sick units.

The Andhra Pradesh State Finance Corporation assisted 10 units viz 4 Mineral and Building material based, each 2 in Agro based and Engineering and Allied based and one each from Forest and Chemical based Categories have fallen sick. 2 each in Mineral and Building material based and Engineering and Allied based units have also got assistance from Commercial Banks for working capital purposes. The State Finance Corporation assisted Rs. 28.83 crores to the 10 sick units i.e. 44.65% for term loan purposes.

One unit from Forest based category and one unit from Engineering and Allied based category are assisted by money lenders with Rs. 23.98 lakhs i.e. 3.71% of the total borrowed capital. 2 units are assisted by friends and relatives to an extent of Rs. 48.32 lakhs i.e. 7.48% of the total borrowed capital. These 2 units belong to Agro based category and Mineral and Building material based category. One unit is assisted by Small Industry Service Institute by way of supply of machinery on hire-purchase scheme to an extent of Rs. 21 lakhs.

Table—6.15 Statement Showing the Reasons for Sickness in Sample Units of Different Strata of Visakhapatnam District

Category of units	*Managerial problems*	*Financial problems*	*Marketing problem*	*Production problem*	*Labour problem*	*Govt. Policy*	*Total no.of sick units*
Agro based	—	3	2	—	—	—	4
Forest based	1	3	2	1	1	2	5
Chemical based	—	1	2	—	—	1	2
Mineral & Building material based	—	5	4	1	2	—	6
Engineering & Allied based	1	5	4	2	2	—	5
Total	2 (9.09)	17 (77.27)	14 (63.63)	4 (18.18)	5 (22.72)	3 (13.63)	22

Note : Figures in brackets indicate percentages to total.

An amount of Rs. 6.45 crores is blocked in the hands of the above 22 units which are fallen sick assisted by the above organised and unorganised agencies. Table 6.15 gives the reasons for sickness in sample units in terms of no. of units.

The table explains that out of 22 sick units 17 units i.e. 77.27%, each five from Mineral and Building material based and Engineering and Allied based and 3 each from Agro based and Forest based and one unit in Chemical based category have fallen sick due to financial crisis.

63.63% of total sick units i.e. 14 units have fallen sick due to problems in marketing their products. Out of these 14 units four units each belong to Mineral and Building material based and Engineering and Allied based and 2 units each belong to Agro based, Forest based and Chemical based category.

5 i.e. 22.72% of the units have fallen sick due to labour problem. Out of the 5 units 2 units each belong to Mineral & Building material based and Engineering & Allied based category and one unit belong to Forest based category.

Except 3 units in Agro based category all the remaining are fallen sick with more than 2 problems in Visakhapatnam district. 4 units in Engineering and Allied based category have fallen sick due to more than 3 reasons. The reasons for sickness in detail have already been discussed in Table 6.12.

—*References*

1. *Department of Industries, Hyderabad*

2. *Source : Report of SLICE, 1996*

CHAPTER—VII

COMPARATIVE ANALYSIS OF PROBLEMS OF SAMPLE UNITS

The main objective of this chapter is to make a detailed comparative analysis of various problems of sample units of Vizianagaram, Srikakulam, and Visakhapatnam districts. Further each problem where consisting different aspects, they are also dealt with in detail. To make a comparative structure of different problems faced by small scale units in these three districts. This type of analysis is made in this chapter. Analysing the problems of small scale units district wise without comparative analysis may not be ful-fledged. Besides that researcher viewed that this comparative analysis is useful to draw a meaningful inferences and conclusions.

The different problems faced by sample units are taken in an order of comparative analysis of three districts. A particular problem of small scale industrial units of Vizianagaram, Srikakulam and Visakhapatnam districts is taken and analysed inserting the information in one table. Before going to the problems, the total no.of units and number of sample units selected for different categories of units in these three districts are portrayed in table 7.1 for a brief and comparative outlook.

For an easy understanding distribution of different categories of sample units of Vizianagaram, Srikakulam and Visakhapatnam districts is shown in the shape of bar graphs given in the page 213.

From the above table it is clear that Visakhapatnam district occupies first place consisting 1116 small scale industrial units as on 31st March 1996. The number of units in Srikakulam and Vizianagaram districts are 484 and 464 respectively. This shows that Visakhapatnam district consists of more than double the number of units in Vizianagaram and Srikakulam districts.

Table—7.1 Total no. of Units and Sample Units of Vizianagaram, Srikakulam and Visakhapatnam Districts as on 31-3-96.

Category of units	*Vizianagaram district*		*Srikakulam district*		*Visakhapatnam district*	
	Total units	*Sample units*	*Total units*	*Sample units*	*Total units*	*Sample units*
Agro based	230 (49.57)	23 (52.27)	304 (62.81)	30 (68.19)	178 (15.96)	18 (18.0)
Forest based	83 (17.90)	8 (18.18)	26 (5.37)	3 (6.81)	224 (20.07)	22 (22.0)
Chemical based	19 (4.10)	2 (4.54)	24 (4.96)	2 (4.54)	132 (11.83)	1.3 (13.0)
Mineral & Building material based	68 (14.65)	7 (15.91)	40 (8.26)	4 (9.10)	220 (19.71)	22 (22.0)
Engineering & Allied based	39 (8.40)	4 (9.10)	50 (10.33)	5 (11.36)	244 (21.86)	25 (25.0)
Textile based	5 (1.07)	—	13 (2.69)	—	40 (3.58)	—
Miscellaneous based	20 (4.31)	—	27 (5.58)	—	78 (6.99)	—
Total	464	44	484	44	1,116	100

Note : Figures are in brackets indicate the percentages to the total.

As already mentioned in second chapter 25 units in Vizianagaram district, 40 units in Srikakulam district and 118 units in Visakhapatnam district are excluded from the study relating to textile and other miscellaneous category units. 439 units of Vizianagaram district, 444 units of Srikakulam district, 998 units of Visakhapatnam district are taken as universe for the random sampling. Out of 439 units in Vizianagaram district and 444 units of Srikakulam district, 44 units each were taken as sample units. In Visakhapatnam district 100 units were taken as sample out of 998. units.

A deeper analysis shows that 23 Agro based sample units of Vizianagaram district consists of 52.27% of the total sample units of the

GRAPH-5 — DISTRIBUTION OF DIFFERENT CATEGORIES OF SAMPLE UNITS IN VIZIANAGARAM, SRIKAKULAM AND VISAKHAPATNAM DISTRICTS

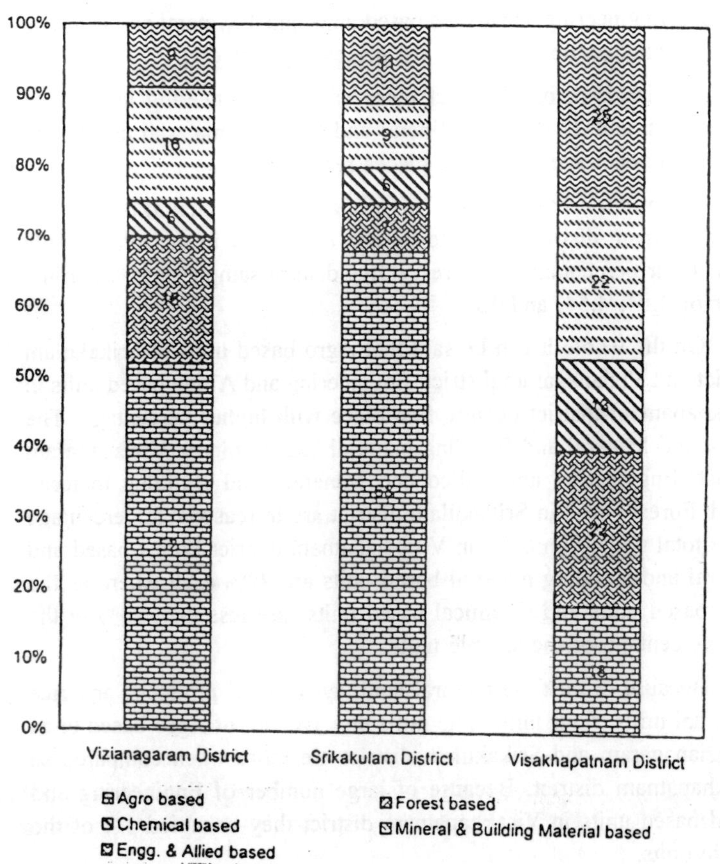

district. In Srikakulam district the number of Agro based sample units are 30 and their percentage in total sample units is 68.9%. But in case of Visakhapatnam district there are only 18 Agro based sample units consisting of 18% in total sample units.

In Vizianagaram district Forest based and Mineral and Building material based sample units are 8 (18.18%) and 4 (15.91%) respectively occupy 2 and 3 places in the sample units of the district. In Srikakulam district 5 Engineering and Allied based units and 4 Mineral and Building material units occupy 2nd and 3rd places respectively.

In Visakhapatnam district there are 25 Engineering and Allied based units, and 22 each of Mineral and Building material and Forest based units occupying 2 and 3 places respectively.

Chemical based units in Vizianagaram, Srikakulam, and Visakhapatnam districts seem to be less in number in the total sample units. Their percentage in the respective district sample units are in the order of 4.54, 4.54, and 13.

On the whole it can be said that Agro based units in Srikakulam district and Vizianagaram district, Engineering and Allied based units in Visakhapatnam district occupy first place with higher percentage. The Forest and Mineral and Building material based units in Vizianagaram district, Engineering and Allied and Mineral and Building material based, Forest based in Srikakulam district are in reasonable percentage in the total units. Similarly, in Visakhapatnam district Forest based and Mineral and Building material based units are 22% each where as the Agro based units and Chemical based units are less than 20% in the total percentage of the sample units.

Because of vast agricultural land, agricultural products, and rice mills, dal mills, flour mills, jute mills etc. The no. of Agro based units in Vizianagaram and Srikakulam district are more when compared to Visakhapatnam district. Because of large number of Engineering and Allied based units in Visakhapatnam district they occupied 1/4 of the sample units.

PRODUCTION PROBLEMS

36 units out of 44 in Vizianagaram district, 38 units out of 44 in Srikakulam district and 78 out of 100 units in Visakhapatnam district are in healthy condition but facing different problems. The remaining

sample units have become sick and they have already been dealt with in the previous chapter. The production problem i.e. First problem of sample units in Vizianagaram, Srikakulam and Visakhapatnam districts are inserted in table 7.2 for comparative analysis.

Table—7.2 Production Problems of Sample Units inVizianagaram, Srikakulam and Visakhapatnam Districts

District	*Total no. of healthy units*	*Units with raw-material problems*	*Units with shortage of power*	*Units with machinery problems*	*Without problem*
Vizianagaram	36	4 (11.11)	13 (36.12)	7 (19.44)	12 (33.33)
Srikakulam	38	10 (26.31)	13 (34.21)	4 (10.53)	11 (28.95)
Visakhapatnam	78	20 (25.65)	25 (32.05)	16 (20.51)	9 (11.54)

For an easy understanding production problems of sample units of Vizianagaram, Srikakulam and Visakhapatnam districts is shown in the shape of bar graph given in the next page.

It can be observed from the table that as high as 26.31% of sample units in Srikakulam district are suffering from the problem of raw-material followed by Srikakulam district with 2565%. In Vizianagaram district only 4 units i.e. 11.11% of sample units are facing the raw-material problem. Around 35% of small scale units in these Vizianagaram, Srikakulam and Visakhapatnam districts are suffering from shortage of power. Around 20% of units in Vizianagaram and Visakhapatnam districts are facing machinery troubles. This percentage is only 10.53% in case of Srikakulam district. 33.33% units of Vizianagaram district, 28.95% units of Srikakulam district and 11.54% units of Visakhapatnam district, 28.95% units of Srikakulam district and 11.54% units of Visakhapatnam district are seemed to be free from production problems. A detailed analysis relating to raw-material problem, shortage of power, and machinery troubles can be seen in the following tables.

GRAPH-6 — PRODUCTION PROBLEMS OF SAMPLE UNITS IN VIZIANAGARAM, SRIKAKULAM AND VISAKHAPATNAM DISTRICTS

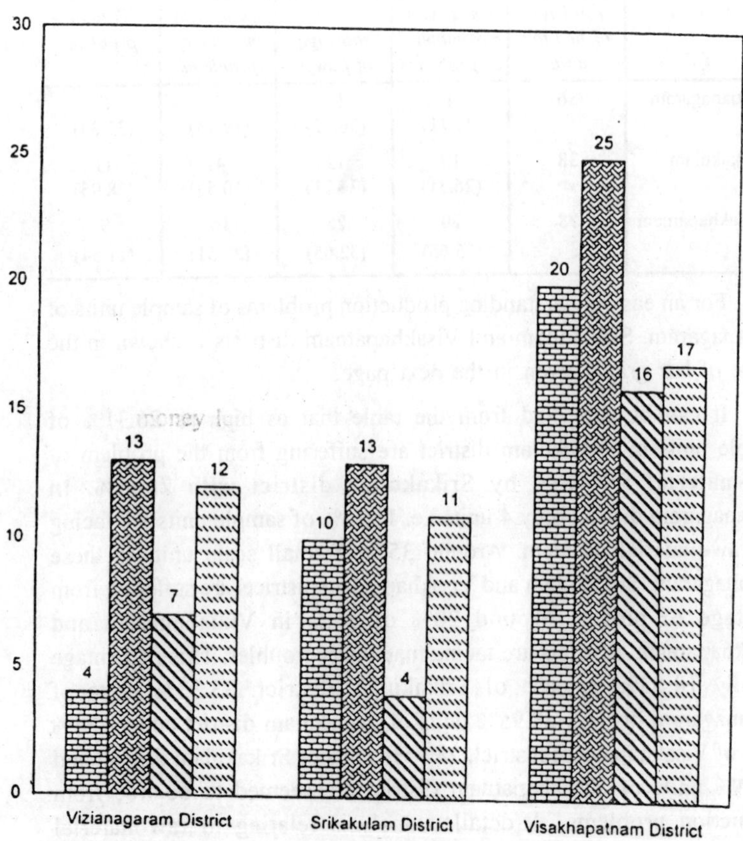

Shortage of Raw-material

Table—7.3 Units Facing Shortage of Raw-material in Vizianagaram,Srikakulam and Visakhapatnam Districts

Category of units	*Vizianagaram district*		*Srikakulam district*		*Visakhapatnam district*	
	Sample units	*Units with shortage of raw-material*	*Sample units*	*Units with shortage of raw-material*	*Sample units*	*Units with shortage of raw-material*
Agro based	19	—	26	6 (60.0)	14	8 (33.33)
Forest based	6	2 (50.0)	3	2 (20.0)	17	9 (37.5)
Chemical based	2	1 (25.0)	2	1 (10.0)	11	4 (16.7)
Mineral & Building material based	6	1 (25.0)	3	1 (10.0)	16	3 (12.5)
Engineering & Allied based	3	—	4	—	20	—
Total	36	4 (11.11)	38	10 (26.31)	78	24 (30.76)

Note : Figures are in brackets indicate the percentage to the total

Table 7.3 shows shortage of raw material faced by different categories of units in Vizianagaram, Srikakulam, and Visakhapatnam districts. 2 Forest based units, one unit each of Chemical, Mineral and Building material based units of Vizianagaram district., 6 Agro based units, 2 Forest based units and one unit each of Chemical and Mineral and Building material units of Srikakulam district and 4 Agro based units, 9 Forest based units, 4 Chemical based units and 3 Mineral and Building material based units of Visakhapatnam district are reported that they are facing shortage of raw-material. As high as 20 units in Visakhapatnam district i.e. 25.65%, 10 units in Srikakulam district i.e., 26.31% and 4 units of Vizianagaram district i.e., 11.11% are facing this problem.

GRAPH-7 — UNITS FACING SHORTAGE OF RAW MATERIAL IN VIZIANAGARAM, SRIKAKULAM AND VISAKHAPATNAM DISTRICTS

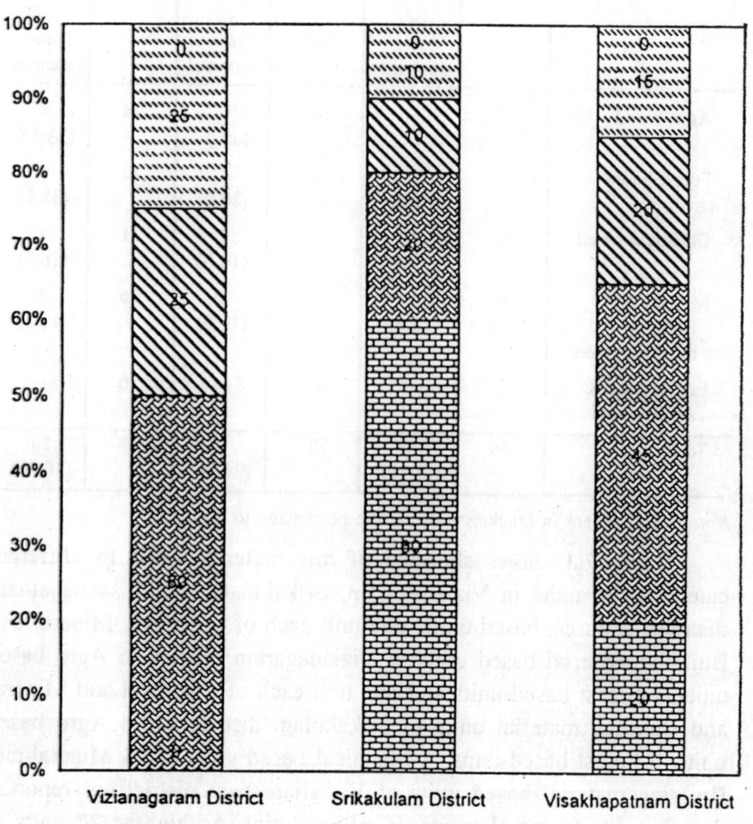

The Agro based units in Srikakulam and Visakhapatnam districts are facing the raw-material problem i.e. Non-availability of quality raw-materials. 9 Forest based units of Visakhapatnam district, 2 units each of Vizianagaram and Srikakulam district of this category are also facing this problem. Under Chemical based category while one unit each in Vizianagaram and Srikakulam district are facing this problem. 4 units of Visakhapatnam district are suffering with this problem. Similarly, one unit each of Vizianagaram and Srikakulam districts under Mineral and Building material based category and 3 units in Visakhapatnam district of this category are facing the shortage of raw-material.

On the whole 20 units of Visakhapatnam district i.e. 25.65% of the total units are facing shortage of raw-material. The units of Vizianagaram and Srikakulam district though facing the problem of raw-material the severity when compared to Visakhapatnam district is less.

For an easy understanding the shortage of raw-material of sample units of Vizianagaram, Srikakulam and Visakhapatnam districts is shown in the shape of bar graph given in page 218.

Shortage of Power

Like finance, now a days power supply can also be said as the life blood of any industry unit. Nearly 1/3 rd of small scale industrial units in Vizianagaram, Srikakulam and Visakhapatnam districts are suffering from power shortage. The following table gives a picture showing this problem relating to three districts with different categories of industrial units.

The table 7.4 shows that 36.11% of small scale units of Vizianagaram district, 34.21% units of Srikakulam district and 32.05% of units in Visakhapatnam district have reported that due to shortage of power and interruptions in power supply badly effected their production. In these 3 districts the Agro based units seemed to be hit severely by this problem. 46.15% of Vizianagaram district, 61.53% of Srikakulam district and 24% of Visakhapatnam district Agro based units faced the problem of power shortage. With 23.07% of the Forest based units in Vizianagaram district reported the power shortage for their units. The Mineral and Building material based units and Engineering and Allied based units each consisting 15.39% of Vizianagaram and Srikakulam districts have experienced the problem of shortage of power. 32% of the

Engineering and Allied based units and 20% of Forest based units in Visakhapatnam district have also experienced the same problem.

Table—7.4 Units Facing Shortage of Power in Vizianagaram, Srikakulam and Visakhapatnam Districts

Category of units	*Vizianagaram district*		*Srikakulam district*		*Visakhapatnam district*	
	Sample units	*Units with shortage of power*	*Sample units*	*Units with shortage of power*	*Sample units*	*Units with shortage of power*
Agro based	19	6 (46.15)	26	8 (61.53)	14	6 (24.0)
Forest based	6	3 (23.07)	3	1 (7.69)	17	5 (20.0)
Chemical based	2	—	2	—	11 (8.0)	2
Mineral & Building material based	6	2 (15.39)	3	2 (15.39)	16	4 (16.0)
Engineering & Allied based	3	2 (15.39)	4	2 (15.39)	20	8 (32.0)
Total	36	13 (36.11)	38	13 (34.21)	78	25 (32.05)

Note : Figures in brackets indicate the percentages to the total

From the above analysis nearly 50% of the small scale units that to Agro based units have faced shortage of power in Vizianagaram district. Similar the case with Srikakulam district where 61.53% Agro based units have experienced the problem. But in case of Visakhapatnam district the 32% of Engineering and Allied units have suffered heavily due to shortage of power and then comes Agro, and Forest based units facing the problem.

The researcher observed that the overall power shortage in the state mainly during the summer season effected many of the small scale industries units in these three districts.

For an easy understanding the shortage of power problem of sample units of Vizianagaram, Srikakulam and Visakhapatnam districts is shown in the shape of bar graph given in the next page.

GRAPH-8 — UNITS FACING SHORTAGE OF POWER IN VIZIANAGARAM, SRIKAKULAM AND VISAKHAPATNAM DISTRICTS

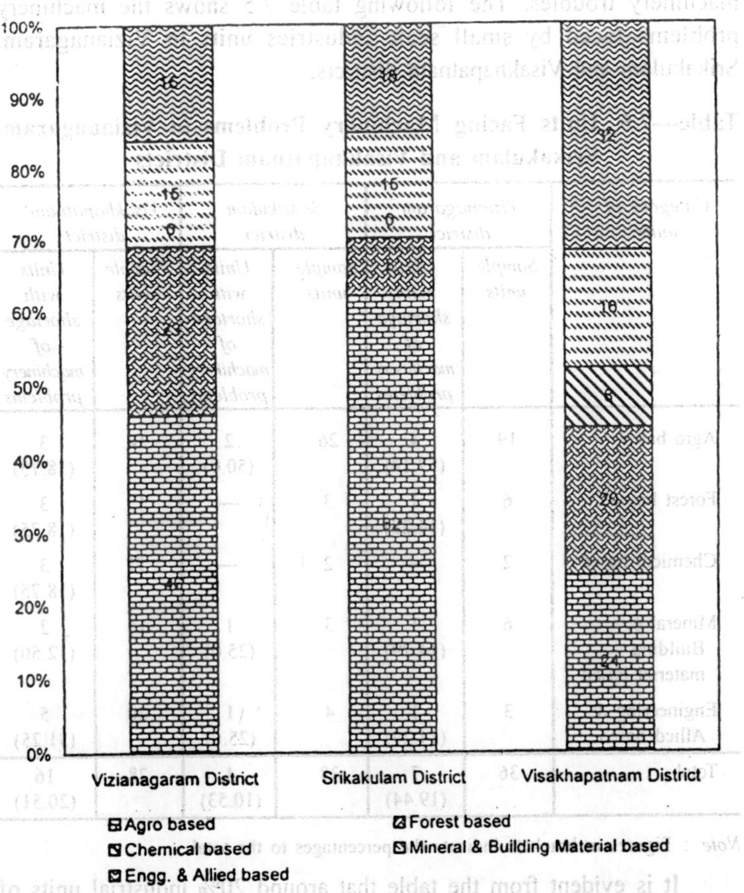

Machinery Troubles

Non-availability of quality raw-material and power shortage may not be controlled by the entrepreneur to a large extent which in turn takes the shape of production problem. The machinery problems which are to a greater extent controlled are also hampering the growth of small scale industries units in these 3 districts to a reasonable extent. As said in the 5th chapter machinery breakdown, non-availability of skilled labour, usage of secondhand machinery, poor maintenance lead to machinery troubles. The following table 7.5 shows the machinery problems faced by small scale industries units in Vizianagaram, Srikakulam and Visakhapatnam districts.

Table—7.5 Units Facing Machinery Problems in Vizianagaram, Srikakulam and Visakhapatnam Districts

Category of units	*Vizianagaram district*		*Srikakulam district*		*Visakhapatnam district*	
	Sample units	*Units with shortage of machinery problems*	*Sample units*	*Units with shortage of machinery problems*	*Sample units*	*Units with shortage of machinery problems*
Agro based	19	4 (57.14)	26	2 (50.0)	14	3 (18.75)
Forest based	6	1 (14.28)	3	—	17	3 (18.75)
Chemical based	2	—	2	—	11	3 (18.75)
Mineral & Building material based	6	1 (14.29)	3	1 (25.0)	16	2 (12.50)
Engineering & Allied based	3	1 (14.29)	4	1 (25.0)	20	5 (31.25)
Total	36	7 (19.44)	38	4 (10.53)	78	16 (20.51)

Note : Figures in brackets indicate the percentages to the total.

It is evident from the table that around 20% industrial units of Vizianagaram and Visakhapatnam districts are 10.5% of industrial units of Srikakulam district are seemed to be suffered from machinery troubles

4 Agro based units i.e. 57.14% in Vizianagaram district have experienced the problem 5 Engineering and Allied based units i.e. 31.25% and 3 units each i.e. 18.75% Agro, Forest Chemical based units of Visakhapatnam district have faced machinery problem 2 Agro based units i.e. 50% have faced this problem in Srikakulam district. When compared to shortage of raw-material and power supply the severity of machinery troubles is not too high. But if the units are free from machinery troubles. There is no doubt that the production small scale units would have been much better.

The agro based units in Vizianagaram and Srikakulam district, the Engineering and Allied based units in Visakhapatnam district on a whole seemed to be suffered reasonably due to machinery troubles.

For an easy understanding the machinery problems of sample units of Vizianagaram, Srikakulam and Visakhapatnam districts is shown in the shape of bar graph given in the next page.

MARKETING PROBLEMS

Establishing an industrial unit and producing good quality product is only one aspect, marketing the product attracting the customer is another and important aspect. Thus marketing now a days occupies prominent place in the life of an industrial unit. Most of the industrial units of Vizianagaram, Srikakulam, and Visakhapatnam district have been facing problems in marketing their products. Lack of demand consisting of competition, seasonal fluctuations and poor quality and government policy are the aspects affecting in marketing the products. Table 7.6 shows the marketing problems faced by sample units in Vizianagaram, Srikakulam and Visakhapatnam districts.

It can be understood from the table 7.6 that 47.22% i.e. 17 units of Vizianagaram district, 42.10% i.e., 16 units of Srikakulam district and 80.77% i.e. 63 units of Visakhapatnam district have faced the problem of selling their products in the market due to competition from among small units and from large units, seasonal fluctuation and poor quality. 8 units of Vizianagaram district i.e. 47.05%, 9 units of Srikakulam district i.e. 56.25% and 34 units of Visakhapatnam district i.e. 53.97% are facing competition in selling their products in the market. 3 units i.e. 17.64% of Vizianagaram district, 3 units i.e. 18.75% of Srikakulam district and 7 units i.e. 11.11% of Visakhapatnam district have unable

GRAPH-9 — UNITS FACING MACHINERY PROBLEMS IN VIZIANAGARAM, SRIKAKULAM AND VISAKHAPATNAM DISTRICTS

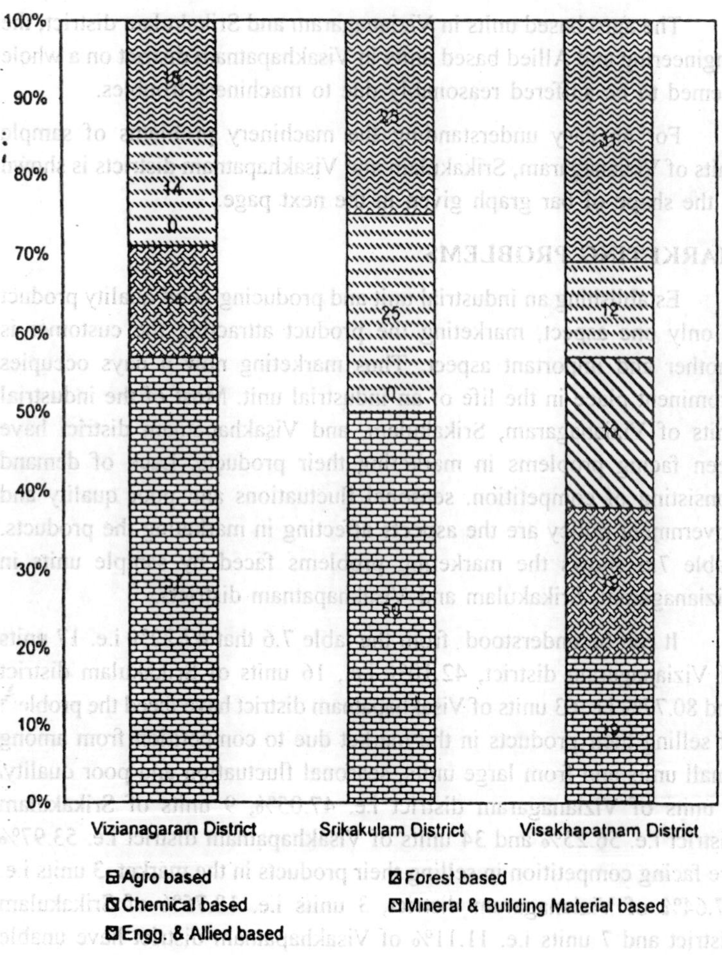

to sell their products due to seasonal fluctuations. 6 units i.e. 35.29% of Vizianagaram district 4 units i.e. 25% of Srikakulam district and 22 units i.e. 34.92% of Visakhapatnam district failed to market their products because of their poor quality products.

Table—7.6 Marketing Problem of Sample Units of Vizianagaram, Srikakulam and Visakhapatnam Districts

District	*Total no. of units*	*Compe-tition*	*Seasonal fluctuation*	*Poor quality*	*Total*	*Govt. Policy*	*Without problem*
Vizianagaram	36	3 (17.64)	3 (17.64)	6 (35.29)	17 (47.22)	13 (36.11)	6 (16.66)
Srikakulam	38	9 (56.25)	3 (18.75)	4 (25)	16 (42.10)	12 (31.59)	10 (26.31)
Visakhapatnam	78	7 (11.11)	22 (34.92)	34 (53.97)	63 (80.77)	5 (6.41)	12 (12.82)

Note : Figures are in brackets indicate the percentage to the total.

The often changing State and Central Government policies have also affected 13 units i.e. 36% in Vizianagaram district, 12 units i.e. 31.59% of Srikakulam district and 5 units i.e. 6.41% of Visakhapatnam district.

On a whole 30 units out of 36 units i.e. 83.37%, 28 units out of 38 units i.e. 73.69% of Srikakulam district and 68 units out of 78 units i.e. 73.69% of Srikakulam district and 68 units out of 78 units i.e. 87.18% in Visakhapatnam district have been facing marketing problems.

The remaining 6 units of Vizianagaram district and 10 units of each in Srikakulam and Visakhapatnam district have reported that have no marketing problems.

From the table it can be said that most of the units in Visakhapatnam district followed by Vizianagaram district and majority of the units in Srikakulam district are facing problems in marketing their products.

For an easy understanding the marketing problems of sample units of Vizianagaram, Srikakulam and Visakhapatnam districts is shown in the shape of bar graph given in the next page.

GRAPH-10— MARKETING PROBLEMS OF SAMPLE UNITS IN VIZIANAGARAM, SRIKAKULAM AND VISAKHAPATNAM DISTRICTS

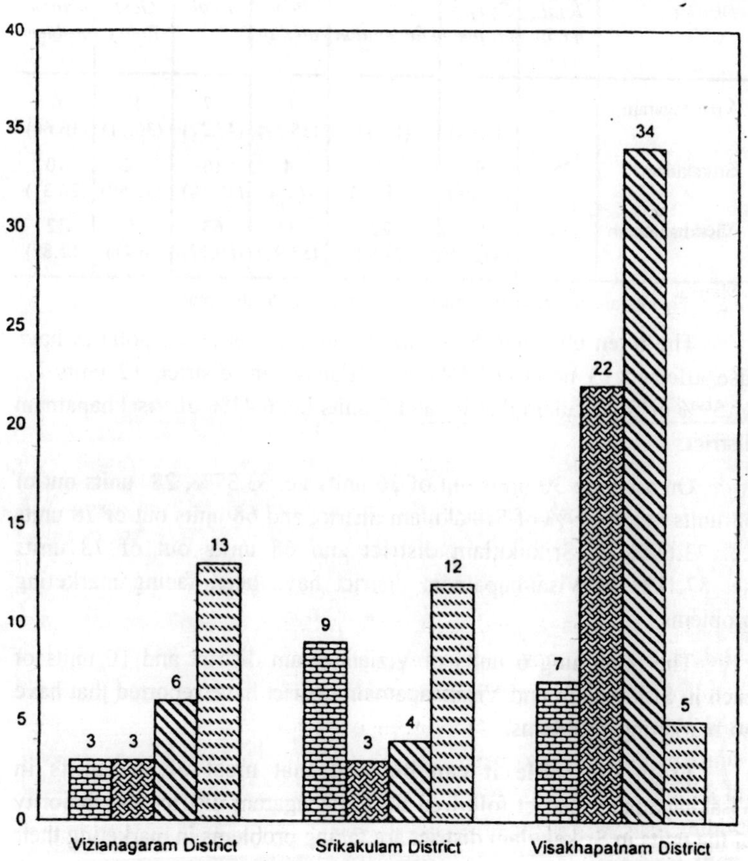

Competition

For an in-depth analysis and comparative study separate tables are formed for every aspect leading to marketing problem.

Table—7.7 Units Facing Competition in Vizianagaram, Srikakulam and Visakhapatnam Districts

Category of units	*Vizianagaram district*		*Srikakulam district*		*Visakhapatnam district*	
	Sample units	*Problem units*	*Sample units*	*Problem units*	*Sample units*	*Problem units*
Agro based	19	2 (25.0)	26	5 (55.55)	14	6 (17.64)
Forest based	6	—	3	—	17	9 (26.47)
Chemical based	2	2 (25.0)	2	1 (11.11)	11	4 (11.76)
Mineral & Building material based	6	4 (50.0)	3	1 (11.11)	16	6 (17.64)
Engineering & Allied based	3	-	4	2 (22.23)	20	9 (26.47)
Total	36	8 (22.22)	38	9 (23.68)	78	34 (43.58)

Note : Figures in brackets indicate the percentages to the total

Table 7.7 shows units that are facing competition in these three districts. Out of 8 units (22.22%) facing competition in marketing the products in Vizianagaram district, out of which 4 belong to Mineral and Building material based category and 2 each belong to Agro and Chemical based category and 2 each belong to Agro and Chemical based units. 9 units i.e., 23.68% facing competition in Srikakulam district 5 units belong to Agro based category, 2 units belong to Engineering and Allied category and one unit each from Chemical and Mineral and Building material category. Out of 34 units i.e. 43.58% facing competition 9 units each belong to Forest based and Engineering and Allied based category, 6 units each from Agro and Mineral and Building material based category and 4 units from Chemical based category.

Mineral and Building material based units of Vizianagaram district, Agro based units of Srikakulam district and Forest and Engineering and Allied based units of Visakhapatnam district are facing more competition when compared to other categories of units in their respective districts.

Nearly 50% of the sample units in Visakhapatnam district and nearly 25% of sample units in Vizianagaram and Srikakulam districts are facing competition in marketing in their products.

For an easy understanding the units facing competition problem in Vizianagaram, Srikakulam and Visakhapatnam districts sample units is shown in the shape of bar graph given in the next page.

Seasonal Fluctuation

Seasonal fluctuations have also effected some units in Vizianagaram, Srikakulam and Visakhapatnam districts. These particulars are given in table 7.8.

Table—7.8 Units Facing Seasonal Fluctuation Problems in Vizianagaram, Srikakulam and Visakhapatnam Districts

Category of units	*Vizianagaram district*		*Srikakulam district*		*Visakhapatnam district*	
	Sample units	*Problem units*	*Sample units*	*Problem units*	*Sample units*	*Problem units*
Agro based	19	2 (66.67)	26	3 (100.0)	14	3 (42.85)
Forest based	6	1 (33.33)	3	—	17	—
Chemical based	2	—	2	—	11	—
Mineral & Building material based	6	—	3	—	16	4 (57.15)
Engineering & Allied based	3	—	4	—	20	—
Total	36	3 (8.33)	38	3 (7.89)	78	7 (8.97)

Note : Figures are in brackets indicate the percentage to the total.

3 units consisting 2 from Agro based and one from Forest based category of Visakhapatnam district have faced the problem of seasonal fluctuations. Around 8% of the sample units in these 3 districts ,is said to be affected due to this problem.

GRAPH-11— UNITS FACING COMPETITION IN VIZIANAGARAM, SRIKAKULAM AND VISAKHAPATNAM DISTRICTS

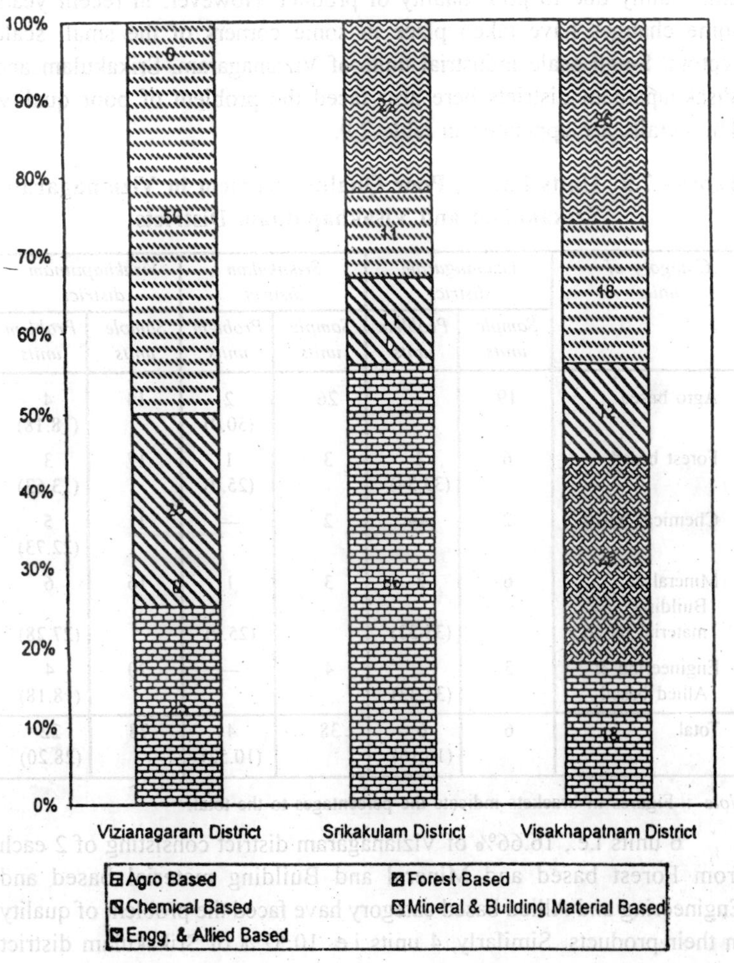

For an easy understanding the seasonal fluctuation problems of sample units of Vizianagaram, Srikakulam and Visakhapatnam districts is shown in the shape of bar graph given in the next page.

Poor Quality

Since independence the small scale industrial units in our country are not in a position to complete with large scale units or medium scale unit mainly due to poor quality of product. However, in recent years some changes have taken place in some corners of the small scale sectors. Small scale industrial units of Vizianagaram, Srikakulam and Visakhapatnam districts here also faced the problem of poor quality. The details are appended in table 7.9.

Table—7.9 Units Facing Poor Quality Problem in Vizianagaram, Srikakulam and Visakhapatnam Districts

Category of units	*Vizianagaram district*		*Srikakulam district*		*Visakhapatnam district*	
	Sample units	*Problem units*	*Sample units*	*Problem units*	*Sample units*	*Problem units*
Agro based	19	—	26	2 (50.0)	14	4 (18.18)
Forest based	6	2 (33.34)	3	1 (25.0)	17	3 (13.63)
Chemical based	2	—	2	—	11	5 (22.73)
Mineral & Building material based	6	2 (33.33)	3	1 (25.0)	16	6 (27.28)
Engineering & Allied based	3	2 (33.33)	4	—	20	4 (18.18)
Total	6	6 (16.16)	38	4 (10.52)	78	22 (28.20)

Note : Figures in brackets indicate the percentages to the total.

6 units i.e., 16.66% of Vizianagaram district consisting of 2 each from Forest based and Mineral and Building material based and Engineering and Allied based category have faced the problem of quality in their products. Similarly, 4 units i.e. 10.52% of Srikakulam district consisting of 2 Agro based units, and one each of Forest based and Mineral and Building material based have also faced the problem. In

GRAPH-12— UNITS FACING SEASONAL FLUCTUATIONS IN VIZIANAGARAM, SRIKAKULAM AND VISAKHAPATNAM DISTRICTS

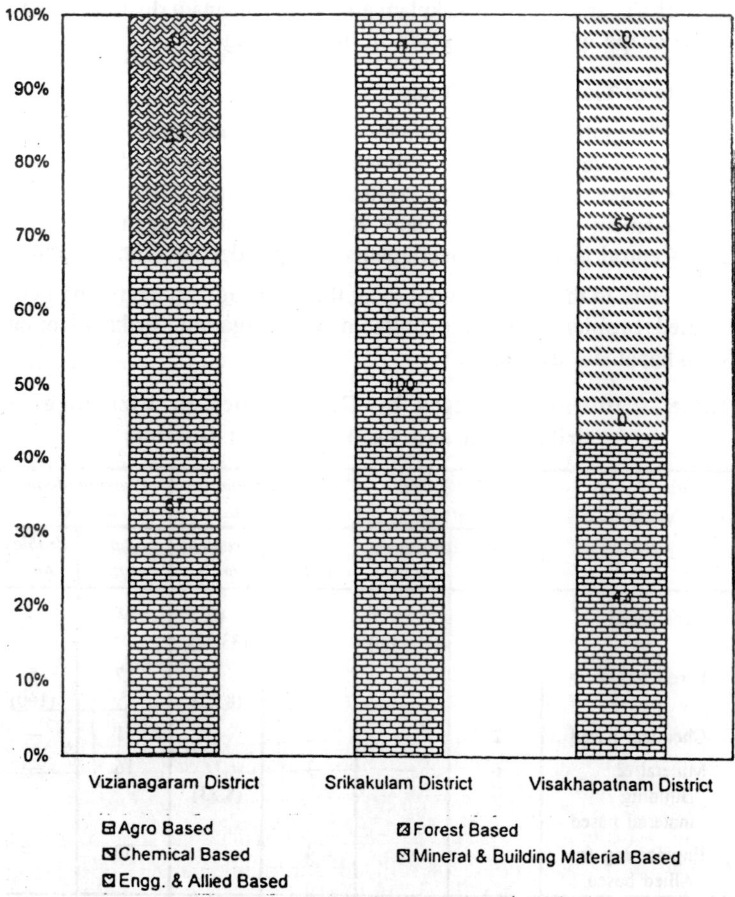

the case of Visakhapatnam district 22 units i.e. 28.20% out of 78 have reported that they are facing lack of demand of their products due to substandard quality. These 22 units consist of 6 from Mineral and Building material based and 3 Agro from Forest based category.

On the whole nearly 30% of the units in Visakhapatnam district are facing this quality problem followed by Vizianagaram and Srikakulam district with 16.66% and 10.52% respectively.

For an easy understanding the poor quality problems of sample units of Vizianagaram, Srikakulam and Visakhapatnam districts is shown in the shape of bar graph given in the next page.

Affects of Government Policy

The policy pronouncements of Central and State Governments have no doubt boosted the growth and development of small scale sector since independence. Industrial policies, Five Year Plans establishment of various finance and non-financial agencies etc., by both Central and State Governments come under government policy.

Here in this study the policy of the State Government in particular created problems to some units in Vizianagaram, Srikakulam and Visakhapatnam districts.

Table—7.10 Units Affected by Govt. Policy in Vizianagaram, Srikakulam and Visakhapatnam Districts

Category of units	*Vizianagaram district*		*Srikakulam district*		*Visakhapatnam district*	
	Sample units	*Problem units*	*Sample units*	*Problem units*	*Sample units*	*Problem units*
Agro based	19	13 (100.00)	26	10 (83.34)	14	—
Forest based	6	—	3	1 (8.33)	17	5 (100)
Chemical based	2	—	2	—	11	—
Mineral & Building material based	6	—	3	1 (8.33)	16	—
Engineering & Allied based	3	—	4	—	20	—
Total	36	13 (36.11)	38	12 (31.59)	78	5 (6.4)

Note : Figures in brackets indicate the percentages to the total

GRAPH-13— UNITS FACING POOR QUALITY PROBLEM IN VIZIANAGARAM, SRIKAKULAM AND VISAKHAPATNAM DISTRICTSS

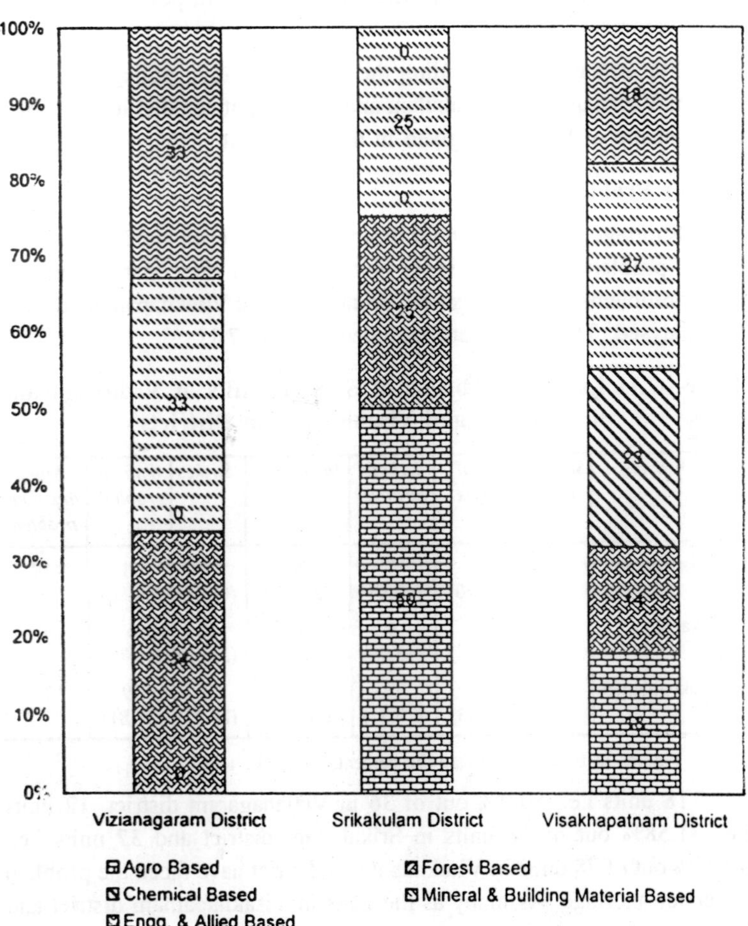

As incorporated in table 7.10, 13 Agro based units out of 36 total units of Vizianagaram district have expressed some problems encountered by them due to policy changes of the State Government. The rice mills, oil mills, flour mills of the district were affected due to leavy policy and changes in essential commodities act. Similarly 10 Agro based units and one unit each from Forest and Mineral and Building material based unit have faced this problem. In case of Visakhapatnam district only 5 units of Forest based category had bitter experience with policy changes of the government.

For an easy understanding the effects of Govt. policy of sample units of Vizianagaram, Srikakulam and Visakhapatnam districts is shown in the shape of bar graph given in the page next.

Labour Problems

Shortage of labour, labour turnover, absenteeism and strikes cause labour problems in small scale units based on there parameters the labour problems of Vizianagaram, Srikakulam and Visakhapatnam district are analysed. The details are included in table 7.11

Table—7.11 Labour Problems of Sample Units of Vizianagaram, Srikakulam and Visakhapatnam Districts

Districts	*Sample units*	*Total units*	*Labour turnover*	*Absenteeism*	*Strikes*	*Without problem*	*More than one problem*
Vizianagaram	36	18 (50.00)	7 (19.44)	8 (22.22)	2 (05.56)	11 (30.56)	10
Srikakulam	38	12 (31.58)	6 (15.79)	8 (21.05)	12 (31.58)	6 (15.79)	6
Visakhapatnam	78	37 (47.43)	16 (20.51)	13 (16.67)	21 (26.92)	29 (37.81)	38

Note : Figures in brackets indicate the percentages to the total

18 units i.e., 50.0% out of 36 in Vizianagaram district, 12 units i.e., 31.58% out of 38 units in Srikakulam district and 37 units i.e., 47.43% out of 78 units in Visakhapatnam district have faced the problem of labour shortage. As many as the units in Visakhapatnam district and Vizianagaram district located in urban areas, nearly 50% of the units have faced this problem.

GRAPH-14— UNITS AFFECTED BY GOVT. POLICY IN VIZIANAGARAM, SRIKAKULAM AND VISAKHAPATNAM DISTRICTS

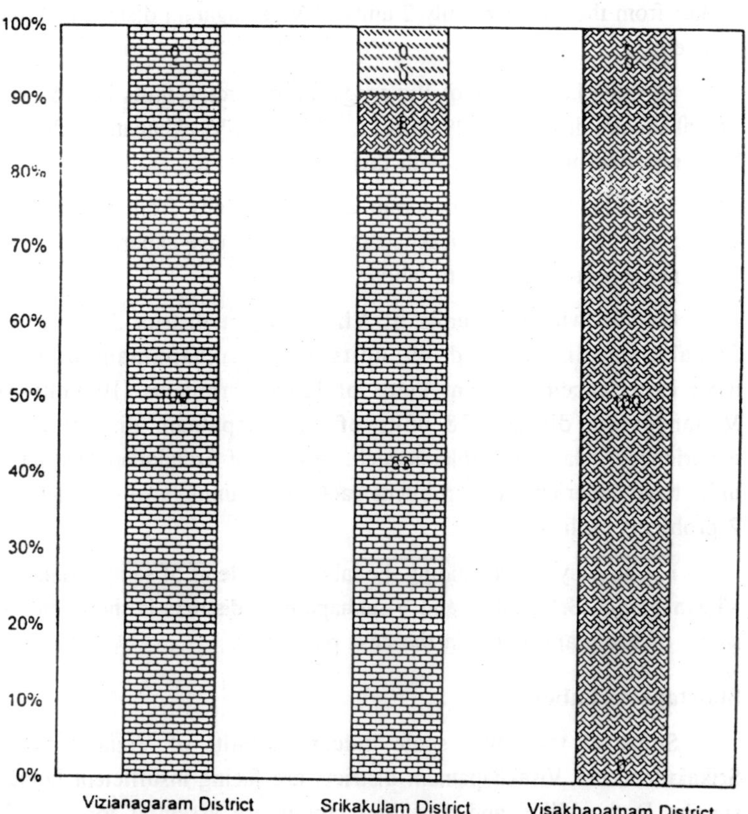

7 units i..e. 19.44% in Vizianagaram district, 6 units i.e. 15.79% in Srikakulam district and 16 units i.e. 20.51% in Visakhapatnam district have experienced the problem of labour turnover. Similarly, 8 units i.e. 22.22% of Vizianagaram district, 8 units of Srikakulam district i.e. 21.05% and 13 units i.e. 16.67% of Visakhapatnam district are facing the problem of absenteeism. 12 units in Srikakulam district i.e. 31.58% and 21 units i.e. 26.92% in Visakhapatnam district have faced strikes from their labour. Only 2 units of Vizianagaram district had this problem.

11 units i.e 30.56% of Vizianagaram district, 6 units i.e. 15.79% of Srikakulam district and 29 units i.e. 37.81% of Visakhapatnam district have reported no problems with their labour.

10 units from Vizianagaram district, 6 units from Srikakulam district and 38 units from Visakhapatnam district have experienced more than one problem relating to labour.

On the whole 25 units of Vizianagaram district 32 units of Srikakulam district and 49 units of Visakhapatnam district have experienced different kinds of labour problems. 10 units of Vizianagaram district, 38 units of Visakhapatnam district have experienced 2 labour problems each. In case of Srikakulam district 2 units have experienced 3 problems each and 2 units have experienced 2 problems each.

For an easy understanding the labour problems of sample units of Vizianagaram, Srikakulam and Visakhapatnam districts is shown in the shape of bar graph given in the next page.

Shortage of Labour

Some of the small scale industries units of Vizianagaram, Srikakulam and Visakhapatnam districts are facing insufficient labour supply. Both skilled and unskilled labour are essential for smooth running of any enterprise. The following table shows the problem of labour supply in these 3 districts and in different categories of units.

GRAPH-15— LABOUR PROBLEMS OF SAMPLE UNITS IN VIZIANAGARAM, SRIKAKULAM AND VISAKHAPATNAM DISTRICTS

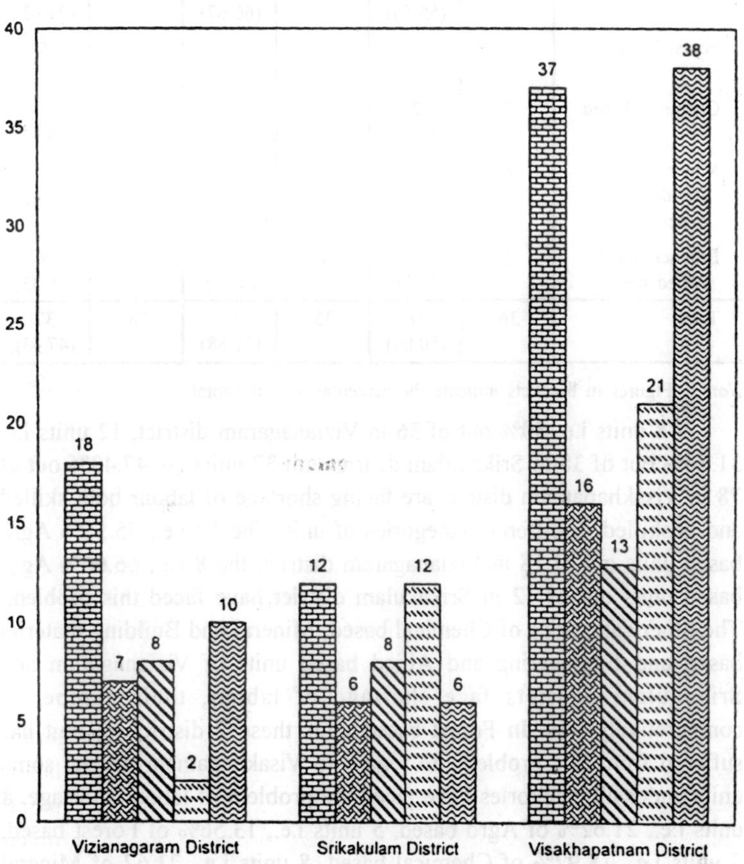

Table—7.12 Units Facing Shortage of Labour in Vizianagaram, Srikakulam and Visakhapatnam Districts

Category of units	*Vizianagaram district*		*Srikakulam district*		*Visakhapatnam district*	
	Sample units	*Problem units*	*Sample units*	*Problem units*	*Sample units*	*Problem units*
Agro based	19	10 (55.56)	26	8 (66.67)	14	8 (21.62)
Forest based	6	—	3	—	17 (13.51)	5
Chemical based	2	2 (11.11)	2	1 (8.33)	11	7 (18.92)
Mineral & Building material based	6	4 (22.22)	3	2 (16.67)	16	8 (21.62)
Engineering & Allied based	3	2 (11.11)	4	1 (8.33)	20	9 (24.33)
Total	36	18 (50.00)	35	12 (31.58)	78	37 (47.43)

Note : Figures in brackets indicate the percentages to the total.

18 units i.e. 50% out of 36 in Vizianagaram district, 12 units i.e. 31.58% out of 38 in Srikakulam district and 37 units i.e, 47.43% out of 78 in Visakhapatnam district are facing shortage of labour both skilled and unskilled in different categories of unit. The 10 i.e., 55.56% Agro based units out of 18 in Vizianagaram district, the 8 i.e., 66.66% Agro based units out of 12 in Srikakulam district have faced this problem. The other categories of Chemical based, Mineral and Building material based and Engineering and Allied based units of Vizianagaram and Srikakulam districts face shortage of labour, their number is comparatively less. In Forest based units these 2 district no unit has suffered from this problem. In regard to Visakhapatnam district some units under all categories have faced the problem of labour shortage. 8 units i.e., 21.62% of Agro based, 5 units i.e., 13.56% of Forest based, 7 units i.e., 18.92% of Chemical based, 8 units i.e., 21.62 of Mineral and Building material based and 9 units i.e., 24.32% of Engineering and Allied based units have faced this problem in Visakhapatnam district.

On the whole 50% of units in Vizianagaram district 47.43% of units in Visakhapatnam district have faced the problem of labour supply.

12 units i.e., 31.58% of Srikakulam district have also experienced this problem. But when compared to the problem in Visakhapatnam and Vizianagaram districts it is some what less.

For an easy understanding the shortage of labour problem of sample units of Vizianagaram, Srikakulam and Visakhapatnam districts is shown in the shape of bar graph given in the next page.

Labour Turnover

Among the labour problems, labour turnover has occupied a considerable part. 7 units of Vizianagaram district, 6 units of Srikakulam district and 16 units of Visakhapatnam district have experienced the problem of labour turnover. The details can be seen in the following table 7.13.

Table—7.13 Units With Labour Turnover in Vizianagaram, Srikakulam and Visakhapatnam Districts

Category of units	*Vizianagaram district*		*Srikakulam district*		*Visakhapatnam district*	
	Sample units	*Problem units*	*Sample units*	*Problem units*	*Sample units*	*Problem units*
Agro based	19	—	26	4 (66.67)	14	3 (18.75)
Forest based	6	3 (42.87)	3	—	17	2 (12.50)
Chemical based	2	1 (14.28)	2	1 (16.66)	11	3 (18.75)
Mineral & Building material based	6	2 (28.57)	3	1 (16.66)	16	4 (25.0)
Engineering & Allied based	3	1 (14.28)	4	—	20	4 (25.0)
Total	36	7 (19.44)	38	6 (15.79)	78	16 (20.51)

Note : Figures in brackets indicate the percentages to the total.

The percentage of labour turnover in these three districts ranges between 15% to 21%. Agro based units in Vizianagaram district, Forest based and Engineering and Allied based units in Srikakulam district have experienced no labour turnover. Except these, the different

GRAPH-16— UNITS FACING SHORTAGE OF LABOUR IN VIZIANAGARAM, SRIKAKULAM AND VISAKHAPATNAM DISTRICTS

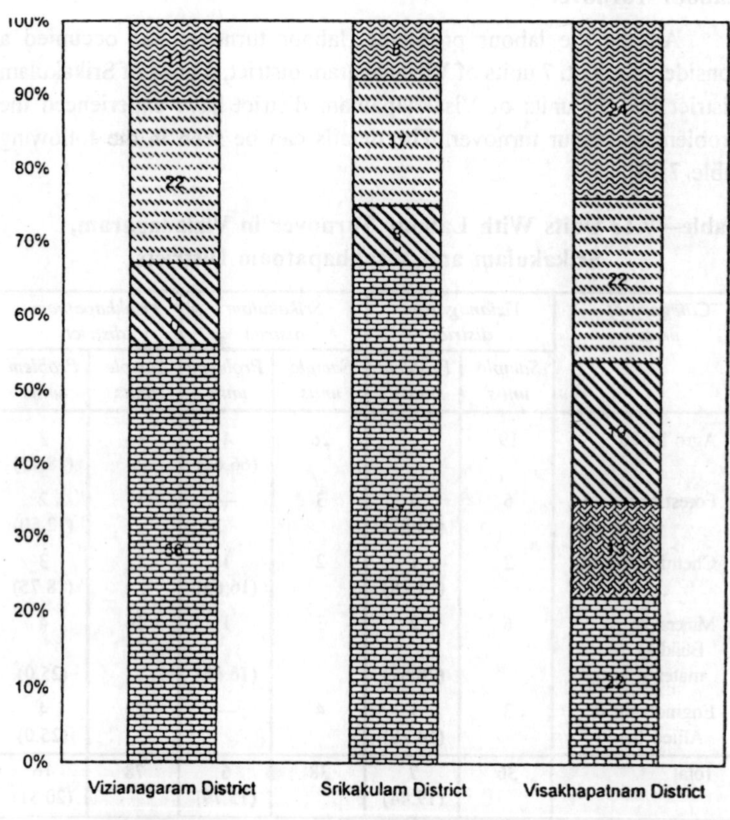

categories of units in these three districts have labour turnover consisting of one to four units in each category as shown in the table.

For an easy understanding the labour turnover problems of sample units of Vizianagaram, Srikakulam and Visakhapatnam districts is shown in the shape of bar graph given in the next page.

Absenteeism

Almost similar to the problem of labour turnover some of the units in the 3 districts have faced the problem of absenteeism. 8 units each in Vizianagaram and Srikakulam district and 13 units in Visakhapatnam district have reported the problem of absenteeism. Except Chemical based units in Srikakulam district all categories of units in these three district here the problem of absenteeism consisting of 1 to 5 units in each category as shown in the table 7.14.

Table—7.14 Units Facing Absenteeism Problem in Vizianagaram, Srikakulam and Visakhapatnam Districts

Category of units	*Vizianagaram district*		*Srikakulam district*		*Visakhapatnam district*	
	Sample units	*Problem units*	*Sample units*	*Problem units*	*Sample units*	*Problem units*
Agro based	19	3 (37.5)	26	5 (62.5)	14	2 (15.38)
Forest based	6	1 (12.5)	3	1 (12.5)	17	2 (15.38)
Chemical based	2	2 (25.0)	2	—	11	2 (15.38)
Mineral & Building material based	6	1 (12.5)	3	1 (12.5)	16	3 (23.08)
Engineering & Allied based	3	1 (12.5)	4	1 (12.5)	20	4 (30.78)
Total	36	8 (22.22)	38	8 (21.05)	78	13 (16.67)

Note : Figures in brackets indicate the percentages to the total.

The rate of absenteeism in these three districts ranges between 16% and 23% when this rate was 22.22% in Vizianagaram district, it was only 16.67% in Visakhapatnam district. The rate of absenteeism in Srikakulam district is 21.07%.

GRAPH-17— UNITS WITH LABOUR TURNOVER IN VIZIANAGARAM, SRIKAKULAM AND VISAKHAPATNAM DISTRICTS

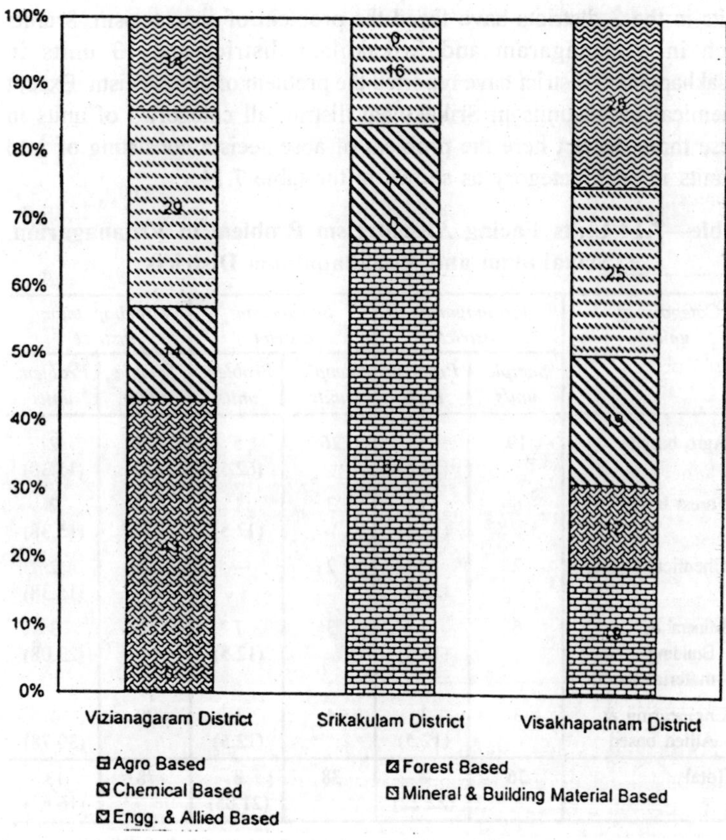

For an easy understanding the absenteeism problem of sample units of Vizianagaram, Srikakulam and Visakhapatnam districts is shown in the shape of bar graph given in the next page.

Problem of Strikes

The small scale industrial units suffer heavily with the workers who go on strike for longer period. The particulars of problems faced by small scale industrial units of Vizianagaram, Srikakulam and Visakhapatnam districts due to strikes of workers are shown in table 7.15

Table—7.15 Units Facing Problems Rose out of Strikes in Vizianagaram, Srikakulam and Visakhapatnam Districts

Category of units	*Vizianagaram district*		*Srikakulam district*		*Visakhapatnam district*	
	Sample units	*Problem units*	*Sample units*	*Problem units*	*Sample units*	*Problem units*
Agro based	19	—	26	9 (75.0)	14	3 (14.29)
Forest based	6	—	3	—	17	2 (9.52)
Chemical based	2	—	2	—	11	4 (19.04)
Mineral & Building material based	6	2 (100.00)	3	2 (16.67)	16	8 (38.10)
Engineering & Allied based	3	—	4	1 (8.33)	20	4 (19.04)
Total	36	2 (5.56)	38	12 (31.58)	78	21 (26.92)

Note : Figures in brackets indicate the percentages to the total.

Fortunately only 2 units i.e., 5.56% of Mineral and Building material based category of Vizianagaram district have experienced the problem of strike. But in case of Srikakulam and Visakhapatnam district it is different. 12 units i.e., 31.58% of Srikakulam district and 21 units i.e., 26.92% of Visakhapatnam district have experienced the problem created by the workers through strikes. Out of 12 units in Srikakulam district 9 belong to Agro based category, 2 belong to Mineral and Building material based category and one belongs to Engineering and

GRAPH-18— UNITS FACING ABSENTEEISM PROBLEM IN VIZIANAGARAM, SRIKAKULAM AND VISAKHAPATNAM DISTRICTS

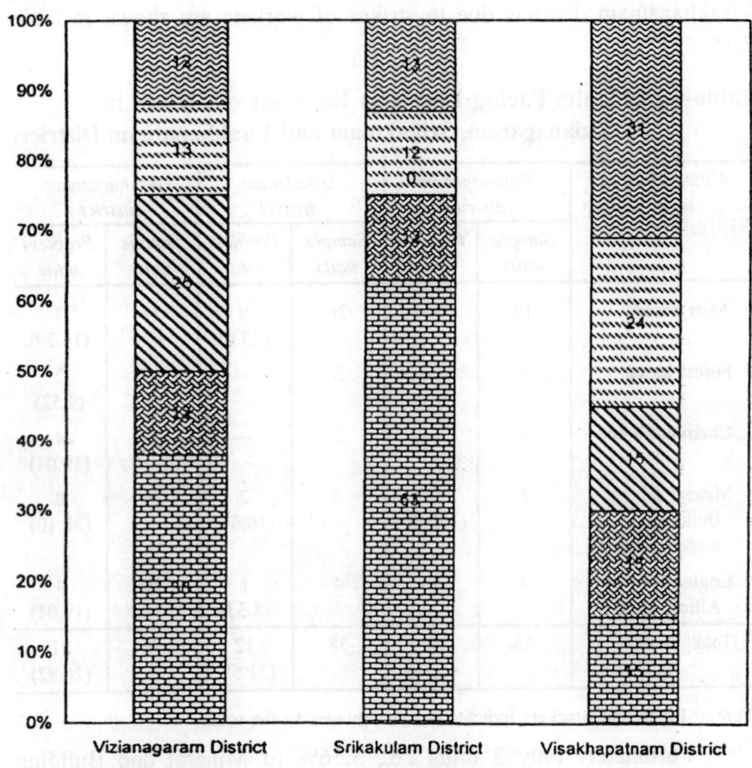

Allied based category,. In Visakhapatnam district out of 21 units 3 are from Agro based category, 2 are from Forest based, Chemical based and 4 each from Chemical and Engineering and Allied based category and 8 are from Mineral and Building material category.

On the whole it can be said nearly 1/3 rd of small scale industrial units in Srikakulam and Visakhapatnam districts have experienced the labour strikes. This problem is negligible in Vizianagaram district. The labour strikes are more in the Mineral and Building material based units of Visakhapatnam district and Agro based units in Srikakulam district when compared to other categories of units.

For an easy understanding the problems raised out of strikes of sample units of Vizianagaram, Srikakulam and Visakhapatnam districts is shown in the shape of bar graph given in the next page.

FINANCIAL PROBLEMS

Any problem of a small scale unit whether it is production problem, labour problem or marketing problem finally turnover to be a problem of finance. That is why the financial problems faced by small scale industrial units occupy prominent place in a study like this. In the following pages the financial problems of sample units of Vizianagaram, Srikakulam and Visakhapatnam districts are comparatively analysed. Table 7.16 shows the brief outlook of sample units financial problems in these three districts.

From the table 7.16 a point to be noted is that all the small scale units in these three districts have not approached the financial agencies like Commercial Banks, Andhra Pradesh State Finance Corporation, SIDBI, friends and relatives, money lenders for financial help. 28 units out of 36 in Vizianagaram district, 26 out of 38 units in Srikakulam district and 59 out of 78 units in Visakhapatnam district have approached different financial agencies for assistance. Because of self-sufficiency, lack of information and lack of interest the remaining units have not approached the agencies. 4 units of Vizianagaram district, 8 units of Srikakulam district and 6 units of Visakhapatnam district are found to be free from any problem while dealing with the financial agencies.

GRAPH-19— UNITS FACING PROBLEM RAISED OUT OF STRIKES IN VIZIANAGARAM, SRIKAKULAM AND VISAKHAPATNAM DISTRICTS

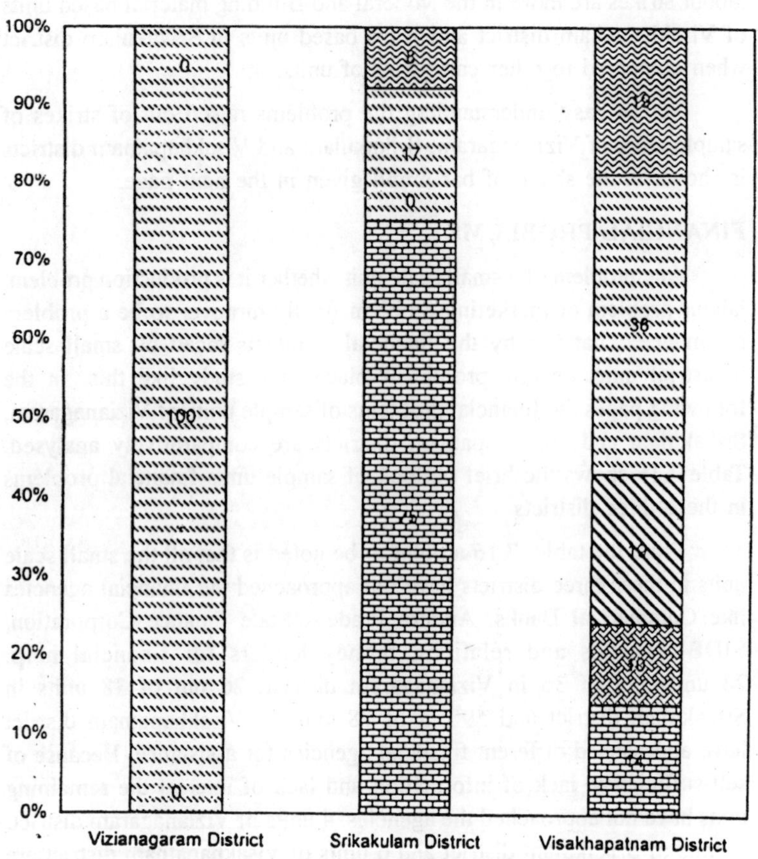

Table—7.16 Financial Problems of Sample Units of Vizianagaram, Srikakulam and Visakhapatnam Districts

District	*Total no.of units*	*No of units approached*	*Secu-rity*	*Delay in sanction*	*Insuffi-cient finance*	*High rate of interest*	*Cumber-some procedure*	*Without problem*
Vizianagaram	36	2 (100.00)	6 (21.42)	8 (28.57)	5 (17.86)	6 (21.42)	4 (14.28)	4 (14.28)
Srikakulam	38	26 (100.00)	9 (34.61)	4 (15.38)	6 (23.07)	5 (19.23	6 (23.07)	8 (30.76)
Visakhapatnam	78	59 (100.00)	14 (23.72)	19 (32.20)	14 (23.72)	1 (01.69)	7 (11.86)	6 (10.17)

Note : Figures in brackets indicate the percentages to the total.

The industrial units have faced the problem of securities, delay in sanction, insufficient finance, high rate of interest and cumbersome procedure while dealing with the financial agencies.

6 units i.e., 21.42% of Vizianagaram district, 9 i.e., 31.61% units of Srikakulam district and 14 i.e., 23.72% units of Visakhapatnam district have experienced the problem of securing while getting as assistance from financial agency particularly the Commercial Banks.

8 units i.e., 28.57% of Vizianagaram district, 4 units i.e., 15.38% of Srikakulam district and 19 units i.e., 32.20% of Visakhapatnam district have experienced the problem of delay in sanctioning financial assistance from financial from Andhra Pradesh State Finance Corporation, Commercial Banks and SIDBI.

5 units i.e., 17.86% of Vizianagaram district, 6 units i.e., 23.07% of Srikakulam district and 14 units i.e., 23.72% units of Visakhapatnam district have felt that the finance received from financial agencies was not sufficient.

6 units i.e., 21.42% of Vizianagaram district, 5 units i.e., 19.23% units of Srikakulam district and one unit i.e., 1.69% of Visakhapatnam district have felt that the rate of interest charged by financial agencies particularly money lenders was high.

4 units i.e., 14.28% of Vizianagaram district, 6 units i.e., 23.07% of Srikakulam district and 7 units i.e., 11.86% units of Visakhapatnam district have opined that the procedure followed by some financial agencies particularly Commercial Banks and Andhra Pradesh State Financial Corporation in sanctioning loans was cumbersome.

For an easy understanding the financial problems of sample units of Vizianagaram, Srikakulam and Visakhapatnam districts is shown in the shape of bar graph given in the next page.

Problem of Security

As said earlier the financial agencies like Commercial Banks Andhra Pradesh State Finance Corporation, SIDBI, demanded security from small entrepreneurs while sanctioning loans. This has become a problem to most of the small entrepreneurs particularly the entrepreneurs with little property. The table 7.17 shows the problem of security faced by the units under the different categories in Vizianagaram, Srikakulam and Visakhapatnam districts.

GRAPH-20— FINANCIAL PROBLEMS OF SAMPLE UNITS IN VIZIANAGARAM, SRIKAKULAM AND VISAKHAPATNAM DISTRICTS

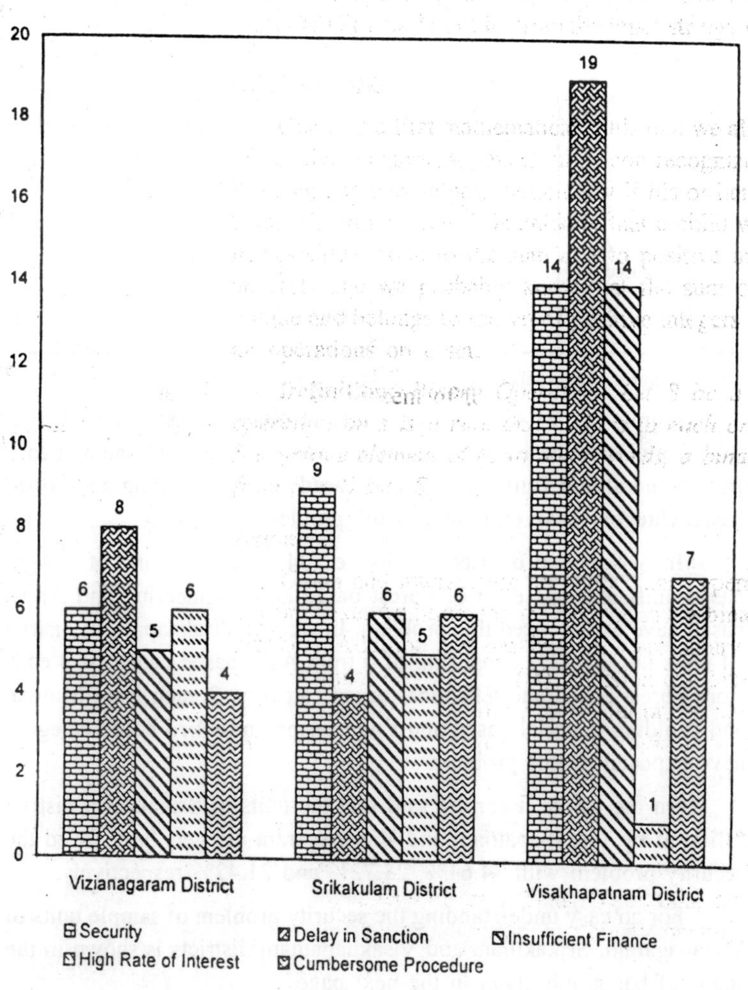

Table—7.17 Security Problem of Sample Units in Vizianagaram, Srikakulam and Visakhapatnam Districts

Category of units	*Vizianagaram district*		*Srikakulam district*		*Visakhapatnam district*	
	Sample units	*Problem units*	*Sample units*	*Problem units*	*Sample units*	*Problem units*
Agro based	16	—	16	7 (77.78)	12	4 (28.59)
Forest based	4	2 (33.34)	2	1 (11.11)	11	3 (21.42)
Chemical based	2	2 (33.34)	2	—	9	3 (21.42)
Mineral & Building material based	4	1 (16.66)	3	—	12	2 (14.28)
Engineering & Allied based	2	1 (16.66)	3	1 (11.11)	15	2 (14.28)
Total	28	6 (21.42)	26	9 (34.61)	59	14 (23.72)

Note : Figures in brackets indicate the percentages to the total.

6 units i.e., 21.42% of Vizianagaram district consisting of 2 units each from Forest based and Chemical based category and one unit each from Mineral and Building material based and Engineering and Allied based category have experienced the problem of security.

In Srikakulam district 9 units i.e., 34.61% consisting of 7 Agro based units and one each of Forest based and Engineering and Allied based have experienced this problem. In case of Visakhapatnam district 14 units i.e., 23.72% consisting of 4 from Agro based category, 3 each from Forest based and Chemical based category, 2 each from Mineral and Building material based and Engineering and allied based category have exposed to this problem.

On the whole it can be said that the units of Srikakulam district followed by Visakhapatnam and Vizianagaram districts have faced the security problem with 34.61%, 23.72% and 21.42% respectively.

For an easy understanding the security problem of sample units of Vizianagaram, Srikakulam and Visakhapatnam districts is shown in the shape of bar graph given in the next page.

GRAPH-21— SECURITY PROBLEMS OF SAMPLE UNITS IN VIZIANAGARAM, SRIKAKULAM AND VISAKHAPATNAM DISTRICTS

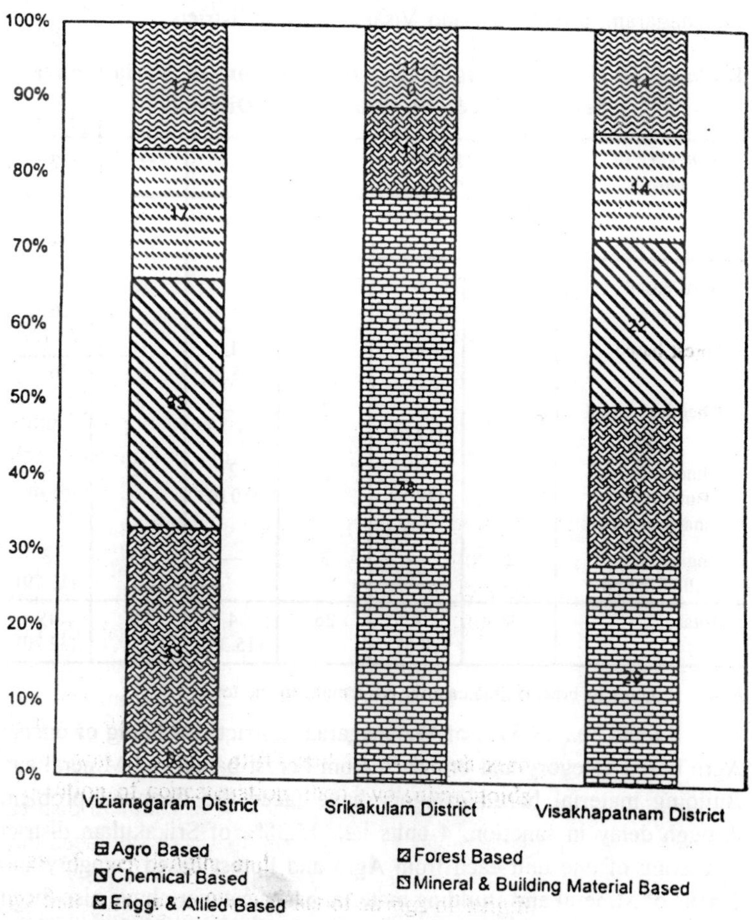

Delay in Sanction

After submitting the applications for financial help by the entrepreneurs some financial agencies particularly Commercial Banks make delay in sanctioning the required amount. This also become a financial problem to the entrepreneurs. Timely finance occupies an important place for smooth running of any plant. The following table 7.18 gives the particulars of this problem faced by the units of the Vizianagaram, srikakulam and Visakhapatnam districts.

Table—7.18 Units Facing Delay in Sanction in Vizianagaram, Srikakulam & Visakhapatnam Districts

Category of units	*Vizianagaram district*		*Srikakulam district*		*Visakhapatnam district*	
	Sample units	*Problem units*	*Sample units*	*Problem units*	*Sample units*	*Problem units*
Agro based	16	6 (75.0)	16	1 (25.0)	12	5 (26.32)
Forest based	4	—	2	1 (25.0)	11	5 (26.32)
Chemical based	2	1 (12.5)	2	—	9	2 (10.52)
Mineral & Building material based	4	1 (12.5)	3	2 (50.0)	12	4 (21.05)
Engineering & Allied based	2	—	3	—	15	3 (15.79)
Total	28	8 (28.57)	26	4 (15.38)	59	19 (32.20)

Note : Figures in brackets indicate the percentage to the total

8 units i.e., 28.57% of Vizianagaram district consisting of 6 from Agro based category and one each from Forest based and Mineral and Building material based category have faced the financial problem through delay in sanction. 4 units i.e., 15.38% of Srikakulam district consisting of one unit each from Agro and Forest based category and 2 units of Mineral and Building material based category have also faced this problem. In case of Visakhapatnam district 19 units i.e., 32.20% consisting of 5 units each in Agro and Forest based category and 2 units from Chemical based category 4 units from Mineral and Building material

based category and 3 units from Engineering and Allied based category have suffered financially due to delay in sanction.

On the whole 32.20% of small scale units of Visakhapatnam district followed by 28.57% units of Vizianagaram district and 15.38% units of Srikakulam district have suffered financially because of delay in sanction by the financial agencies.

For an easy understanding the delay in sanction of sample units of Vizianagaram, Srikakulam and Visakhapatnam districts is shown in the shape of bar graph given in the next page.

Insufficient Finance

Most of the times all most all the financial agencies used to sanction only a part of the required finance to the small scale industrial units. Similar the case with the units of these three districts. Table 7.19 shows the number of units of different categories of Vizianagaram, Srikakulam and Visakhapatnam districts facing the problem of insufficient finance. Though these units got financial help from the agencies they felt that the finance received by them was not sufficient for their requirement.

Table—7.19 Units Facing Insufficient Finance in Vizianagaram, Srikakulam and Visakhapatnam Districts

Category of units	*Vizianagaram district*		*Srikakulam district*		*Visakhapatnam district*	
	Sample units	*Problem units*	*Sample units*	*Problem units*	*Sample units*	*Problem units*
Agro based	16	3 (60.0)	16	4 (66.68)	12	3 (21.43)
Forest based	4	—	2	—	11	3 (21.43)
Chemical based	2	1 (20.0)	2	1 (16.66)	9	4 (28.58)
Mineral & Building material based	4	—	3	—	12	2 (14.28)
Engineering & Allied based	2	1 (20.0)	3	1 (16.66)	15	2 (14.28)
Total	28	5 (17.86)	26	6 (23.07)	59	14 (23.72)

Note : Figures in brackets indicate the percentages to the total

GRAPH-22— UNITS FACING DELAY IN SANCTION IN VIZIANAGARAM, SRIKAKULAM AND VISAKHAPATNAM DISTRICTS

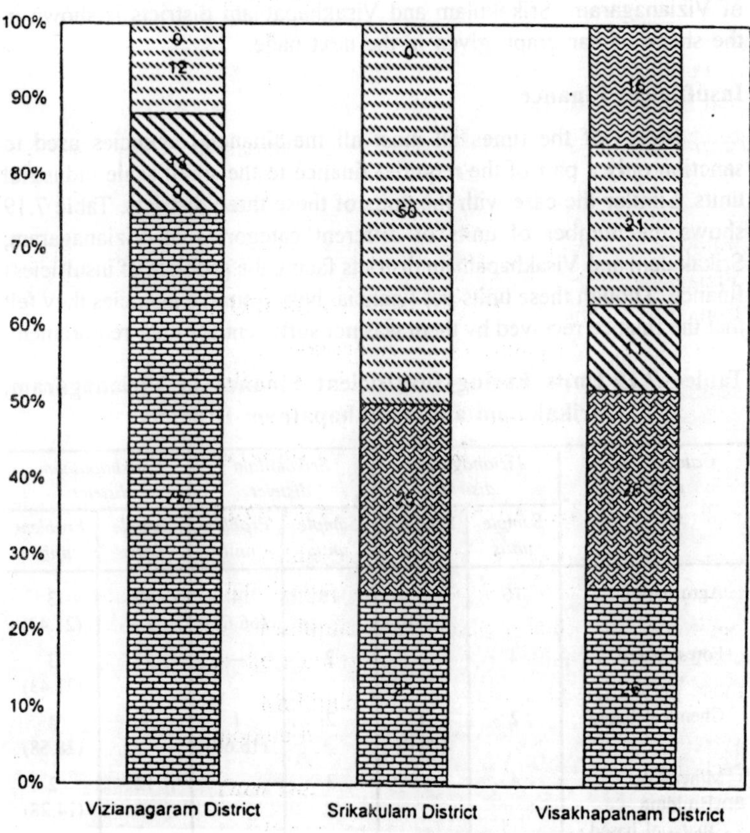

5 units i.e., 17.86% of Vizianagaram district consisting of 3 from Agro based category and one each from Chemical and Engineering and Allied based category have opined that the financial loans received by them were not after with their requirements. 6 units i.e., 37.5% in Srikakulam district consisting of 4 units of Agro based category and one each from Chemical and Engineering and Allied based category have expressed the feeling of insufficient finance received by them from financial agencies. Similarly 14 units i.e., 23.72% of Visakhapatnam district consisting of 3 each from Agro based and Forest based category, 4 units from Chemical based category and 2 units each from Mineral and Building material based category and Engineering and Allied based category have also felt that the loan amounts sanctioned by the financial agency is not sifficient for their requirement.

On the whole it can be said 23.72% units of Visakhapatnam district followed by 23.07% units of Srikakulam district and 17.86% units of Vizianagaram district have experienced insufficient financial sanctions from their financial agencies.

For an easy understanding the insufficient finance problem of sample units of Vizianagaram, Srikakulam and Visakhapatnam districts is shown in the shape of bar graph given in the next page.

High Rate of Interest

High rate of interest charged by financial agencies particularly the money lenders also create financial problem to the small scale units. As said in the 5th chapter the m-2 charge exorbitant rate of interest on this loans. At times the Andhra Pradesh State Finance Corporation also charge heavy penalties in case of delay in repayments. Table 7.20 gives these particulars.

6 units i.e., 21.42% of Vizianagaram district consisting of 2 units each from Agro based and Mineral and Building material based category and 1 unit each from Forest based and Engineering and Allied based category have felt that the rate of interest charged by the financial agencies were exorbitant.

5 units i.e., 19.23% of Srikakulam district consisting of 3 Agro based units and one unit each from Chemical and Engineering and Allied based category have also felt on similar lines. Only one unit of Mineral and Building material based category of Visakhapatnam district

GRAPH-23— NITS FACING INSUFFICIENT FINANCE IN VIZIANAGARAM, SRIKAKULAM AND VISAKHAPATNAM DISTRICTS

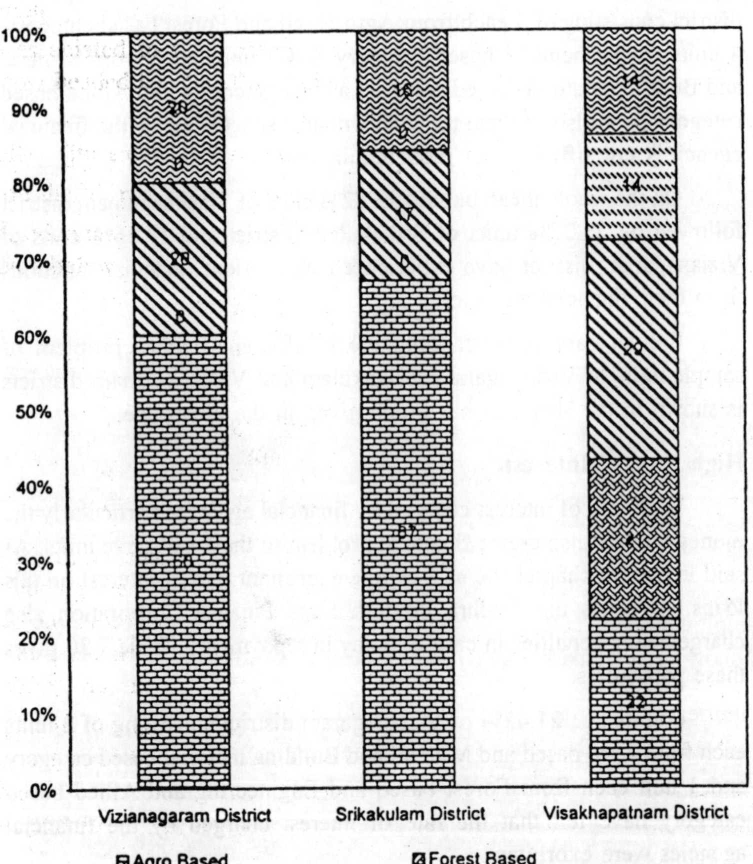

was in the opinion (1.69%) of high rate of interest on its loan taken from money lenders and friends and relatives. On the whole 21.42% units of Vizianagaram district, followed by 19.23% units of Srikakulam district and only one unit of Visakhapatnam district have felt high rate of interest that are charged by money lenders in particular.

Table—7.20 Units Facing High Rate of Interest in Vizianagaram, Srikakulam and Visakhapatnam Districts

Category of units	*Vizianagaram district*		*Srikakulam district*		*Visakhapatnam district*	
	Sample units	*Problem units*	*Sample units*	*Problem units*	*Sample units*	*Problem units*
Agro based	16	2 (33.34)	16	3 (60.00)	12	—
Forest based	4	1 (16.66)	2	—	11	—
Chemical based	2	—	2	1 (20.00)	9	—
Mineral & Building material based	4	2 (33.34)	3	—	12	1 (100.00)
Engineering & Allied based	2	1 (16.66)	3	1 (20.00)	15	—
Total	28	6 (21.42)	26	5 (19.23)	59	1 (100.00)

Note : Figures in brackets indicate the percentages to the total

For an easy understanding the high rate of interest problem of sample units of Vizianagaram, Srikakulam and Visakhapatnam districts is shown in the shape of bar graph given in the next page.

Cumbersome Procedure

The small entrepreneurs some times felt that the procedure to be followed while applying for financial assistance from organised sources like Commercial Banks, State Finance Corporations, SIDBI and NSIC was cumbersome. Table 7.21 gives the details of small scale industrial units of three districts facing the problem, because of cumbersome procedure adopted by financial agencies.

GRAPH-24— UNITS FACING HIGH RATE OF INTEREST IN VIZIANAGARAM, SRIKAKULAM AND VISAKHAPATNAM DISTRICTS

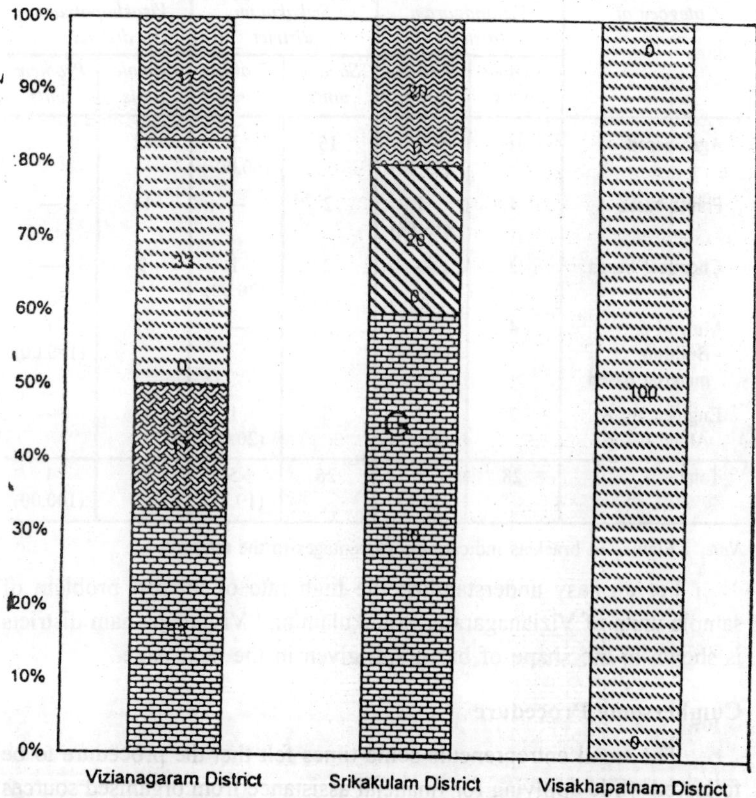

GRAPH-25— UNITS FACING THE PROBLEM OF CUMBERSOME PROCEDURE IN VIZIANAGARAM, SRIKAKULAM AND VISAKHAPATNAM DISTRICTS

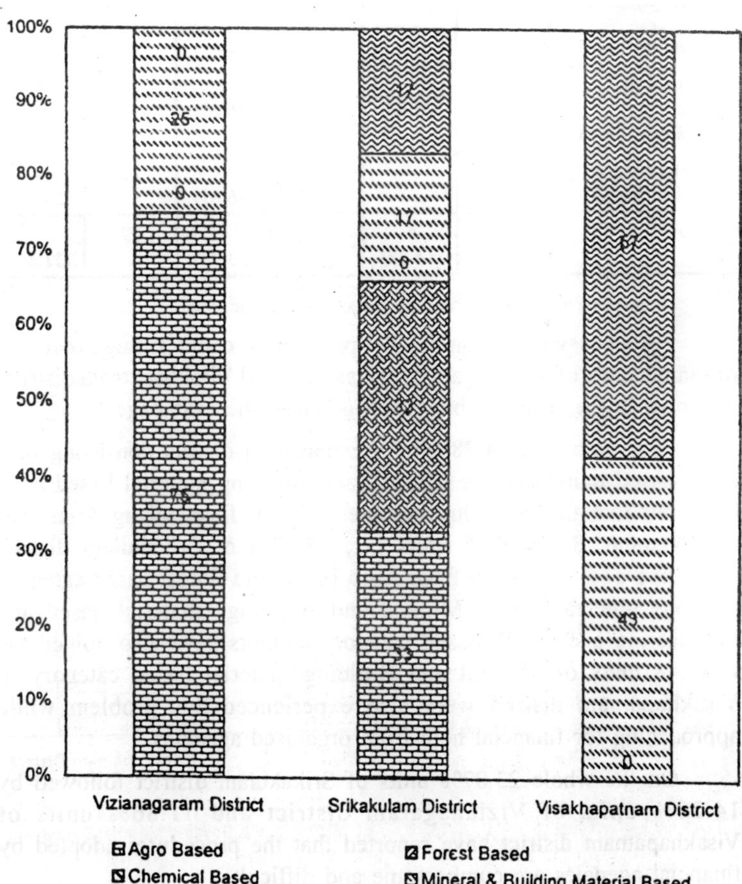

Table—7.21 Units Facing the Problem of Cumbersome Procedure in Vizianagaram, Srikakulam and Visakhapatnam Districts

Category of units	*Vizianagaram district*		*Srikakulam district*		*Visakhapatnam district*	
	Sample units	*Problem units*	*Sample units*	*Problem units*	*Sample units*	*Problem units*
Agro based	16	3 (75.00)	16	2 (33.33)	12	—
Forest based	4	—	2	2 (33.33)	11	—
Chemical based	2	—	2	—	9	—
Mineral & Building material based	4	1 (25.00)	3	1 (16.67)	12	3 (42.86)
Engineering & Allied based	2	—	3	1 (16.67)	15	4 (57.14)
Total	28	4 (14.28)	26	6 (23.07)	59	7 (11.86)

Note : Figures in brackets indicate the percentages to the total

For an easy understanding the problem of cumbersome procedure of sample units of Vizianagaram, Srikakulam and Visakhapatnam districts is shown in the shape of bar graph given in the next page.

Four units i.e., 14.28% of Vizianagaram district consisting of 3 Agro based units and one Mineral and Building material based units have felt that the procedure adopted by the financial agencies was cumbersome. Similarly 6 units i.e., 23.07% of Srikakulam district consisting of 2 units each from Agro based and Forest based category and one unit each from Mineral and Building material based and Engineering and Allied based category of units have also opined the same. 3 units of Mineral and Building material based category in Visakhapatnam district were also experienced this problem while approaching for financial help from organised agencies.

On the whole 23.07% units of Srikakulam district followed by 14.28% units of Vizianagaram district and 11.86% units of Visakhapatnam district have reported that the procedures adopted by financial agencies are cumbersome and difficult.

CHAPTER—VIII

FINDINGS, CONCLUSIONS AND SUGGESTIONS

The various purposes of this chapter are to draw major findings and conclusions of the study and to suggest suitable measures to the small entrepreneurs and other relevant agencies based on the findings and conclusions made out in the study.

MAJOR FINDINGS

The major findings of the study are as follows:

1. The growth of small scale industrial units in the state of Andhra Pradesh in the recent past has been significant. The available literature on the industrial front of Andhra Pradesh denotes that the state has a sound infrastructural facilities. These facilities are not only adequate for the existing industrial units but also sufficient to the units to be setup in the near future.

2. The state ranks fourth in industrial investment in the country. There are also a good number of small industry promoting agencies functioning in the state. They have made a mark in the development of the state industrially.

3. The state government of Andhra Pradesh is offering attractive incentives to the enthusiastic small entrepreneurs in establishing and running the units.

4. From the analysis of the data obtained from sample units, it is found that the growth was different in different categories of small units in Vizianagaram, Srikakulam and Visakhapatnam districts.

In Vizianagaram district the growth of small scale industrial units doubled and reached to 464 in a short span of one and half decades.

Srikakulam district though a backward one, the growth of small scale units is almost at par with Vizianagaram district. This is mainly due to benefits given by the Central Government declaring it as a backward district up to year 1993.

Total number of small scale units in Visakhapatnam district had more than what Vizianagaram and Srikakulam districts together have. Availability of infrastructure facilities in the district as a whole and in Visakhapatnam district in particular and concentration of many large industries fetches a lot for establishment of more small scale units in Visakhapatnam district when compared to other two districts.

5. Because of vast agricultural land, agricultural products and the rice mills, dall mills, jute mills, floor mills etc are established, and the number of Agro based units in Vizianagaram and Srikakulam districts are more when compared to Visakhapatnam district. Because of concentration of large number of Engineering and Allied based units in Visakhapatnam district they occupied 1/4th of the total sample units.
6. Capital structure of small scale units in Vizianagaram, Srikakulam and Visakhapatnam districts witnessed vast variances. The differences in size of total capital exist not only different category of units but also between different units in the same category.
7. In Vizianagaram district 15 units (41.66%) out of 36 healthy units have more than Rs. 75 lakhs investment.

   In Srikakulam district 25 units i.e. 65.78% out of 38 healthy units have below Rs. 50 lakhs investment category.

   In Visakhapatnam district 47 units i.e. 60.25% out of 78 healthy units have investment in the range between Rs. 50 lakhs and Rs. 75 lakhs.
8. The ratio of total fixed capital in total productive capital is high in Agro based units of Vizianagaram and Srikakulam districts and in Mineral and Building material based units of Visakhapatnam district.

9. The ratio of fixed capital to total capital is high in Engineering and Allied based units of Vizianagaram, Srikakulam and Visakhapatnam districts, and the ratio of working capital to total capital is high in Chemical based units of Vizianagaram, Srikakulam and Visakhapatnam districts.
10. The borrowed capital plays an important role in the development of small scale industrial units in Vizianagaram, Srikakulam and Visakhapatnam districts with 40 per cent, 30 per cent and 51 per cent respectively.
11. It is observed that capacity utilisation is varied in different category of units in different years. Much of the capacity is found to be idle in several units.
12. The capacity utilisation was as its maximum in all categories of units in Vizianagaram and Srikakulam districts during 1991-92 . In Visakhapatnam district this type of situations was observed during 1995-96. The capacity utilisation of Chemical based units in these three districts ranges between 50-60 per cent.
13. Almost all the small scale industrial units in Vizianagaram, Srikakulam and Visakhapatnam districts have been facing one problem or the other and thus they are not working to their fullest capacity.
14. Shortage of finances, lack of demand, labour problems, shortages of raw-materials, shortages in power supply, etc., are found to be the major reasons for the idle capacity in small scale industrial units of these three districts.
15. During the period of the study more than 50 per cent of total production was contributed by Agro based units in Vizianagaram and Srikakulam districts. In Visakhapatnam district the Agro based units contributed similarly in the last two years only.

    The Mineral and Building material based units and the Forest based units have contributed much to the total production when compared to other categories of units during the first two years and third year of the study respectively.
16. The average production is found to be the highest in Mineral and Building material based units during the period of the study in Vizianagaram, Srikakulam and Visakhapatnam districts.

Whereas in Visakhapatnam district the average production of Mineral and Building material units was high during the first two years.

The average production in Engineering and Allied based category units of these three districts was lower when compared to other category of units in the respective districts.

17. It is found from the study that small scale industrial units of these three districts have been suffering from several problems which hamper their growth. It is found that no single unit is free from problems and every unit is hit by some problem or the other based on its size and structure.
18. The important problems experienced by them are production, labour, marketing, finance and sickness.
19. It is found that 66.66% of units in Vizianagaram district, 68.42% of units in Srikakulam district, and 79.21% of units in Visakhapatnam district have suffering from shortage of inputs such as raw-materials, power supply and breakdown in machines and equipment.
20. 24% of the total units in Visakhapatnam district are facing shortage of raw-materials. The units of Vizianagaram and Srikakulam districts though facing the problems of raw-material the severity when compared to Visakhapatnam district is less.
21. The overall power shortage in the state mainly during the summer season affected many of the small scale industrial units in these Vizianagaram, Srikakulam and Visakhapatnam districts.
22. The Agro based units in Vizianagaram and Srikakulam districts, the Engineering and Allied based units in Visakhapatnam district on a whole seemed to be suffered reasonably due to machinery troubles.
23. Most of the industrial units of Vizianagaram, Srikakulam and Visakhapatnam districts have been facing problems in marketing their products. Lack of demand consisting of competition, seasonal fluctuations and poor quality and government policy are the aspects affecting in marketing their products.
24. Nearly 50% of the sample units in Visakhapatnam district and nearly 25% of sample units in Vizianagaram districts are facing competition in marketing their products.

25. Mineral and Building material based units of Vizianagaram district Agro based units of Srikakulam district and Forest and Engineering and Allied based units of Visakhapatnam district are facing more competition when compared to other categories of units in their respective districts.
26. Around 8% of the sample units in Vizianagaram, Srikakulam and Visakhapatnam districts are said to be affected by seasonal fluctuations.
27. On the whole nearly 30% of the units in Visakhapatnam district are facing the quality problems followed by Vizianagaram and Srikakulam district with 16.66% and 10.52% respectively.
28. Shortage of labour, labour turnover, absenteeism and strikes cause labour problems in small scale units of Vizianagaram, Srikakulam and Visakhapatnam districts.
29. 10 units from Vizianagaram district, 6 units from Srikakulam district and 38 units from Visakhapatnam district have experienced more than one problem relating to labour.
30. 50% of units in Vizianagaram district, 47.43% of units in Visakhapatnam district and 31.58% of units in Srikakulam district have faced the problem of labour supply. In Srikakulam district when compared to Vizianagaram and Visakhapatnam districts the severity of the problem is some what less.
31. The percentage of labour turnover in these 3 districts ranges between 15% to 21%.
32. Except Chemical based units all the units in these three districts have the problem of absenteeism.
33. Nearly 1/3rd of small scale industrial units in Srikakulam and Visakhapatnam districts have experienced the labour strikes. The labour strikes are more in the Mineral and Building material based units of Visakhapatnam district and Agro based units in Srikakulam district when compared to other categories of units.
34. The small industrial units have faced the problem of security, delay in sanction, insufficient finance, high rate of interest and cumbersome procedure while dealing with the financial agencies.

35. The units of Srikakulam district, followed by Visakhapatnam and Vizianagaram districts have faced the security problem with 36.41%, 23.72%, and 21.42% respectively.
36. 32.20% of small scale units of Visakhapatnam district followed by 28.57% unit of Vizianagaram district and 15.38% units of Srikakulam district have suffered financially because of delay in sanction by the financial agencies.
37. 23.72% units of Visakhapatnam district followed by 23.07% units of Srikakulam district, 17.86% units of Vizianagaram district have experienced insufficient finances from their financial agencies.
38. 21.42% units of Vizianagaram district, followed by 19.23% units of Srikakulam district and only one unit of Visakhapatnam district have felt high rate of interest that are charged by unorganised financial agencies.
39. The procedure to be followed while applying for financial assistance from organised sources like Commercial Banks, State Finance Corporation and SIDBI was cumbersome.
40. It is observed that sickness has assumed in alarming proportion in small scale sector. And it has become a big challenge not only to the management but also to the Government, trade unions, banks and other financial agencies.
41. The rate of sickness in the country in general and the state of Andhra Pradesh in particular is about 11%.
42. The sickness in small scale sector in Visakhapatnam district is in alarming proportion with 22% followed by Vizianagaram district with 18.18% and Srikakulam district with 13.63%.
43. The highest percentage of sickness in Vizianagaram district is in Forest based and Engineering and Allied based category with each 25%, in Srikakulam district the highest percentage of sickness in Mineral and Building material based category with 25%, whereas in Visakhapatnam district also the highest sickness is in Mineral and Building material based category with 27.27%.
44. Out of the total capital of sick units 45.56% and 55.81% were blocked only in Agro based units of Vizianagaram and Srikakulam districts respectively.

45. The sick units of these Vizianagaram, Srikakulam and Visakhapatnam district borrowed funds from Commercial Banks, Andhra Pradesh State Finance Corporation, moneylenders, friends and relatives.
46. The main reason for sickness in Vizianagaram, Srikakulam and Visakhapatnam districts are financial problems followed by marketing, labour and production problems.

CONCLUSIONS

From the above major findings of the study the following conclusions are drawn:

1. The growth of small scale industrial units in the state of Andhra Pradesh in the recent past has been significant.
2. The growth was different in different categories of units in Vizianagaram, Srikakulam and Visakhapatnam districts.
3. Availability of infrastructure facilities and concentration of many large industries fetches a lot for establishment of more small scale industrial units in Visakhapatnam district when compared to Vizianagaram and Srikakulam districts.
4. The capital based of small scale industrial units on an average is high in Visakhapatnam district followed by Vizianagaram and Srikakulam districts.
5. The borrowed capital plays an important role in the development of small scale industrial units in Vizianagaram, Srikakulam and Visakhapatnam districts.
6. Considerable amount of installed capacity is idle in many industrial units of these districts due to the problems of shortage of finance, lack of demand labour problems, shortage of raw-materials, shortage of power supply etc.,
7. The small scale industrial units of Vizianagaram, Srikakulam and Visakhapatnam districts have been suffering from problems like production, marketing, labour, financial and sickness. Every unit is hit by some problem or the other.
8. The small scale industrial units of these three districts faced production problems due to shortage of raw-materials, shortage of power supply and machinery breakdowns.

9. Lack of demand consisting of competition, seasonal fluctuations and poor quality, and Government policy are the aspects affecting in marketing the products of small scale industrial units of Vizianagaram, Srikakulam and Visakhapatnam districts.
10. Shortage of labour, labour turnover, absenteeism and strikes cause problems in small scale units of Vizianagaram, Srikakulam and Visakhapatnam districts.
11. Most of the small scale industrial units of these three districts have been facing financial problems mainly due to security, delay in sanction, insufficient finance, high rate of interest and cumbersome procedure.
12. The sickness in small scale industrial units of these three districts is in alarming proportion ranging from 13-22% when compared to state average of 11%. This sickness was caused due to financial, marketing, labour, production and managerial problems.

SUGGESTIONS

The following suggestions are made to resolve the various issues of small scale industrial units. The suggestions are given categorically to the government, to the financial agencies, and to small entrepreneurs.

To the Government

1. Both the Central and State Governments should give wide publicity so as to reach the information to all the small entrepreneurs about policies, incentives, schemes, programmes, etc., relating to small scale units.
2. The small industry promoting agencies should take care of the well being of small enterprises and they should initiate such measures which would result in the further promotion and smooth functioning of small scale industrial units.
3. The reorientation programmes, workshops and seminars should be organised at district level to provide latest information, and training to the small entrepreneurs on small scale industries.
4. The industries department may appoint *a specialised small industries task force* at every Mandal headquarters level consisting of 3 or 4 technically qualified experts for continuous monitoring of small industrial units.

5. The district industries centers should be restructured in such a way that they are suitable for changing requirements of the present small scale enterprises. The raw-material servicing centers, and entrepreneurs guidance cell should be made more effective.

6. The government may think of giving concessions to small entrepreneurs in regard to licence fees, land conversion fees, electrical line fixation charges, etc.

Sickness

7. The Government may appoint a special task force specially for diagnose the symptoms of sickness at district level consisting of 3 or 4 technically, financially and professionally qualified people for continuous monitoring the poor performance of small industrial units.

8. The Government should take proper and speedy steps to revive the viable units which have fallen sick.

To Banks and Financial Agencies

9. The Commercial Banks and financial agencies may establish more small scale industrial specialised branches atleast one in every mandal headquarters either independently or in association with SIDBI to cater the financial needs of small entrepreneurs.

10. The banks may follow liberal procedures in regard to security while sanctioning loans to small scale industrial units.

11. The banks and financial agencies may reduce the cumbersome procedure and also reduce the processing fees, other servicing charges like valuers fees, documentation charges, legal consultants fees etc., to a reasonable extent. For easy understanding the banks and financial agencies should supply all types of loan applications in regional languages.

12. The banks and financial agencies must provide timely, needy and sufficient finance to the small entrepreneurs.

13. The banks and financial agencies must reduce the delay in sanction and disbursement of loan amounts to small scale industrial units.

To Entrepreneurs

14. The small entrepreneurs should develop a proper business plan before starting a unit.
15. The small entrepreneurs should employ latest techniques of production, skilled labour so as to improve the quality of the product and marketing. They always initiate such measures which would protect the well-being of the workers so as to avoid labour troubles.
16. The entrepreneurs should take proper training through the government agencies before starting a unit, this enables the entrepreneurs to protect their units from sickness.
17. As the competition is found to be a major problem in may units, the small entrepreneurs should try to divert to less competitive areas and before they venture they should analyse the demand. They should make feasibility studies before they finalise their products. In a nut shell they should undertake only such projects which are technically competent, operationally feasible, and economically viable.
18. Severe penalties may be levied on entrepreneurs found misusing the funds or otherwise seeking financial assistance by underhand means, preventive measures should be taken to provide a check on the malpractices of small units.

SELECT BIBLIOGRAPHY

BOOKS AND RESEARCH WORKS

Apparao.B., *Small Enterprise Promotion in Andhra Pradesh: Role of Andhra Pradesh State Financial Corporation.* 2V. 1981. 828, 144P Thesis: Andhra University, Nassdoc.

Bakshi, B.S., *Problems of Innovations in Small Scale and Cottage Industries of J & K State*, 1980. 209P. Thesis : Jammu University, Nassdoc.

Balakrishna, G., *Financing Small Scale Industries in India*, 1950-52. Poona, Gokhle Institute of Politics and Economics, 1972.

Brahmi, S., *Modern Small Industry: A Whell within a Wheel*, 1979, 295P. Research Project Sponsored By Icssr Nassdoc

Bell, D., *Coming of Post-Industrial Society: A Venture in Social Forecasting.* New Delhi, Arnold Heinemann, 1974. 507P, Nassdoc

Carr, Marilyn, *Developing Small Scale Industries in India: An Integrated Approach: The Experience of the Birla Institute of Technology's Small Industry Scheme.* London, Intermediate Tech. Pub., 1981, 1x, 87P

Desai, Vasant, *Problems and Prospects of Small Scale Industries in India.*, Bombay, Himalaya, 1983. 338P

Deshpande, M.U., *Small Scale Industrial Entrepreneurship in a Developing Region*, 1979. 440P. Thesis: Marathwada University, Nassdoc.

Gopal Swaroop, *Advances to Small Industries and Small Borrowers (A Practical Guide).* New Delhi, Sultan Chand, N.D. 475P

Hattangdi, Anil, *Bankers Handbook on Small Scale Industries. Bombay, I.B.H.* New Delhi 197P

India. Cantral Small Scale Industry Organization. *Financing of Small Scale Industries in India (With Special Reference Second Plan Period)*, New Delhi, The Author, 1964. 170P.

Iyer, T.N. Krishna, *Guidelines for Financing of Small Scale Industries*, Bombay, 1976, 147P

Jain, O.P., *Small Industries Exports. A Study into Promotional Techniques*, Delhi, S. Chand, 1970. 326P. *Small Industry Exports*, Delhi, S. Chand, 1971. 842P

Jain, S.C. , *Institutional Finance for Small Scale Industries in U.P*, Since 1956, 1971, 438P. Thesis: Agra University

Kaveri, V.S., *Financial Ratios as Predictors of Borrowers Health with Reference to Small Scale Industries in India,* New Delhi, Sultan Chand, 1980. 232P

Krishna Iyer, T.N., *Guidelines for Financing of Small Scale Industries*, Bombay, Vora, 1976.

Mishra, J.N., *Small Scale and Cottage Industries in Saugar District. Saugar*, University of Saugar, N.D. 159P

Murthy, P.L.N.V.S.S.G.K., *Financing of Small Scale Industry in Rayalaseema*, 1980, 483P. Thesis: Sri Venkateswara University

Navrang, Suderan Lal, *Loans to Small Industries and Small Borrowers*, Bombay, Asia, 1976. 222P

Nanjundan, S. and Others, *Economic Research for Small and Industry Development Illustrated by India's Experience*, New Delhi, Asia, 1962. 316P. Nassdoc

Oommen, M.A., *Small Industry in Indian Economic Growth: A Case Study of Kerala, Delhi*, The Author, 1972. 193P. Nassdoc

Pareek, H.S., *Financing of Small Scale Industries in a Developing Economy*, New Delhi, National, 1978, 279P, Nassdoc

Panchaskaraiah, Hire Nath, *Problem of Sickness in Small Scale Industry: A Comparative Sociological Study of Eight Small Industrial Units in Bangalore*, 1981, Xxii, 208P. Thesis: Indian Institute of Technology, Kanpur.

Pareek, H.S., *Financing of Small Scale Industries in a Developing Economy,* New Delhi, National, 1978. 279P, Nassdoc

Parikh, Suryakant M., *How to Finance Small Business Enterprises*, Delhi, Maconillan, 1977. 335P.

Ramana, K.V., *Report on Structure and Working of Unorganised Sector in the Visakhapatnam City*, N.D. 369P. Research Project Sponsored by ICSSR

Rao, R.V., *Small Industry and the Developing Economy in India*, New Delhi, Concept, 1979, 210P.

Roy, P.N. and Chattopadhyay, R., *Small and Big Industries, their Relations and Inter Relations*, 1979, 27P. Research Project Sponsored by ICSSR

Ramakrishna, K.T., *Finances for Small Scale Industry in India*, Bombay, Asia, 1962. Xii, 77P

Tulsi, S.K., *Incentives for Small Scale Industries: An Evaluation*, Delhi, Kunj, 1980 Xii, 134P.

Sudershan Lal, *Loans to Small Industries and Small Borrowers*, Delhi, Navrang, 1976, 222P.

ARTICLES :

Acharya, Dhanraj, *Sick Industries in Small Sector,* Mainstream 15(33) 16 April, 1977, P. 11-12.

Ambastha, C.K., **Small Scale Industries,* Rural India 34(5) May 1971 P 76-79.

Banik, Sunil, *Small Industry and Decentralised*, Janata (Republic Day Number) 34 (1), 1979, P.27-29.

Bedbak, H.K.,*Export Strategy of Small Scale Industries in India,* Indian Journal of Commerce, 33(4), December, 1980, P 25-36.

Bhargava. R.K., *Importance of Small-Scale Industry,* Commerce (Supplement), 124 (3190), 24 June, 1972, P 31-32.

Big Ideas on the Tiny Sector, Editorial, Capital 179 (4493), 15 December, 1977, P 818-19.

Buchale, Robert. B., *Role of Small Business Entrepreneur,* Productivity 12(1), April-June, 1971, P 27-33.

Credit Facilities for Small Scale Industries, Economic Trends, B(22), 16 November, 1979, P 5-8.

Exports by Small Scale Units, Link 19(37), 24 April 1977, P20,

Ghosh, Biswanath, *The Role of Low Investment, High, Employment: Small Industries in our Development,* Yojana, 17(9), 1 June 1973, P 371-76.

How to Help Small Units to Promote their Exports, Capital, 168 (4209), 13 April 1972 P 1054-55.

Institutionalisation of Small Industry Exports, Foreign Trade Review, 13(1), April-June 1978, P 1-24.

Large Vs Small Scale Industries, Financial Express, 21 July, 1979, P4: 3-8

Kumar, M., *Small Industries Policy Needs National Thinking.* Mainstream, 17(2) 18 November 1978 P 15-17.

Let Small Units Proliferate. Eastern Economist 72(16) 20, April 1979 P 802-04.

Parameshwaran, K.P., *Some Basic Problems in the Way of Development of Small Scale Ancillary Industries.* Productivity 15(2) July-September 1974, P 194-98.

Ramachandaran, C., *Development of Small Industries in Tamil Nadu.* Journal of Industry and Trade 28(11-12) November-December 1978, P 55-56.

Rao, M.N., *Rural and Small Scale Industries in Indian Economy.* Kurukshetra 25(12), 16 March 1977, P14-15.

Rele, Subhash J., *Small Scale Sector: Barriers to Growth.* Eastern Economist, 73(7) 17 August 1979, P 53-54.

Shetty, P. Bhoja, *Promising Scope for Small Industries.* Commerce (Supplement) 139 (3562) 22 September 1979, P 20-21.

Small Scale Industries. Eastern Economist (Supplement) 55(16) October 1970 P 57-60.

Small Scale Industries in Andhra Pradesh. Thought 24(32), 5 August 1972, P 9.

Bundaram, C.R., *The Story of Small-Scale Industries.* Integrated Management Vol. 75, July 1972, P 19-23.

Vankata Reddy, M. And Vasudeva Rao, D., *The Progress of Small Scale Industries.* Eastern Economist, 62(15) 12 April 1974, P 740-50.

Ambastha, A.V., *Small Scale Industries vis-a-vis Property, Unemployment and Inequality in India.* Economic Studies 12(11) May 1972, P 585-87: 12(12) June 1972, P 640-44.

Jolan, Bimal, *Production in Tiny, Small and Large Scale Sectors: A Note.* Economic and Political Weekly 13(20) 20 May 2978, P 852-54.

Ramanathan, N.L. and Mathew, Thomas, *Small Industries and the Environment.* Indian Management, 17(8) August 1978 P 9-12

Shaligram, K.R., *Economic Performance of Small and Ancillary Units.* Productivity 22(1) April-June 1981 P 63-70.

Asthane, A.R., *Sickness in Small Scale Industries.* Management Acciybtabt, 15 (6) June 1980 P 253+

Bharadwaj, V.P. and Upadhyaya, D.V., *Some Employment Aspects of Small Scale Industries in India: A Cross Sectional Analysis.* Anvesak 11(1-2) June-December 1981, P 415-25.

Chandha, Chetan, *The Growth of Small Scale Industries.* Yojana 22(21) 16, November 1978, P 21-22.

Dalmia, S.N., *Development of Small Scale Industries.* Management Accountant 17(3) March 1982 P 163-64.

Hashim, S.R., *Input and Output Structure of Small-Scale Industries.* Artha-Vikas 15 (1) January-June 1979 P 15-26.

How Large is Small? Economic and Political Weekly 15(31), 2 August 1980, P. 1287-88.

Institutionalization of Small Industry Exports. Foreign Trade Review 13(1) April-June 1978, P 1-24

Jha, S.M., *Promoting Small Industries to Reduce Rural Poverty.* Kurukshetra 30(4) 16 November 1981, P 12-14.

Lodi, M.A.K., *Nucleus Industrial Complexes: The Concept and Challenge.* Economic Times (Supplement) 28 April 1982 P2: 1-4: Sedme 8(3) September 1981 P 167-82.

Mishra, G.P. and Mishra, P.N., *Government Policies for Promoting Small Scale Industries.* Goa Chamber of Commerce and Industry Bulletin 10 October 1979 P 9-21.

Mitra, S. and Ganguly, P.K., *Role of Small Units.* Capital 186(4649) 23 March 1981 P 2-4.

Mukherjee, Neela and Mukherjee Amitave, *Economics of Small Scale Industries: Emphasis On Efficiency Dimension,* Yojana 24(7) 16 April 1980 P 24-37.

Narain, Ram and Bhojwai H.R., *Technological Needs of Small Scale Industry.* Eastern Economist 74(14) 4 April 1980 P 681-95.

Pillai, P.P., *Scale and Efficiency of Small Scale Industries in India.* Asian Economic Ravie 20(1) April 1978, P 21-37.

Rajula Devi, A.K., *Small is Viable: A Critical Study of Small Industries.* Eastern Economis 79(2) 11 July 1982 P 77-81.

Reddy, G. Raghava, *Bank Finance for Village and Small Industries.* Eastern Economist 76(10), 6 March 1981, P 607-09.

Reddy, I. . Subbi and Reddy, M. Bhaskara, *Role of Small Industry in a Developing Economy.* Southern Economist (Annual Number) 20(1) 1 May 1981, P 33-35.

Shetty, K.S., *How Small Industries are Murdered in Socialist India.* Organiser 33(47) 11 April 1982, P 11-12.

Sinha, I.C., *Improvement in Quality of Product Through Standardisation in Small Scale and Ancillary Industries.* ISI Bulletin 30 September 1978 P 315-19.

Sivaraman, B., *Role of Rural and Small Industries.* Productivity 19(4) January-March 1979 P 441-56.

Small Sector Can Export More. Eastern Economist 75 (10) 5 September, 1980, P 589-90.

Varghoso, K. Goorgo and Ramachandran, K., *Investment Allowance and Small Scale Industries.* Charteredaccountant, 28(11) May 1982, P 1035-39

Vepa, Ram K., *Doubling Exports from the Small Sector.* Man and Development. 2(4) December 1980 P 61-66.

Baput, L.G., *Credit Needs of Small Industries.* Swarajya 11 September 1971 P 13-14.

Bilgrami, Izhar, A., *Bank Assistance for Small Sector.* Indian Finance 101(25) 24, June 1978 P 500-503.

Taleyarkhan, J.H., *Promotion of Projects: Importance of Timely Financing.* Economic Times (Supplement), 20 December 1980 P1: 6-8+

Bhat, A.R., *Development of Small Industries in Free India.* Commerce 125 (3196) 19 August 1972 P 68-72.

Bhatt, R.S., *Growth of Entrepreneurship in Small and Medium Sectors.*

Indian Journal of Public Administration 20(3) July-September 1974, P 453-65.

Kapoor T.N. and Others, *Marketing Problems of Small Industries.* Productivity 23(4) January - March 1983 P 361-69.

Lal, Sundarshan, *What Do We Mean by Small Industries? They Must be Defined Again.* Yojana 17(23-24) 1 January 1974, P 893-94.

Lingaraj, B.P. and Giri Kumar, T., *Problems of Small Industries in a Developing Country.* Decision 9(4) October 1982 P 179-88.

Pennathum K.,' *Productivity Problems of Small Industries.* Khadi Gramodyog 13(3) December 1966, P 229-31.

Chattoadhyaya, Amal, *Prospects and Problems of Small-Scale Industry.* Radical Humanist 45(5) August 1980 P 53-58.

Jain, S.K., *The Role of Small Scale Industries in Creating Employment Opportunities.* Development Policy and Administrative Review. 4(2) July-December 1978 P 9-10.

Kasbekar, S.R., *SSI's : Incentives not a Major Force.* Economic Times (Supplement)17 September 1980 P1:1-4+

Mishra G.P. and Mishra, P.N., *Government Policies for Promoting Small Scale Industries. GCCI Bulletin* 10 October 1979 P 9-21.

Ram Narain and Bhojwani, H., R., *Technological Needs of Small Scale Industry.* Eastern Economist 74(14) 4 April, 1980 P 681-95.

Deshmukh, S.B. and Kumar, Suresh, M., *Banks and Sick Small-Sick Units.* Economic Times, 24 January 1978 P 5: 3-8

More Liberal Finance Needed for Small-Scale Industries. Capital 167 (4175) 5 August 1971 P 274

Financing of Small Scale Units. Banker N. 25(1) March 1978, P 24-26.

Role of Financial Institutions in Rural Industries Projects. Kurukshetra 22(18) 1974 P 2.

Subba Rao, S.R., *SFC's and Small Industry Development,* Southern Economist 17(23) 1 April 1979 P 29-30.

Bilgrami, Izhar A., *Bank Assistance for Small Sector.* Indian Finance 101(25) 24 June 1978 P 500-03.

Chattopadhayay, P., *Why Small Units are Still not Getting Adequate Bank Finance?* Capital 167(4179) 2 September 1971 P 484-86.

Chopra, Kailash C., *Advance to Small Scale Industries : Supervision and Follow Up,* Banker (India) 21(7) May 1974 P 44-48.

Choudhury, R.P., *Changing Pattern of Small Business Finance in India.* Indian Journal of Commerce 33(4) December 1980, P 101-06.

Gupta, A.P., *Problem of Credit Management for Small Manufacturing Business. Indian Journal of Commerce* 16(3) September 1973, P 665-69.

Small Industry: Many Allurements. Economic and Political Weekly 16 June 1979, P 978-79.

Small Unit Face Many Hurdeals in Getting Bank Credit. Capital 1985, 11 August 1980 P 2.

Rale, Subhash J., *Small-Scale Sector Barriers to Growth.* Eastern Economist 73(7) 17 August 1979 P 33-54.

REPORTS AND PUBLICATIONS

— Government of India, Development Commissioner, Small Scale Industries, Report on the Census of Small Scale Industries, 1976.

— Sido Reports—1980-84, 1984-85.

— Financing of Small Scale Industries in India, 1963.

— Government of India, Development Commissioner, Facilities for Small Industries, 1964.

— Facilities for the Development of Small Scale Industries, February 1982.

— Profile on Entrepreneurship Development Programmes in Andhra Pradesh, 1978.

— Planning Commission, Draft five-Year Plans. 1st to 7th.

— Report of Indian Industrial Commission, 1918.

— Report of Fiscal Commission, 1949-50.

— Report of Stores Purchase Committee.

— Report of the Japanese Delegation on Small Scale—Industries.

— Report of the Village and Small Industries Committee, 1955.

— Report on Small Industries in India, International Planning Team, The Ford Foundation, 1955.

— Report on Hyderabad Conference on 'Social Research on Small Industries in India.

— Industrial Policy Statement, 1980.

— Government of Andhra Pradesh, Bureau of Economics and Statistics 1981-82 to 1985-86.

— Brochure on Industries and Infrastructure on Andhra Pradesh, 1980.

— Report on Annual Survey of Industries, 1978-79.

— Guidelines for Setting up Small Scale Industries in Andhra Pradesh, 1985.

JOURNALS AND PERIODICALS

ICSI Herald

Laghu Udyog

Main Stream

Sedme

Journal of Commerce

Capital

Yojana

Productivity

Indian Journal of Commerce

Eastern Economist

Indian Journal of Labour Economics.

Organiser

Journal of Industry and Trade

Kurukshetra

Thought

Economic and Political Weekly

Khadi Gramodyog

Foreign Trade

Man and Development

Organiser

Southern Economist.

Banker

Management Accountant.

INDEX

Abid Hussain Committee, 15-, 32
Absenteeism, 241-43
Acharya Sarthi, 51
Agarwal, 55
Agarwal, Manik Chandra, 51
Agarwal, Radharaman, 50
Agrobased, 42
Agro Horticulture, 66-67
All India Manufacturers Organisation, 27
Ancillary Development Programme, 31
Andhra Pradesh, 62
Andhra Pradesh Assistance Centre for Entrepreneurs, 77
Andhra Pradesh Electronic Development Corporation Ltd. 75
Andhra Pradesh Industrial and Technical Consultancy Organization, 76-77
Andhra Pradesh Industrial Development Corporation Ltd., 70-71
    Activities, 70-71
    Objectives, 70
Andhra Pradesh Industrial Infrastructure Corporation Ltd., 71
Andhra Pradesh Mineral Development Corporation Ltd., 76
Andhra Pradesh Small Scale Industrial Development Corporation, 71-72
    Activities, 71-72
Andhra Pradesh State Agro Industries Development Corporation Ltd., 75-76
Andhra Pradesh State Electricity Board, 68
Andhra Pradesh State Financial Corporation, 51, 72-74, 165
    Schemes of, 73-74
Andhra Pradesh State Trading Corporation, 77
Anselm, Mercy, 51
Apparao, Balla, 51
Asthana, BR., 52
Athreya, Nagan Harihar, 51
Atomic Minerals's Complex, 97
Average production, 133-36
Azmat Ali, 5, 51
Backward Integration Project, 69
Bahader Singh, 51
Balachandan Committee, 52
Balakrishna, G, 51
Balmohandas, Y, 51
Banerjee, Naresh Chandra, 50
Banerjee, Sabita, 51
Barooah, Hem Kanta, 57
Basanta Kumar, 52
Bhandari, Aravind, 52
Bhat Committee, 52
Boiton Committee, 1
Brahmanadham, G. N., 51
Brahma, S, 50
Building material based, 43-44
Camera, Nirmal, 50
Capacity utilisation, 119-23

Capital structure, 193-98
Captive Power Plants, 69
Central Footwear Training Centres, 27
Chemical based, 43
Composite loans, 73
Common Production Programme, 7
Confederation of Indian Industry, 27
Credit policies, 29
De Hann, H., 50
Desai, Vasant, 50
Deshpande, Manohar Uttam Rao, 51
De, Sushil Kumar, 51
Development of Small Scale Industry, 60-97
    Growth and development of Small and tiny sector in AP, 60-62
    Growth and working of industries, 77
    Incentives to, 67
    Infrastructure facilities, 63-65
    Large and medium industry, 62-63
    Opportunities, 66-67
    Resources, 67
Dey, Kikhil Bhushan, 51
Dhameja, N.L, 51
Direct taxes, 28-29
Diversification Forward Integration Projects, 69
Domman, MA, 50
Engineering and Allied based, 44
Entrepreneurship Development Programmes, 31-32
Excise Duty Exemption Scheme, 28
Expansion Project, 68
Export Processing zone, 96-97
Farooq Khan, A, 52
Federation of Association of Small Industries of India, 13, 27
Federation of Indian Chamber of Commerce and Industry, 27
    Financial, 33-34
Financial Problems, 161-67, 245-60
    Financing, 165-67
    Sources of finance, 162-65
Five year plan, 7-10
    1st, 7
    2nd, 7
    3rd, 8
    Annual plan, 1966-69, 8
    4th, 8
    5th, 8
    6th, 8-9
    7th, 9
    8th, 9-10
Fixed vs working capital, 107-11
Forest, based, 42-43
Gadgil, Prabhakar Gopal, 51
Gambhir, Gurubachan Das, 51
Gandhian thought, 5-6
Gandhiji, 5
Gangole, Arun Kumar, 50
Garg, Shubhra, 52
Germany, 1
Gopal, DK, 50
Gopal Swaroop, 51
Growth and organisation of sample units, 98-138
    Average production, 133-36
    Capacity, 113-19
        Installed vs utilised, 113-19
    Capacity utilisation, 119-23
    Fixed vs working capital, 107-11
    Growth of total units, 98-99
    In Srikakulam district, 101-102
    In Visakhapatam district, 102-04
    In Vizianagram district, 100-01
    Reasons for idle capacity, 123-28
    Share of fixed and working capital in total capital, 111-13
    Structure of Capital, 104-07
    Total production, 128-33
    Trends of total and average production, 136-38
Growth Centre Scheme, 30
Gupta, Vipin Chandra, 50

Gurucharan Kaur, 51
Human, resources, 67
ILO, 1
Incentives and facilities, 28-29, 67
Indian Council of Small Industries, 27
Indian Federation of Tiny Enterprises, 27
Industrial Estate Programme, 30
Industrial policy, 1948, 10
Industrial policy, 1956, 11
Industrial policy, 1977, 11-12
Industrial policy, 1980, 12
Industrial policy, 1985, 12
Industrial policy, 1991, 12-13
Industrial Association, 27
Infrastructural Development Schemes and Special programmes, 29
Infrastructure facilities, 63-66
Integrated Infrastructural Development Scheme, 30
Iyer, T. N. Krishan, 51
Jagri, Syed Amin, 52
Jain, 50
Japan, 1
Joshi, N., 50
Kapardikar, S.D., 51
Kaveri, V.S, 51
Labour problems, 147-55, 234-36
Large and medium industry, 62-63
Liberalisation, 15-16
Lokandham Committee, 52
Mahila Udyog Nidhi Scheme, 74
Managerial, 33
Manjundhar, Soumendu, 50
Marketing, 33
Marketing problems, 155-61, 223-45
Mathur, S.P., 50
Mineral based, 43-44, 66-67
Mishra, Gaya Prasad, 51
Mitra, Lalit Kumar, 51
Mohammed Sayed, 51
Mohanty, Bedabati, 50
Mussa Baker, A, 50
Murthy, P.L.N.V.S. GK, 51
Namdeo, R.S., 51
National Equity Fund Scheme, 29
National Institute for Entrepreneurship and Small Business Development, 25
National Institute of Design, Ahmedabad, 26
National Institute of Small Industry Extension and Training, 26
National Productivity Council, 26
National Small Industries Corporation, 7, 24
Navrang, Sudhershanlal, 51
Niranjundun, S., 50
Nisar Ahmed, 51
Objectives and methodology, 35-39
    Limitation, 54
    Methodology, 37-38
    Objectives, 37
    Period of Study, 38
    Problem of Study, 36-37
    Profile of respondents, 45-50
    Selection of sample, 38-44
        Agro based, 42
        Chemical based, 43
        Engineering Allied based, 44
        Forest based, 42-43
        Mineral and building material based, 43-44
    Significance of study, 53
    Survey of literature, 50-53
Oommen, M.A., 50
Padmanabhan, D., 51
Panda, Ganasyam, 51
Pareek, Hanuman Sahai, 51
Parikh, Suryakant M., 51
Patel, C.R., 51
Patwardhan, M.S., 52
PHD Chamber of Commerce and Industry, 27
Port based industrialisation, 66
Power, 65

Problems of sample units, 139-85
  Financial problems, 161-85
    Financing, 165-67
    In Srikakulum district, 170-78
    In Visakhapatnam district, 178-85
    In Viziangaram district, 162-70
    Source of finance, 162-65
  Labour problems, 147-55
  Marketing problems, 155-61
  Production problems, 139-47
Problems of Sample units-comparative analysis, 211-60
  Financial problems, 245-60
    Cumbersome procedure, 257-60
    Delay in sanction, 252-53
    High rate of interest, 255-57
    Insufficient finance, 253-55
    Problem of security, 245-51
  Marketing problems, 223-45
    Absenteeism, 241-43
    Affects of govt. policy, 232-33
    Competition, 227-30
    Labour problems, 234-36
    Labour turnover, 239-41
    Poor quality, 230-32
    Shortage of labour, 236-39
    Strikes problems, 243-45
  Objectives of, 211
  Production problems, 214-23
    Machinery troubles, 222-23
    Power shortage, 219-21
    Raw material shortage, 217-19
Product-cum process development centres, 26
Production, 33
Production problems, 139-47, 213-14
Quality Certification Scheme, 32
Raj, P.R., 51
Ramakrishna, K.T., 51
Ramandaham, V.V., 51
Rao, R.V., 50
Rao, Uma Maheswar, 50
Rastogi, Chandramohan, 50
Rastogi, K.P., 51
Raw materials, 32-32
Reasons for ideal capacity, 123-28
Resources, 67
Sandesara, J.C., 50
Satyapal, 51
Saxena, K.K., 51
Schemes for Physically Handicapped and SC/ST Entrepreneurs, 73
Self-employment Scheme for young entrepreneurs, 74
Sharma, Anil Kumar, 51
Sharma, Dandayal, 51
Sharma Deo Raj, 51
Sickness, 34, 186-210, 269
  Capital Structure, 199-210
  Extent of, 186
  In Andhra Pradesh, 187-91
    Causes of, 190
    External factors, 190
    Internal factors, 190
  In Srikakulam district 198-203
    Capital structure, 199-203
  In Visakhapatnam district, 204-10
    Capital structure, 206-10
  Symptoms of 192-93
Singh, Navnihal, 51
Singh, Shamboo Prasad, 50
Singh, Y.R., 52
Single, Window Scheme, 73-74
Sinha, R., 52
Sinha, SLN, 52
Siya Ram, 51
Small Industries Development Bank of India, 25-26
Small Industries Development Organisation, 7, 23-24
Services of, 23-24
Small Industries Service Institutes, 24

Small Industries Board, 10, 27-28
Small Scale Sector, 1-34
Advantages of, 3-4
Contribution to Indian Economy, 18-23
To employment, 18-21
To export, 22-23
To output, 22
Credit policies, 29-30
Definition of, 13-17
Liberalisation, 15-16
Reservation of items, 17
Strength, 16
SWOT, 16
Threats, 17
Weakness, 16
Development in India, 4-7
After independence, 6-7
Gandhian thought, 5-6
Pre-Independence, 5
Five year plans and, 7-10
Importance of, 2-3
Incentives and facilities to, 28-29
Industrial policies, 10-13
Institutional setup and, 23
Major findings, 261-67
Problems of, 32-34
Suggestions, 268-70
Sickness, 269
To Banks and Financial Agencies, 269-70
To the government, 268-69
Software, 66
Sohgal, Jag Mohan Lal, 51
Srikakulam district, 37, 83-89
About the district, 83
Agricultural and horticulture resources, 83
Average production, 134-35
Banking, 89
Capacity utilisation, 121-22
Finance, 170-78
Fixed vs working capital, 109-10
Growth and working of industry in, 83-89
Growth of sample units in, 101-02
Infrastructure facilities, 85
Installed vs utilised capacity, 116-18
Labour problems in, 150-52
Large and medium industry, 85
Marketing problems in, 157-59
Power, 87
Production problems, 142-64
Railways, 87
Reasons for idle capacity, 125-26
Roadways, 87
Share of fixed and working capitals in total capital, 112
Sickness in, 198-203
Small and tiny unit in, 83-85
Structure of capital, 105-06
Total production, 130-31
Water supply, 87
Staly, 50
State Aid to Industries Act, 10
Strike, 243-45
Structure of capital, 104-07
Sundershran Lal, 51
Suryanarayana, CVAS, 51
Switzerland, 1
SWUT, 16
Target 2000 Scheme, 67-68
Tax Holiday Scheme, 29
Technical Consultancy Organisations, 32
Tele Communications, 65, 66-67
Textiles, 66
Tool rooms, 26
Total production, 128-31
Transport, 65
Transport Subsidy, 30-31
UK, 1
Upadhyaya, DV, 50

USA, 1

Varma, NS, 50

Venkatswamy, G. 51

Village and Small Industries Committee, 52

About the district, 89-91

Agricultural resources, 91

Atomic minerals complex, 97

Average production, 135-36

Banking, 96

Capacity utilisation, 122-23

Export Processing Zone, 96-97

Financial problems of sample unit, 178-85

Finacing, 181-83

Sickness, 204-10

Sources of finance, 178-81

Fixed vs working capital, 110-11

Growth and working of 89-91

Growth of sample units, 102-04

Infrastructure facility, 94

Installed vs utilised capacity, 118-19

Labour problems, 152-55

Large and medium scale industry, 94

Marine resources, 95

Marketing problems, 159-61

Petro-chemical complex, 97

Power, 95-96

Production problems, 144-47, 214

Railways, 95

Reasons for idle capacity, 126-28

Roadways, 94

Share of fixed and working capital in total capital, 113

Small and tiny, units, 91

Structure of capital, 106-07

Total production, 135-36

Water, 96

Waterways, 95

Vizianagaram district, 37, 77-82

About the district, 77

Agricultural resources, 79

Average production, 133-34

Banking, 87

Capacity utilisation, 120-21

Financial problems, 167-70

Fixed vs working capital, 108-09

Growth and working of industries, 73-82

Growth of sample units, 100-01

Infrastructure facilities, 80

Infrastructure facilities by APCTC, 81-82

Installed vs utilised capacity, 114-16

Marketing problems, 155-57

Power, 81

Production problems, 139-42, 214-15

Railways, 80

Reasons for idle capacity, 123-24

Roadways, 80

Share of fixed and working capitals in total capital, 111-12

Small and tiny units in, 79-80

Sources of Finance, 162-65

Structure of Capital, 104-05

Total production, 128-30

Water, 81

Water, 65

Women entrepreneur scheme, 74

World Association of Small and Medium Enterprises, 27